SPORTS AFIELD
OUTDOOR
SKILLS

SPORTS AFIELD
OUTDOOR
SKILLS

Edited by Frank S. Golad

HEARST BOOKS
NEW YORK

Library of Congress Catalog Card Number: 91-71812
ISBN: 0-688-10415-0

Printed in Verona, Italy
First U.S. Edition
1   2   3   4   5   6   7   8   9   10

Designed by Dirk Kaufman and Diana Russo
Edited by Charles A. de Kay
Produced by Smallwood and Stewart, Inc.
New York City

CONTENTS

INTRODUCTION

Samples of reader opinion, which are taken monthly at *Sports Afield*, give the editors a real feel for what these outdoor-oriented people expect in a magazine—what they want more of and what they can do without. Two features stand out as consistent winners: the *Sports Afield* Almanac and articles on outdoor skills. It didn't take a genius to come up with the idea of combining the two into one book.

Collecting all the bits and pieces and organizing them into a reader-friendly environment between two covers was a gargantuan task undertaken by Almanac editor Frank S. Golad. The monthly *Sports Afield* Almanac is an eight-page section that has been running since May 1972. It is a potpourri of hiking, camping, fishing, and assorted outdoor lore, and Frank was the perfect choice to compile this book because he, too, has a wide range of such interests and expertise.

What are outdoor skills and why should we want to acquire them in such high-tech times? For one thing, outdoor people are almost without exception the most practical conservationists and environmentalists. It becomes clearer every day that Planet Earth is in deep trouble and needs all the constructive help it can get. Outdoor people are forming the basis of this new constituency since they already possess a knowledge of water, earth, insects, animals, trees, and so forth. In cities residents are pretty much in charge of their environment—except for natural disasters such as earthquakes, hurricanes, and blizzards. Perhaps it would be better to say that in cities people have been able to create the illusion that they are in charge. In the "boonies" there are few such illusions.

The fact is that in urban areas we are very much dependent upon the many services provided. For warmth we turn up the heat. For transportation we drive on paved streets. For light we flick a switch. Not so in the woods. In the woods we do it ourselves. For warmth we gather wood and build a fire. For transportation we place one foot in front of the other. For light we ignite a lantern. What we haven't brought with us we do without.

The benefits we derive from our out-of-doors experiences are a wonderful, can-do feeling of self-reliance and a linkage to our forebears. There is not much tradition in cable television, and there is little satisfaction in following road signs to get someplace. Finding our way by compass and stars not only offers us plenty of self-gratification but also lets us feel we are in step with the past.

Here then, in these pages, you will find useful information on clothing, gear, tents, wild foods, hiking, fire making, weather forecasting, dealing with insects or shock, fording a river, and sharpening a knife. You will learn how to tie things and how to buy things; how to make things and bake things; how to boat and float; how to camp in the woods or tote in the goods. You'll learn how to fish and forage. You'll learn the joys of being on your own and providing for yourself.

But, above all, I hope you'll be inspired to spend some time in the great outdoors and become reacquainted with wild places and wild things, and that this new inspiration will make you active in helping to preserve our natural world.

Tom Paugh
Editor in Chief
SPORTS AFIELD

CHAPTER ONE

BE PREPARED

Preparing for a trek into the wilderness or onto untraveled waters should not turn out to be an adventure in itself. This chapter is devoted to those matters that outdoors people should take into account before leaving the house. With more than 100 helpful suggestions on what to bring along—from what to consider when selecting a tent or sleeping bag to what common household items to take along that might save a life in a survival situation—and how to pack and secure your gear to give you the greatest freedom afield, this chapter is a valuable collection of sound advice on how to make your next camping, fishing, or other wilderness journey safer and more enjoyable.

In addition to suggesting valuable equipment to have on hand in the wilderness, a special section discusses ways of modifying everyday items to work more effectively afield. Reliable information about such matters as protecting your watch and customizing your daypack, along with other hints, may help you extend the life of your equipment.

ESSENTIAL CLOTHING AND GEAR

Plan to Fish or Hike? Visit Your Library

Before you take that expensive hiking or fishing trip, do some scouting in the library. Most large libraries contain phone book collections, so if you're bound for steelhead in Oregon or the forests of the Adirondacks, you can look up the local tackleshops, tourist bureau, or chamber of commerce and call for information about guides, bait and tackle, boat rentals, restaurants, and hotels. Many libraries also carry road and tourist maps, which they often lend out. Finally, a librarian can recommend background reading to help you cut costs and improve your chances of finding just what you're looking for—at the right price—afield.

Choosing a Personal Tent

Backpackers' tents have come a long way in recent years. They are more durable, more resistant to weather extremes, and, possibly best of all, very lightweight. All of these traits are attributable to innovative fabrics not available a few years ago. If you intend to pack your camp in great distances, the lightweight models of three to six pounds are perfect.

In order to keep the weight down, however, many concessions had to be made. For this reason, a small backpacker's tent would be a poor selection for a family that drives to within a few feet of camp.

As a rule of thumb, 15 to 18 square feet are necessary to sleep one person and another 3 square feet would be required for his or her gear. This is the absolute minimum.

All tents, whether for backpacking or family camping, should be equipped with no-see-um bug netting, screened windows, and zip-down door flaps. The ventilation provided by these screens is very important in summer and winter to prevent condensation, which can cause mildew, food spoilage, and warped gear.

Fluorescent Not Just for Hunters

Fluorescent garments work for deer hunters, but there are two other groups of people who do get shot at during deer season—backpackers and anglers. The backpacker does a lot of ducking and stooping, and the small-stream angler also often seems to be a low-level contortionist.

During deer season, backpackers and anglers would be well-advised to wear blaze orange as well.

Customize Your Day Pack

Day packs are great, but you can always find something you need that won't fit into this carryall. I've yet to embark on an ambitious day afield for hunting, fishing, hiking, or whatever when mine would hold everything I needed.

By adding sturdy, slotted leather tabs at strategic points around the pack, you can double or even triple its carrying capacity. Depending on your activity, you can then tie a slicker and rainpants to the outside. Or you might want to

roll up your stocking-foot waders and tie them alongside your pack rod. If you're a photographer, it might be a tripod. The possibilities have no end. I often tie on a shorty pad and a light down bag in its

stuff sack, turning my day pack into a weekend pack.

The best rule is to be liberal: Put tabs wherever you think they will be useful. If you don't want to do the sewing yourself, take the pack to a cobbler. Mine sewed on eight tabs for just a few bucks.

You can use buckled straps to cinch down large items such as sleeping bags. I use nylon bootlaces for most things, leaving them tied to the tabs until I need them.

EMERGENCY GEAR

Accidents and emergencies will happen, particularly to people who expose themselves to the capriciousness of nature. Here are a few suggestions on what you should carry in the way of emergency gear.

• Jack and lug wrench. It's a good idea to practice with your jack at home to see how it works.
• Tire chains. A must for wintertime travel.
• Tire pump. There are all kinds, from hand pumps to foot pumps. You can even buy a pump that can be plugged into your cigarette lighter. Some drivers also carry canned air.
• Flashlight. Flares are helpful in highway emergencies.

• Fire extinguisher. Buy the all-purpose type and check the pressure indicator on it from time to time.
• First-aid kit. Include compress, gauze and adhesive bandages, first-aid cream, and other items you favor.
• Booster cables. Check your car manual on how to hook them up.
• Hand tools. Open-end wrenches, pliers, and screwdrivers should get you by, but you may want to add to that assortment. A shovel comes in very hand at times.
• Gas can. Some motorists also carry a siphon
• CB radio. Channel 19 provides information on highway conditions from other motorists.

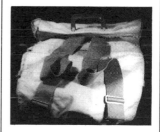

Convertible Backpack

A handle added to the top of a knapsack or backpack converts it to a suitable piece of luggage for packing extra clothes, blankets, and other accessories.

Here, a handle removed from a carpet-sample book has been riveted to the upper portion of the flap. A thin strip of plywood placed on the underside of the material keeps the rivets from pulling through.

WHAT IS WILDERNESS?

From the time the Pilgrims landed at Plymouth to well after the Declaration of Independence was signed, pioneers to the New World found neither the temperate nor the flowering land they had expected. They found, in the baldest terms, a wilderness. To appreciate what the word meant to them, one might, today, climb to the treeless, granite summit of Saddleback Mountain in Maine and gaze across thousands of square miles of New England. Try to imagine this landscape of hardwood and evergreen hills without fences or orchards, towns or roads; then imagine this country rolling into the unknown west for another 3000 miles—much of it inhabited by bears, wolves, cougars, hostile Indians, and the snows of winter. The pioneer, ax in hand, did not extol the silent and vast beauty we choose to praise. In fact, he or she called it "dismal," "terrible," and "howling."

Early humans left that dark forest and chose instead to use their keen eyesight to avoid predators on the savannas. Thus was handed down our primal love of open spaces and fear of timbered country. This inheritance is still expressed by our need to clear woodlands, to build our homes with a view and, until only 100 years ago, to cultivate nearly every acre of the land.

Around 1870, however, the historically unprecedented idea that some wild country should not be developed began to take shape. Finding its roots in two phenomena—the urbanization of the eastern United States and the formation of a class of people who viewed hunting and fishing as sports rather than as tools of survival—the nascent conservation movement was husbanded.

By the time Theodore Roosevelt left office in 1909, the nation had 13 national parks, 150 million acres of national forest, plus the still largely unexplored territory of Alaska. Wild country, to be sure, but within all of it there wasn't an acre of what might be called official wilderness—lands managed with the preservation of their primitive characteristics in mind. Indeed, what constituted "primitive," "wilderness," or "undeveloped" proved obscure and debatable for a number of decades.

Over the years, many attempted to define these terms. Robert Marshall, the explorer of central Alaska and the chief of the Forest Service's Division of Recreation and Lands during the late 1930s, called wilderness a place you couldn't walk across in a day (and Marshall could walk 35 miles a day). Aldo Leopold, ecologist, Forest Service ranger in the Arizona Territory, and author of the inspirational wilderness text, A Sand County Almanac, maintained that a wilderness had to be able to absorb a two-week pack trip. More recently, Ed Abbey, minstrel of Utah's canyon country, has called wilderness a

place where a person can be killed and eaten by a wild animal.

In September 1964 the U.S. Congress, after years of hearings, enacted the Wilderness Act, which took a precise look at the elusive word: "A wilderness, in contrast with those areas where man and his own works dominate the landscape, is hereby recognized as an area where the earth and its community of life are untrammeled by man, where man himself is a visitor who does not remain." The landmark legislation went on to state that a wilderness was at least 5000 acres in size and would be permanently devoid of roads, commercial enterprises, and motorized equipment, motorboats, and aircraft, except where they had been traditionally used for access (as in Alaska, for example).

The Wilderness Act has helped to lay aside 3.5 percent of the entire United States—land for backpacking, fishing, canoeing, hunting, mountaineering, cross-country skiing, horsepacking. Is this enough wilderness? Is it too much? Should

Congress try to incorporate more lands into the wilderness system? These are difficult questions to answer, but three arguments for an expanded and healthy wilderness system present themselves. These are the recreational, the ecological, and for want of a better term, the unselfish.

The recreational motive is easy to grasp. Living in urban and suburban environments, as most of us do, we welcome the chance to refresh ourselves in the quiet of primitive settings that our pioneer grandparents might have chosen to clear and citify.

The ecological reason for preserving wilderness is also straightforward. René Dubos, the renowned microbiologist and writer of natural history and anthropology, calculated that wilderness accounts for a large part of the planet's photosynthetic energy. Giving clean air into the atmosphere and clean water into our oceans, wilderness balances those areas of the planet that we've polluted.

Last, we may consider that by preserving as yet unprotected wilderness areas and impacting minimally those wild lands that have become overcrowded, we are participants in the unselfish spirit of Grinnell, Roosevelt, and Muir. By camping gently, we can maintain the cleanliness and uniqueness of our wilderness areas. And in today's world the remaining wilderness, with its great variety of fish and wildlife, deserts, lakes, and rivers, becomes a measuring stick for the future—an irreplaceable reference point by which free-thinking people can evaluate their progress and their peace of mind.

Selecting the Correct Family Tent

For a family, the cabin and umbrella tent designs offer the best weight-to-size ratios, floor plans, and overall features.

Where wind is a problem, lower resistance is offered by the umbrella; but the cabin type, with its vertical sides, is better if double-decker-type cots are used. Otherwise, choosing a tent style is a matter of preference.

Many manufacturers overrate tents. You may see advertisements for a 10 × 14-foot (140 square feet) tent for sleeping up to eight. No way! Each person, including children, needs 25 square feet, which allows space for a cot or sleeping bag, a suitcase or clothes bag, and room for moving around. A family of four needs a 100-square-foot tent with a floor plan of 10 × 10 feet minimum.

If the family is larger than four, or if adults prefer to sleep away from children, consider a second tent for sleeping only, based on 18 square feet for each child.

If you cannot find a tent with exactly the right floor space, go up to the next size larger, not down to the next one smaller.

Don't worry about the tent's construction. Quality manufacturers use the very best materials available.

Shop around. A high-quality family-sized tent from a reputable manufacturer is the best buy.

Look for these features: outside frames for more inside room; floors that prevent moisture from entering at ground-level seams; adequate headroom; at least three windows; and a sizable door—one that does not require bending double to get through. All windows must have bug screens and flaps that zip closed. Make sure zippers are well constructed and sturdy.

For hot-weather camping a double-roof construction (with a top fly) helps minimize condensation and keeps the inside of the tent cool under direct sunlight.

Select a good tent that is easy to assemble, flame-resistant (they're not fireproof!), pleasing in color, roomy, dry, and acceptable to the whole family.

NEW TENT CARE

Two days after setting up camp it rained, and our first-time-out brand-new tent spouted a few leaks. Brand-new and already leaking like the *Titanic!*

Indignantly I took the offending canvas structure to the sporting-goods store where I bought it. Tears flowed as I explained what happened (I was careful not to let them fall on the offending tent). As I went on, the store manager's grin grew wider and wider and I got hotter and hotter. To cut this tale of woe very short, he gave me a valuable tip.

A canvas tent should be set up on the lawn first and not at the campsite. Then it should be thoroughly hosed down with water. After it is completely dry, hose it once more. This sets the shape of the tent and shrinks the fabric to prevent the entry of rain. Now it's no problem to stay dry.

When selecting a sleeping bag intended for cold-weather use, look for one that provides a positive seal at the zipper. A gasket-type strip of weather seal running along both the inside and outside of the zipper keeps out cold air. In addition, the weather seal prevents the chilled metal zipper from coming in contact with a sleeper's bare arm.

THE CLASSIC PACK

The early Americans whose wilderness life most closely approached that of modern backpackers and canoe campers were the timber cruisers of Wisconsin and Minnesota. Their work required journeys of a week to six months in canoes or by packing through the woods, with equipment that was both light and rugged.

The cruiser's crowning piece of equipment was the packsack. The Porier packsack (named for its maker, the Porier Tent and Awning Co. of Duluth, Minnesota), came to be known as the Duluth pack.

The original was made of a single piece of canvas with an end folded back and sewed along the sides. About 20 inches was left free to form the flap, which was fastened over the filled pack with three leather straps. When loaded, it snuggled into the small of the back and onto the hips, and it held close to the shoulders with a head strap or tumpline.

Today, the Duluth Tent and Awning Co. carries on the tradition. It may have adapted the original, but it has scarcely improved it.

Shape Up

Sports lovers are aware of the need for daily exercise before strenuous outdoor activities, but most neglect the needs of their dogs and unfairly expect top-notch, day-long performance from a fat or out-of-condition animal.

Long, brisk walks on a regular basis through the local park or around the block will tone up leg and heart muscles and increase general levels of fitness—for both of you.

Jogging, running, swimming or bicycling will help, but consult your physician first. Work into condition gradually: You didn't get out of it in a day, and you can't regain your former stamina and trimness as easily as you lost them.

Dogs decondition just like humans, though usually not to so great an extent. A walk, a swim, or a few retrieves will increase your dog's endurance and help assure his constant attention to his duties on opening day.

BUYING BINOCS

When choosing binoculars for field use, don't buy more power than you need. The higher the magnification, the more difficult it becomes to keep the image steady without using a rigid support. Hand-holding high-power binocs tires eyes quickly. Eight power is most people's upper limit. Zoom models let you pick the power you actually need. But zoom glasses don't transmit as much light as fixed-power binocs.

Like zoom glasses, armor-clad and waterproof binocs have their niches. The trade-off here is added bulk: Do you really need these special features?

Spend five minutes actually looking through an intended purchase. Some less expensive binocs are much better than others. Look first to see if what you focus on is sharp and bright. If so, keep looking. If the lenses are misaligned, they may cause you to develop a headache or a sick stomach within minutes.

Eyeglass wearers should first try new binocs without wearing their glasses. The focus adjustment is often sufficient to correct vision.

Madake, a Japanese bamboo, blossoms only once about every 120 years.

BE PREPARED

When day hiking to your favorite mountain lake or trout stream, keep in mind the changeability of weather at high altitudes. What begins as a sunny summer day can often end in a chilly rain or even a snowstorm. Be prepared with warm clothing, raingear, and matches stored away in a waterproof container.

Heavy rain, snow, or fog can also impede navigation, so take along topographic maps of the area as well as a compass. If you're in a strange area, check in with a ranger or local fire department and then be sure to check out with them when you return. It's easy insurance against inconvenience, or worse, later.

Cleaner and Drier

By spraying your pant cuffs and seat area with a fabric protector such as Scotchgard,™ you'll stay drier and cleaner on hiking and fishing outings. This spray-type waterproofing should be renewed after every washing.

FELT LINERS

The various brands of "snow pack" boots that feature removable felt liners are among the warmest and most comfortable footgear you can wear. However, to insulate properly the felt liners must be removed after a day's use and allowed to dry. The felt ab-sorbs moisture from perspiration, and after a long day of hiking it will be damp. Always buy an extra pair of liners so you won't have to wait for the original pair to dry. Don't buy snow packs that have felt liners that already have been sewn into the boots.

TUMMY WARMERS

Plummeting temperatures can put an unpleasant edge on outdoor activities. A cold-weather item I've come to rely on as much as my vest is a waistband. It can be handknit or a wide, warm scarf. To hold the band in place and make it easy to put on and take off, attach Velcro fasteners.

Face Saver

With modern clothing, it is possible to stay relatively warm even on the coldest of days. Polypropylene undergarments complemented with layers of wool and newfangled raingear are fine, but they still leave one vital area exposed— your face. Being warm all over and having your cheeks sting from cold winds can be unpleasant. You could wear a mask or balaclava, but they ice up from your breath.

An alternative solution to the problem is to spread a thin film of Vaseline over your face. Just a small amount applied with your fingertips provides amazingly good protection against the bite of harsh winds.

GIANT PACKS

Average-sized backpacks can handle food and gear for about a week-long trip. But when used on longer excursions, or on trips that require extra gear—like climbing ventures—these 4000-cubic-inch-volume packs simply lack sufficient room. You're forced to strap your equipment to the outside or top of your pack, which means that the balance of the pack is compromised, you'll become more tired while on the trail, and your gear stands a better chance of getting wet.

If you're planning a big trip, you may want to consider one of the large-volume or "giant" backpacks described below, all of which will handle 6000 or more cubic inches of gear. Deciding between an external frame model or one with an internal frame is easy. If you plan to do nothing but hike, and at times must carry very heavy loads (in excess of 60 pounds), choose an external frame pack. It will be more comfortable. If you plan to ski or if you have to negotiate steep terrain where you'll be doing a bit of scrambling (actually touching the rock for support), choose the internal frame pack. It has a lower center of gravity and will ride better. Thanks to compression straps that create a package that fits closer to your back, an internal frame pack will also carry small loads more conveniently.

When it comes time to choose an internal frame pack, your most important consideration is fit. Although some manufacturers claim that their packs will adjust to "fit all," this is simply not the case. Shoulder straps, waist belts, and pack tapers vary. Hikers who don't have average builds—thin hikers, stout hikers, women, and small men—will find that they get excellent fits in some models and mediocre fits in others. Try several.

In addition, remember that some pack designers don't go to the drawing board with the public in mind. They design for themselves. The way a zipper opens, how pockets attach to the pack, and the very shape of the pack itself—slim and tapered or square and roomy—often represent the designer's opinion about how gear should be loaded and carried. Naturally, the designer's opinion may not be similar to your own. So, besides testing a pack for comfort, try loading and unloading it with clothes, a tent, and cooking equipment. Does the pack accommodate gear easily? Buy the pack that fits your needs.

HANDY ITEMS FOR THE TRIP

Swiss Army Knife: 100 Years of Service

The year 1984 marked the 100th birthday of the venerable Swiss army knife, the knife with so many gadgets that it's like a mini tool chest. New York's Museum of Modern Art has acclaimed the jumbo version, which has 15 separate blades and features tucked into one compact five-ounce package.

The man credited with inventing the direct ancestor of the knife is Carl Elsener, who founded the firm, Victorinox, in the Swiss Alps in 1884. His first success was a pocketknife good enough for the Swiss army. In 1897 he patented a knife that opened on both sides, contained six separate blades, and which required only two springs.

So was born what Victo-rinox, now owned and run by a third generation of Elseners, calls its officer's knife. It comes in 98 variations, priced from $8 to more than $50, depending on size and features. It is the most popular of the 250 different pocketknives produced by the firm.

The company sells a million Swiss army knives annually in the United States alone. It produces approximately 15,000 Swiss army knives and 24,000 other assorted knives on a daily basis.

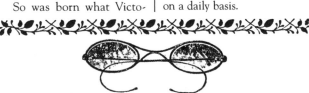

Don't Leave Home Without It

A small applicator of superglue is smaller than a pocketknife, weighs a fraction of an ounce, and can fix rod guides, sunglasses, and scores of other outdoor paraphernalia. Keep a dispenser with you. If you ever have an accident with prescription glasses, you'll be glad to have it with you.

SURVIVAL FOOD

A well-stocked survival kit can mean the difference between an uncomfortable situation and a life-threatening one. Now, the Amway Corporation has come up with an important addition to your survival kit: Nutrilite snack bars. These provide 100 percent of the required daily allowance of all vitamins and 100 percent of the minerals iodine and iron. Each serving also provides 15 to 20 percent of protein and 30 percent each of calcium, phosphorus and magnesium requirements.

A serving usually consists of two bars sealed in an airtight, watertight foil pouch weighing 2½ ounces. The bars are high in calories (around 300 per serving), a plus in a survival situation.

Nutrilite snack bars come in different flavors: peanut butter, raisin and honey, cocoa almond, creamy almond, maple and fruit, and apple cinnamon.

Animal Repellent

Campers and camp owners are often plagued with stray dogs and wildlife—bears, raccoons, skunks—getting into the trash.

To prevent this, try spraying or sprinkling full-strength household ammonia on the trash container or bag.

REPAIR IT WITH MONO

Monofilament can be used to repair many camp items, from backpack to tent or trailer. It is strong, quite easy to work with, and can be wound around many broken items, even some fairly large ones. In fact, when I coupled it with a two-shot epoxy, I have even repaired a broken chair leg on a campstool. The mono is simply wrapped around and around the broken part and then the glue is worked deeply into the patch. The mono and glue, when properly bonded, will make a good temporary repair until more permanent fixing can be made.

BAKING SODA USES

Common baking soda has a variety of practical uses outdoors.

When camping, it pays to have a box on hand. Baking soda is an excellent toothpaste substitute, and it can be used as an antacid by mixing half a teaspoon in a cup of water. Or you can form a paste with it for insect bites. Used as a foot powder, baking soda will keep feet dry and prevent blisters.

For the angler, baking soda works well as a deodorizer. Scrub your cooler out with soda to eliminate odors, and

leave a little in the cooler to keep it fresh. Rinsing hands with soda after cleaning fish will remove the odor.

When storing canteens or RV water containers, sprinkle in a little baking soda to avoid stale odors that sometimes collect in them.

If you still have any left after all these applications, you can use it for baking.

Pocket-Sized Survival

A hiker once turned up missing. On the third day a search was started. It had been drizzling steadily for those three days, with the temperature hovering around the 30°F mark the whole time. Late in the evening they found him— cold, wet, suffering from exposure and hunger, and very close to death. He had grown up in the area yet somehow became lost.

The more time you spend in the outdoors, the greater the chance of finding yourself in such a survival situation. Being prepared can make the difference between surviving or not. Assemble and carry a well stocked survival kit that can be made from household items. Inside a tin or plastic box that is small enough to fit in your pocket, place the following: wooden matches in a waterproof container or a small butane lighter; cottonballs in a sandwich bag (for tinder); a thick candle; instant soup or bouillon cubes; some sort of concentrated food or candy bars; a small folding knife; a small compass; Band-Aids; several feet of heavy fishing line (20- or 30-pound test); a selection of fishhooks and one or two jigs or flies.

You can add a survival instruction booklet, a field guide to edible plants, a snake-bite kit, and aluminum foil.

Versatile Trash Bags

I've been carrying a box of plastic trash bags in the trunk of my car ever since I had to change a tire on muddy ground. Now when changing a tire, I spread one on the ground to keep my clothing clean and dry.

Other good uses: Cut a hole in the top and sides for your head and arms, and you have an emergency raincoat. Put your fish in one, tie the top, and you won't get fish smell all over the trunk of your car. Put muddy boots in a bag to protect the interior of your car.

You will find a hundred other uses for those handy trash bags—if you have them with you.

Lighter for Safety

A cigarette lighter is a handy item to have outdoors. Modern anglers and backpackers usually carry matches in a weatherproof containers, but they are often hard to light in wet or windy weather. That's when an ordinary disposable lighter comes in handy. These throwaway butane lighters are very reliable, and some even have an adjustable flame control, enabling you to light a fire when the weather is windy.

BEAR REPELLENT

Outdoorsmen threatened by bears may have a new means of protecting themselves without harming the animals. Lynn Rogers, a wildlife researcher with the U.S. Forest Service, has discovered that a well-known repellent could prevent tragic camper/bear confrontations. It is capsaicin spray, used by mail carriers to repel overly aggressive dogs.

Although the spray has been tested previously on several species of caged bears, Rogers focused on free-ranging black bears that were attracted by bait. They rubbed their eyes and retreated after being sprayed. Indeed, they stayed away for several days.

Rogers is a former mailman in Grand Rapids, Michigan, and he had used the spray to control aggressive dogs. To-day, he is one of the most renowned black bear researchers in North America. His work, initiated in 1969, is the longest ongoing black bear research project ever undertaken.

It is important to be aware of the limitations of the spray. It *must* hit an eye to be effective, and it has a typical range of *only* three to six meters. Rogers reports that most bears approached him from downwind, which gave the spray additional range.

Although the U.S. Forest Service does not endorse any specific product, this repellent may be a worthwhile purchase for anyone involved in outdoor activity in bear country. Capsaicin sprays are generally available from sporting goods and government surplus stores.

RABIES REMINDERS

Rabies has reached epidemic proportions throughout much of the country, particularly in the heavily populated states. Typical carriers are raccoons and skunks, but woodchucks, bats, foxes, and even white-tailed deer have been implicated, along with domestic dogs, cats, and livestock. Here are some common-sense tips:

• Make sure all pets and working dogs have up-to-date rabies shots.
• Avoid unknown dogs and cats.
• Don't let dogs and cats run loose in areas where rabies is reported.
• License your dogs so they can be identified if they stray.
• Report any strange-acting animal to police or game commission.
• Never handle a wild animal even though it seems normal. It could be incubating the disease.
• If bitten by any animal, wash the wound thoroughly with soap and water and see a doctor immediately. If the animal is a pet, confine it for 10 days to see if rabies develops. If the animal is wild, try to destroy it so its brain tissue can be examined.
• Wear gloves and use tongs or a shovel to remove any dead animal from your property.

Cutting Board in Bear Country

When in bear country, bring along a square of Plexiglas™ to use as a cutting board. Plastic does not retain blood or food odors after proper washing. It should be packed away every day, along with all camp food. Plexiglas is light and can be cut with a hacksaw to any size. The cutting board can also be used as a drawing board or a convenient surface for writing letters. A good way to avoid splinters in your soup, too.

OUTDOOR CANS

Today the supermarket shelves are filled with cans of every size and shape with reusable plastic lids that are suitable for worms and countless other things:

COFFEE CANS: The reusable plastic lid has made the coffee can a treasure. By saving cans in different sizes (from one pound up to five) you'll have a complete outdoor canister set for storing flour, sugar, coffee, and other staples at camp.

Coffee cans can also be used to hold face soap, dish soap, washcloths and small towels, or any other small gear you want to keep dry. Toilet paper in a coffee can will be kept clean and dry even if stored outside. Pack all small kitchen goods in coffee cans to keep them organized.

INSTANT-COFFEE CANS: Cans of imported coffees offer a variety of new sizes and shapes. The rectangular cans will hold three small spice cans. They can be used in tackleboxes to hold weights, leaders, lures, hooks, or other loose gear.

SMOKELESS-TOBACCO CANS: These small, flat cans have been used by anglers for generations to hold leaders, flies, hooks, weights—just about anything carried in a tacklebox or fishing vest. These cans are also great for keeping extra fuses and small lights for vehicles and trailers.

How to Handle a Vacuum Bottle

Many sports lovers keep a stainless-steel vacuum bottle close at hand when afield or afloat. The bottle will keep drinks hot or cold, and it will not break as a glass bottle will. All vacuum bottles are awkward to handle, especially when you're wearing gloves. The handy steel vacuum can be made even handier, however, if you fix a handle on it.

This can be made from a thin piece of aluminum or stainless steel. Put the strip in a vise and bend into a handle. Use automobile hose clamps to secure the handle to the bottle. Make sure to keep the screw clamps facing up so there will be less chance of them denting the bottle if dropped.

The Indispensable Cork

One of the handiest items to have when you are outdoors is a supply of different-sized, ordinary corks:

• Campers find them a great emergency substitute for caps lost off canteens, insect repellent bottles, etc.
• Trappers hollow them out to hold bait, then wedge them near sets.
• Hikers burn them to make trail markings.
• Corks make great emergency fishing floats when sliced halfway through so line can be slipped in, then held in place with a toothpick or twig.
• Dry corks burn fiercely, so they make ready fire-starters used whole, shaved, or broken in pieces.
• Corks in a tacklebox serve as hook holders or as hook guards, preventing dulling and injury, when placed on hooks.
• A tiny cork hung from light fishing line on a branch is a good wind-direction indicator.
• A little quick carving or sanding can transform small corks into effective bass and panfish poppers.
• Corks can be used as temporary plugs for punctures in plastic water jugs, boats, etc.
• A cork comes in handy when you drop a lantern filler plug in a snowbank.

SURVIVAL FISHING KIT

Anyone spending time in the outdoors should carry a survival kit that includes gear to catch fish for food. A simple kit should contain a few hooks of various sizes and styles, maybe a couple of trout flies (Woolly Worm patterns in size 6 or 8 are excellent choices), 10 feet of monofilament line of at least 10-pound test and some rubber bands.

These items will fit nicely inside a 35mm-film container, which can double as a float. Just wrap the rubber band around it to secure it to the fishing line.

Burn Classifications

First-aid kits usually provide directions for the treatment of first-, second-, and third-degree burns. However, do you know what each is? Here are the official classifications:

First—The outer skin is reddened and slightly swollen.

Second—The underskin is affected, and blisters form.

Third—The skin is destroyed, and tissues underneath are damaged.

Learn these so you can identify each and administer the proper treatment.

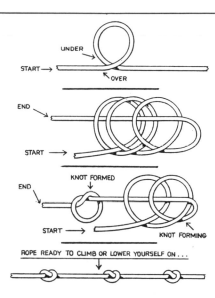

ROPE READY TO CLIMB OR LOWER YOURSELF ON . . .

MONKEY ROPE

A 20- or 30-foot length of climbing rope can be an asset on trips in country not totally familiar to me.

I am not an accomplished climber, so I do not, as I would suggest you don't, attempt scaling sheer cliffs. But a 10- or 15-foot drop-off or steep incline can easily be traversed by utilizing a climbing rope. Since I do not have the greatest hand strength in the world, I use a knotted rope. Knots tied every two feet or so make it much easier to lower or raise equipment and afford a much better hand grip.

Tying knots every two feet in a 20- or 30-foot length of rope can be a tedious and monotonous task, so try this:

Lay your rope out its full length. Allow approximately four feet for securing to a tree, rock, etc. Grasp the rope in each hand, make a circle approximately eight inches in diameter by looping the rope portion in your *right hand under* the portion of rope in your *left hand.* An eight-inch loop will, when the rope is ready for climbing, leave you with knots 24 inches apart.

Continue the procedure until you have looped the entire rope, stacking each new loop atop the preceding ones.

Thread the rope end in your right hand through the center of all the loops. Holding all the loops together with your right hand including the starting end, take the end of the rope running through the loops, and with your left hand begin slowly pulling the entire length of the rope through the loops. You will see the knots forming on the rope as you pull it tight.

POLYPAPER PADS

If you are an angler who occasionally likes to jot down a note or two, or if you write a full report for your outdoor log after each outing, you will be interested in polypaper notebooks. They contain totally synthetic pages on which you can even write underwater. I've used them for several seasons now and have found them to be nothing short of fantastic. No amount of rain, snow, or sleet prevents you from taking notes or destroys them once written.

The pages can be written on with pen or pencil. These pads cost a little more than regular notebooks, but you can erase and reuse them if you have written in pencil. They can also be quite handy for canoeists, rafters, backpackers, or anyone else who needs to take notes in the field.

They are available through many different scientific supply houses.

LOOSE TABLE

Because of space restrictions, campers often take folding bridge tables on their trips. Unfortunately, these are so light that if you don't remember to add ballast (a well-placed rock), the first time a gust of wind blows through the campground the table upsets.

Solve this problem by carrying along two three-foot-long steel rods and a roll of electrical tape. After setting the table up, drive the rods into the ground alongside two of the table's legs at opposite corners. Secure legs to rods with several wraps of electrical tape.

When you break camp, remove the tape, knock out the rods, and store them for your next trip.

Twist Ties

A handful of twist ties belongs in everyone's pocket or pack. The cores of these common household objects are thin, strong, malleable wires that can be a big help in minor emergencies.

Peel the paper off and the wire can be used as a substitute for a screw missing from your eyeglasses. A few quick twists and you've got a temporary fix for the line guide that's falling off your favorite rod. The ties are also helpful in clearing a clogged generator on your stove or lantern.

Keeping Warm with a Space Blanket

A valuable item of camping equipment that has been on the market for some time is called a space blanket. Mine looks like a 7 × 4-foot piece of aluminum foil and weighs about two ounces. It can easily be folded and tucked into a jacket pocket.

In cold weather the space blanket can be placed on top of an air mattress or ground cushion to reflect the body's heat. I have used mine in 20°F temperatures on top of an inflated rubber mattress, and it felt like an electric blanket radiating heat. It should not be used on top of your sleeping bag at very low temperatures, however, because moisture will condense under the space blanket and saturate the bag.

In summer where sweating isn't a critical problem, the foil can be used as a lightweight emergency blanket or rain shelter. Once while I was camping, a thunderstorm flattened my tent, but I stayed warm and relatively dry by covering up with my space blanket.

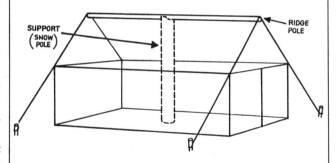

TENT SNOW POLE

Hunters and campers in snow country often fail to prepare for unexpected snow. The result is a lot of work in setting them up again. Sometimes the tent is badly damaged.

To minimize the likelihood of a snow collapse, install a 5- or 6-inch-diameter snow pole under the ridgepole when you leave the tent. It will hold a much greater snow load.

Reusable Plastic Containers

Reusable plastic containers— even big buckets and jugs— are free for the asking from most small businesses that use them.

Restaurants now buy all their cooking oil in 5- or 10- gallon containers. When cleaned with detergent, these make excellent water jugs for camping or all-day fishing trips. Restaurants also receive many food items in five-gallon buckets. These have reseal- able, watertight lids and pro- vide convenient storage for cameras and other gear need- ing protection from water. They also make fine seats around a camp.

Many businesses dispose of these containers in the daily garbage. A friendly conversa- tion with the manager will usually put you on to all the plastic containers you can use.

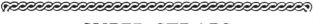

SUPER STRAPS

Straps, versatile and quick to use, are replacing ordinary ropes in many situations. The best are made of heavy nylon webbing with tough buckles. You can choose between cam action buckles and quick- release ones (these have a "push-button" release), and various lengths are available.

Creative lovers of the out- doors customize their straps by simply sewing one end of a webbing strip to the type of buckle they want. Ready-made straps can be purchased at many outdoor stores. Because straps are popular with rafters, a whitewater boating shop or mail-order house is a reliable source.

The most obvious use for straps is to fasten down gear, which they do admirably well. Cam-action buckles are best for this task. Straps have long been used to fasten gear to

rafts to prevent loss of equip- ment in case of an upset; boaters now also use them for strapping rafts to trailers, gear to the backs of pickup trucks, and tarps over the loads of roof racks. Rowing frames can be secured to the raft's D-rings with short, heavy straps.

In camp try suspending a lantern from a tripod created by strapping three oars or poles together. Straps can hang tarps from convenient trees. When the weather turns cold, ropes can be hard to un- tie, but straps open at the touch of a thumb.

Bamboo Tent Bottom

Bamboo beach mats serve as an excellent flooring for a tent bottom. The mats help insu- late one from cold ground and moisture but allow for the pas- sage of air. A bonus is that the mats can be unfurled any- where along the trail or next to a campfire as an instant lounging surface. Mats can be purchased at beach areas, lakes, or sporting goods stores.

Quick Emergency Repair

There is a quick-fix product on the market that is not only strong, flexible, and water- proof, but also inexpensive and easy to use. It will help repair anything from torn waders to leaky canoes, and fits easily into a coat pocket or tacklebox. Its use is not lim- ited to outdoor problems.

The magic cure is none other than ordinary duct tape, the kind sold for less than a dollar per 60-foot roll in most plumbing and hardware stores. Just apply to a clean, dry surface and smooth out any bubbles that may form.

Duct tape will last long enough to let you finish a trip or until permanent repairs can be made. It takes only a matter of a second to apply it.

CONVERTING GEAR FOR FIELD USE

HAT STRINGS

There's nothing so aggravating as a hat that blows off in the wind or gets knocked off in the brush. And there's no hat in the world that is more susceptible to this than a hiker's favorite felt crusher.

There's a simple way to moor such a hat, and it doesn't get in the way when you don't need the hat tied down.

When you buy a new hat, use a paper punch to make holes in the inside leather band, just ahead of each ear.

Now cut two feet of cord. Use old flyline; it could just as well be nylon string or leather bootlace. (You can buy your hat oversized, and thick lace will make it fit. Later, when the hat gets wet and shrinks, use thinner cord, and it will be sure to fit again.)

Run one end of the cord through a hole in the band, tuck it under the band, and run it around back to the other side. Pull it through the other hole and out until the two ends are equal in length. Now double the two loose ends back on themselves and tuck them, also, around the back of the band.

The hat strings will stay right where they are, neatly tucked out of the way, until you need to tie them under your chin to keep the hat on.

A Reminder

When wearing glasses afield, it's a good idea to get an elastic cord or band that fastens across the back of your head. On a boat, for example, glasses can fall off while you lean out over the water to land a fish. Losing your glasses while in the field can turn a memorable trip into a disaster.

Easy-Pour Water Can

Large five-gallon plastic cans are popular water containers for camping, but are heavy and bulky. To make pouring easier, place the can in the center of a section of an old tire. The container can then be rocked forward with one hand for pouring, leaving the other hand free to hold cup, pan or other receptacle. When finished, just let go and the can will rock back into place.

Use a hacksaw with a fresh blade to cut the tire section. Most tires have a small core of about 12 steel wires near the inside rim. These must be severed before you can cut through the tire.

Anchor the can to the back of the tire with a piece of rope to stop it from tilting too far forward when pouring.

Simple Food Security For Backpackers

As legions of campers in wilderness areas have learned the hard way, bears, raccoons, and other wildlife can short-circuit an otherwise carefully planned trip by ravaging food supplies. The standard advice is to suspend food at least 10 feet aboveground and four or more feet from the nearest post, tree trunk, or limb.

The problem is: How do you achieve such security? Wet trees and rope that tends to bind on bark, a precarious climb, and also the difficulty of lifting even a moderate amount of foodstuffs to the proper height can all be frustrating impediments. Including three or four small pulleys and slick nylon rope in your camping gear will overcome these obstacles.

Experienced backpackers normally carry rope anyway, and suitable pulleys made of lightweight plastic and metal alloys constitute no appreciable extra burden for load-conscious campers.

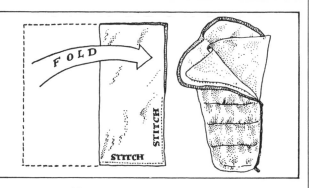

Sleeping Bag Sheet Liner

While many sleeping bags provide comfort against extremely cold conditions, the clammy feel of an unlined nylon bag is unpleasant. Prevent it with a simple cotton liner, easily made from a common flat twin-sized sheet.

Just fold the sheet lengthwise and sew the bottom and halfway up the side.

Unzip the bag, install the liner so the half-sewn side is on the zipper side of the bag, and then rezip the bag. That's all there is to it.

The sheet liner can be removed for cleaning and when you're airing out the bag. The weight the liner adds is minor and more than worth it.

CRYSTAL CLEAR

To protect your wristwatch when hiking in thick cover, paint the crystal with clear fingernail polish. Tiny scratches that normally accrue from contact with brush will affect only the coating, leaving the glass unharmed. Wipe the polish off with remover when scratches become noticeable.

SURVIVAL SAW

You can make a pair of compact saws for backpacking and such by locking a standard 21- or 23-inch bucksaw replacement blade in a vise and snapping it in half.

With each half, snap the teeth off the first three inches of one end and then slip a piece of three-eighths-inch automotive fuel hose over it as a grip. A sheath can be made from a scrap of leather or canvas. This is a very efficient, nearly unbreakable tool.

TIGHTENING AXHEADS

Soaking an axhead in water will swell the wooden handle—but only temporarily. As the handle dries out, the head will loosen again. Instead, rough up the end grain of the handle (where it shows through the eye of the head) with sandpaper. Then soak the end with several coats of Chair-Loc, available at hardware stores. The syrupy liquid, intended for tightening loose rungs of chairs, will swell the handle, effectively locking the head into place.

FLASHLIGHT LIGHTS

The dilemma is how to find the flashlight in the dark, when you most need it. Paint a band of glow-in-the-dark paint around it. Half-ounce bottles can be found at arts-and-crafts or hobby stores. A little goes a long way, but do not paint anything else with it, or you may reach for a desperately needed light and get a handful of something else. Also, avoid getting this stuff on your clothes or other fabric, since the glow never seems to fade.

GLOW IN THE
DARK PAINT

Pickups and Pulleys

When you're cutting heavy firewood on steep hillsides, lack of vehicle access is often a major problem. Sporting people don't usually carry powered winches to drag log segments down or up to an existing road. But you can turn your truck into a lightweight tractor.

Take along 100 to 200 feet of three-eighths-inch steel cable and two or three heavy pulleys. If the narrow mountain road won't let you get a straight-line pull at the log, rig one or more pulleys to angled stumps or trees, route the cable accordingly, and before you know it, that immovable log will be on or near the road, ready for cutting and easy loading.

To double your pulling power on heavy log segments, set one pulley on the log itself, then fix the cable end to a solid point—the old block-and-tackle principle used horizontally. It helps to have your pickup at least partly loaded with wood for better traction.

Pocket-Sized Repair

Have you ever been stuck with a hole in the knee or elbow, or missing a button? Well, a matchbook can be transformed into a small sewing kit.

First cut the matches from the book. Now cut notches along the edges of the back side of the book. Make a small slit up the notches on one side. Wrap thread around the notches in the sizes, colors, and amounts needed. Secure the loose end of each kind of thread in the slits.

Next, cut a small patch of cloth and glue it to the upper half of the matchbook. This is a pincushion for needles and safety pins.

Place the kit in the pocket of your favorite field shirt or jacket until the next time you are 50 miles from nowhere with a torn shirt or pantleg.

Binocular Hold-downs

If you like to carry a pair of binoculars on your backpacking trips or while hunting, you've probably experienced the discomfort of having them bounce on your chest at every step. When you are crouching, or crawling during a stalk, they swing and flop, and may hit the ground.

A remedy is the kind of harness used by professional photographers. These devices usually have a shoulder strap and a chest strap, with the camera held in place by Velcro, or flexible bands. Remove the standard neck strap from the binoculars, and install the harness as on a camera.

Cooler Coolers

Most ice chests and coolers are red, blue, or green, colors that don't reflect the sun's rays; sooner or later, all that expensive ice and food will melt, thaw, and spoil. Parking the cooler in the shade isn't enough. Invariably, that once-shady spot will be the hottest and sunniest place around by the time you return.

On your next trip pack along a large white beach towel and an old white tablecloth. Before leaving in the morning, soak them in water. Cover the cooler with the towel first and then the tablecloth under the corners so a breeze won't blow it off.

The now-white color will reflect the sun's rays, and the water in the towel will evaporate slowly, cooling the ice chest's surface. The principle is the same as that applied in those canvas water bags popular in the Southwest and in canvas and plastic fish creels.

COOLER CARE

• Freeze tap water in clean milk cartons; as it melts it will give you ice water to drink. Need more ice on your trip? Buy it in blocks and place in a sturdy plastic garbage bag; seal it before putting it in the cooler.
• Wash and dry your cooler before you fill it.
• When packing the cooler, put the ice in first. Stand cartons upright to reduce the chances of spills. Pack cold drinks next to the ice. Place bottled and tightly sealed items as props on the bottom layer. Place vegetables, fruits, etc., in waterproof containers or sealed plastic bags, then pack them as a second layer. Often-used items, such as butter, should form a top layer. Pack the cooler tight, but avoid forcing the lid.
• Much of the cold loss from a cooler takes place at the lid-to-body seal. If your cooler has a

cam latch in good condition, this is no problem. If not, use a short piece of rope around the cooler to keep the lid down so it will stay tight.
• Avoid opening and closing cooler unless necessary. Open it once, get all needed items out or in, and shut it again as quickly as possible.
• Keep the cooler in the shade or throw a sleeping bag over it.
• Use a cooler in winter to keep bottles, vegetables, etc., from freezing.
• Check your ice daily. At the same time drain any water that might have collected as the ice melted at the bottom of the cooler.
• Before storing, wash the cooler thoroughly. Then dampen a few paper towels with vinegar and wipe down the inside. This removes soap or scouring powder residue and leaves the cooler smelling sweet and fresh.

Over 75 percent of the earth's fresh water is locked in permanent ice fields.

GOING LIGHT

Camping gear was originally designed for use on mountaineering expeditions where fierce winds, bitter cold, and remote settings demand that equipment be practically bombproof. Not many of us take our gear to these rigorous limits, however, and our sore feet, bruised shoulders, and aching lower backs—all from carrying heavy packs through the wilderness—could do with less engineering.

Quite a few outdoor-gear manufacturers have begun to build equipment more suitable for shorter excursions in the type of summertime conditions in which most of us do our hiking and fishing.

To test the performance and durability of this lightweight gear, I recently assembled a complete outfit and took it on a hike over the Appalachian Trail. Below is a list of what I carried. Some of the items are self explanatory; others I'll comment upon, illustrating how a friend and I managed to reduce our usual 42- to 45-pound seven-day packs to a more pleasant 32 pounds.

My experiment began with the pack. I chose an Alpenlite Superlite for this test. Sewn from thin Ripstop nylon, it has a reinforced Cordura bottom (where most of the wear occurs) and smaller Fastex buckles and straps than those on a standard backpack. Holding 2600 cubic inches, it was large enough for all my gear

except the pad, which was strapped on. The Superlite shaved three pounds from the load that I usually carry on my back.

Likewise, I looked for a sleeping bag that would be warm but also light in weight. This meant choosing a down model over a man-made fiber one. The Marmot Ptarmigan that I took along, rated to about 5°F, saved me another pound. This bag also has a Gore-Tex cover, and I was able to stay dry even when our lean-to's roof leaked. The pad that complemented my bag was a Therm-A-Rest Ultralite. It was a pound lighter than the open cell model I had been using, and was far more compact when rolled up. In respect to finding a shelter, the choice was clear; a tarp. The Chouinard Pyramid is spacious, stable in the wind, and two to three pounds lighter than a tent with equal room.

I found a very fine stove. The Evernew Pack-In that we used is one of the lightest and most innovative around. It's really a burner head supported by tripod legs; folded down, it fits in the palm of your hand. It uses Husch Minigas cartridges, which in the 300-ml size burn for three and a half hours. The stove I tested boiled water in five to eight minutes, but it would also simmer well at low settings. The Evernew cut nearly one and a half pounds from the weight of the white-gas stove that I normally take with me.

Food came out of local grocery and health food stores, and by concentrating on dry mixes and carrying no fresh or canned food, we were able to keep our rations to two pounds per person per day.

What did these dozen odd pounds taken from our backs actually mean? Well, we hiked 10 to 13 miles a day, gaining and losing thousands of feet in elevation. By dinnertime my spine felt tired but not fused from the constant Neanderthaloid hunch one adopts when carrying a heavy soft pack. While on the trail I found a spring in my step, and the chance, even on the uphills, to admire the passing views.

How durable is this light gear? Frankly, some of it isn't as sturdy as standard backpacking equipment. For instance, the Alpenlite pack, made of Ripstop nylon, will not stand being dragged over rocks. However, I've used mine for six months now, hiking, mountaineering, and cross-country skiing, without putting a hole in it. The Marmot sleeping bag I used is every bit as well made as heavier bags, and the Pyramid tarp is as stout as a good tent. The Evernew stove is not designed to support a dutch oven; but it's good for two-quart camping pots.

Perhaps one of the most important concepts to keep in mind when trying to camp light is that it's the diligent pairing of a couple of ounces here and there which eventually takes 12 or 15 pounds off your back. Conversely, throwing in extras—food, clothing, first-aid items, and so on—quickly builds a load that may enhance your character but certainly not your fun.

Camping Gear
Pack—1 lb. 15 oz.
Sleeping Bag—2 lbs. 10 oz.
Pad—1 lb. 3 oz.
Shelter—2 lbs. 9 oz.
Stove—9 oz.
(windscreen, 2 oz.)
Fuel—4 cartridges, 2 lbs. 4 oz.
—2 lighters, 2 oz.

Cooking Gear
1-liter stainless-steel pot, 12 oz.
wooden bowl, 3.5 oz.
plastic cup, 2 oz.
plastic spoon, .5 oz.
1-liter plastic water bottle, 4 oz.
TOTAL WEIGHT CAMPING GEAR—
12 lbs. 12 oz.

First-Aid Kit and Toiletries
Moleskin, gauze, adhesive tape, iodine
for water purification, Chap Stick,
codeine, toothbrush, toothpaste, floss
TOTAL WEIGHT FIRST AID AND
TOILETRIES—11.5 oz.

Miscellaneous Gear
3 candles, 2 oz.
Swiss Army knife, 2 oz.
compass and maps, 1.5 oz.
headlamp and lithium battery, 9 oz.
1 notepad and 2 pens, 6 oz.
1 paperback novel, 8 oz.
FM2 with 35mm fl.4 lens, 2 lbs. 4 oz.
4 rolls film, 4 oz.
TOTAL WEIGHT MISCELLANEOUS
GEAR—4 lbs. 4.5 oz.

Clothes Carried For Inclement Weather
1 pair wool/nylon knicker socks, 3 oz.
pile cardigan, 1 lb. 10 oz.
silk balaclava, 1 oz.
hat, 2.5 oz.
wool liner gloves, 3 oz.
nylon overmitts, 2.5 oz.
coated nylon rainpants, 9 oz.
coated nylon rain anorak, 10 oz.
cotton T-shirt (for warm weather), 6.5 oz
TOTAL WEIGHT CLOTHES CARRIED—
3 lbs. 15.5 oz.

Food
I carried 10 lbs.
TOTAL WEIGHT OF PACK—32 lbs.

PACKING TIPS

Duffel Bag Packing Tips

Ever get tired of making countless trips from car to camp hauling pots, pans, charcoal, and other gear?

With a little planning, a GI duffel bag can accommodate a lot of cooking gear in just one trip. One bag, 12 inches in diameter and three feet long, can hold a dutch oven and lid; fry pans; a single-burner, bottled gas stove; a sack of charcoal, starter, and matches; a coffee pot and other cooking utensils—plus a grill.

The dutch oven lid should be placed in the bag first to prevent the sharp, pointed legs on the dutch oven from punching a hole in the bottom of the bag. Then stand the folded grill up in the middle of the bag. The sack of charcoal, the stove, and a bottle of gas go in next (on either side of the grill) along with the coffee pot. Fill small empty spaces with towels, hot pads, matches, starter fluid, and as many utensils as will fit.

The bag's shoulder strap frees hands to carry other items as well.

Cheap, lightweight bags are available, but the heavier, waterproof duck bags found in army/navy surplus stores last for years.

Sign in a sporting goods store: "Compasses—With Complete Directions"—

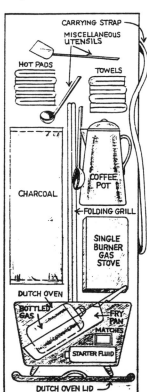

CAMPING BOXES

Minimize the risk of breaking glass containers on camping trips by packing them in impact-resistant boxes. These come in many different sizes, with compartments to fit everything from small jars to large bottles. Ask for them at your local food or liquor stores.

Raingear

Rain or a dunking in a lake or stream can spell disaster for the contents of leather or Cordura day packs.

To solve this problem, I simply pack all my gear in a rubber, waterproof sack such as those used by white water rafters, and stuff it into my day pack. Matches, socks, food, fire starters, and all the gear that you really don't need until you're soaking wet and far from camp will always be at your disposal, dry and ready to use.

Packing your poncho and a survival blanket between the contents of the bag-within-a-bag and your back will ensure a comfortable, dry carry.

Stuff It and Tape It

Large tents are a problem to transport and store. Even when folded they are heavy, bulky, and come with cumbersome poles and stakes. The best answer may well be the military duffel bag. A folded family-size tent will easily fit into one of these bags, including poles and stakes.

Duffels are made of a very heavy canvas that will not be damaged by either the poles and stakes inside or the elements outside. They close securely (may even be padlocked) and can be carried by a handle or a shoulder strap.

Tents supported by sectional aluminum poles often have another problem: The loops that hold the supporting poles have a tendency to slide, which causes the roof to sag. This can be solved by using adhesive tape to hold the loops in place. The tape will also keep the bows (the best knot to use when attaching the loops to the support) from coming untied. Taping the loops only takes a few minutes. time well spent. The duffel bag should have a pocket for storing tape as well as a stick of water-proofing wax.

A Convenient Tackle Caddy

For short fishing trips on familiar water, five-quart plastic ice-cream buckets make ideal tackle caddies. They are wide and deep enough to hold a flashlight and a can of bug repellent. You can keep them lidded in transit. They are reasonably stable. Hang a half-dozen lures along an inside edge and toss in some hooks and sinkers, a small whetstone, and a pair of pliers—and you'll have plenty of room left over for plastic worms and jigs, a sandwich, and other incidentals you'd like to include.

The earliest local weather map in the United States was compiled in February 1870 by the Cincinnati Weather Observatory. It used information from 31 weather stations in the east-central United States sent by Western Union.

THE ORDINARY TRUNK

An ordinary trunk can be of great benefit outdoors. In it you can carry extra food, a down-filled sleeping bag, a small stove, and utensils. Tools, first-aid and sewing kits, socks, boots, candles—the list is as long as the imagination or as short as you want it to be.

A trunk holds a great many essentials—all in one place, easy to get to, protected, and dry. They come in all sizes and price ranges.

Natural Refrigerator

Peat, or sphagnum, moss is usually found in compact green and purple mats along the banks of streams, the surface of the bogs, and around small lakes. It has long been valued for its sponge-like ability to retain water. Peat also has a preservative ability. Bodies recovered from peat bogs as long as 100 years after death were still in good shape.

The moss maintains a uniform temperature all year long and is often used as a natural refrigerator. Food will keep underground for long periods under the moss.

COOL A BALLOON

To keep the contents of an RV refrigerator in place, use toy balloons. They can be inflated to fit any size space. Close the neck of each balloon with a string tied in a bowknot; you can deflate them easily at the end of the trip for storage.

Balloons work better than empty bowls or cans because they can be adjusted to fit snugly and don't bounce and rattle around. If you can't get balloons, inflate plastic bags to different dimensions, tie them off, and push them in place in the refrigerator.

WATERPROOF MINIBAGS

Jumbo-sized toy balloons make excellent waterproof storage bags for camping, backpacking, and boating. They protect medical supplies, matches, and other important items from moisture. Roll the neck portion of a balloon down and insert the item. Unroll the neck and tie a loose knot in it to secure. Jumbo balloons are not hard to come by; they can be found in the toy section of most variety stores.

Make a Case for It

The transport of rods, whether in the back of a pickup or in the trunk of a car, carries with it a potential for possible damage. All quality fishing rods should be transported in a rod case.

Rod cases can be custom-made, inexpensively, from PVC plastic plumbing pipe. The smaller diameters are suitable for individual rods, while larger sizes can accommodate and store a number of rods. End caps are available. One end cap can be secured with glue and the other tethered. PVC pipe is reasonably priced and is available cut to the lengths you need in plumbing supply houses and also many hardware stores.

GEAR PROTECTOR

Don't throw away that old bedraggled sleeping pad.

Cut to fit and placed on a cooler, Ensolite™ helps make a comfortable camp stool, which has the added advantage of extra insulation.

A strip of Ensolite wrapped around a lantern provides protection for the glass.

Those who backpack will find it useful for padding pack frames, cameras, flashlights, binoculars, and other equipment that is easily broken.

Added as an insole to damp boots or shoes, Ensolite furnishes dry, extra comfort while hiking.

Due to its closed-cell construction, Ensolite keeps moisture away from gear while at the same time maintaining its cushioning effect.

TAKING THE DOG

EASY DOG BED

You can make an excellent beanbag dog bed with about two yards of vinyl plastic, some nylon netting, a 12-inch length of one-inch-wide fabric tape, and some plastic foam chips used in packaging. These will guarantee a dog bed that is waterproof, light-weight, insectproof, and easily cleaned. Furthermore, it floats, so if you throw it into the boat, you can use it as an emergency life preserver. Toss it into the back of a truck for a comfortable ride for the dog. It also serves as combined camp groundsheet and mattress.

First, using nylon net, make a bag long and wide enough for whatever size dog you have in mind. The netting can be purchased at any fabric department. Use at least a double thickness. Fill the net bag with enough plastic chips so that when flattened, it will keep the dog off the ground (no need to make it too bulky). Sew up the top of the bag. Use this to keep chips from escaping if the outer covering becomes torn. Spilled plastic chips are not biodegradable.

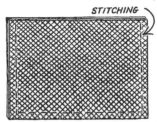

1. MAKE MESH BAG, LEAVING OPENING IN TOP.

2. FILL BAG WITH CHIPS. SEW UP OPENING.

3. HANDLE INSERTED BETWEEN 2 LAYERS OF VINYL FABRIC, SEW SIDE SEAMS AND HANDLE ENDS. TURN BAG INSIDE OUT.

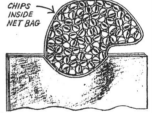

4. STUFF NET BAG INTO VINYL BAG, THEN SEW UP 6" OPENING.

Now make a second bag using heavy vinyl plastic. Sew the edges together, stitching in a carrying handle on one side (use the tape for this). Leave an opening about six inches long on one side. Turn right-side out. Insert the net bag filled with chips through that opening, then sew it up.

Variations: You get a sturdier (but not quite so easily cleaned) outer envelope if you use Ripstop nylon. Or you can use an old piece of tarpaulin or tent canvas. If the outer covering is strong enough, dispense with the inner net bag. For the carrying handle substitute a piece of rope.

DOG-TIRED

A comfortable air mattress bed for your dog can be easily made from an auto inner tube and an old blanket. Simply sew the blanket to form a bag, insert the tube into it, inflate until the cloth is drum tight, then release just enough air to form a soft bed with a hollow center. Tie the bag shut to finish. You can make a round, oval, or rectangular bed.

Heartworm Disease Is Spreading

Heartworm disease (dirofilariasis) in dogs, once common only in the southern United States and the Mississippi Basin, has spread northward and westward and is taking the lives of thousands of animals annually.

Mosquitoes transmit the disease from infected to healthy dogs. The heartworm larvae mature into adult worms, 10 to 14 inches long, in about 200 days. They collect in the dog's right heart chamber and major pulmonary blood vessels, and begin producing more microfilariae, which circulate in the bloodstream. The parasites increase the heart's work load and restrict the flow of blood to vital organs, eventually causing the dog's death.

Ridding a dog of heartworms is a lengthy, expensive, and extremely ticklish procedure. Two drugs must be given over a period of several days, and the dog must be kept inactive to give its body time to absorb the dead worms. If an improper dosage is administered, or if the dog exerts itself, worms may become dislodged and block the pulmonary artery, causing death.

The solution to the heartworm problem lies in prevention. First, a veterinarian must check a blood sample to make certain your dog is not infected. Then, for pennies a day, you can administer a preventative compound (diethylcarbamazine citrate) in wafer, pill, or liquid form throughout mosquito season that will keep your dog free of heartworms.

A *note of caution:* Before selling a dog, some unscrupulous dealers will give it a drug that temporarily clears the bloodstream of microfilariae but leaves adult worms in the heart. When the potential buyer has the dog tested, it appears to be free of heartworms. If you are planning to buy a dog from someone you don't know or whose reputation you cannot verify, ask your veterinarian to also run an antiheartworm antibody test.

Dog Health and Care

Many hazards threaten a dog's health. Learn to recognize the problems:

Distemper: Like influenza in humans, distemper is an airborne disease. There is grave danger from secondary invaders, which can cause pneumonia. If your dog loses its appetite and suddenly becomes sluggish, get it to a vet. It pays to have your dog immunized at a young age.

Worms: Hookworms, heartworms, whipworms, tapeworms, and roundworms all pose a threat. Americans have become so worm-conscious, however, that many young dogs are overdosed with worm medicine. Owners think that every time their dogs become indisposed, worms are the culprit. If you suspect worm infestation, take the dog to the vet.

Ear Mites: Clean ears are a sure sign of a healthy canine. However, cleaning the visible part of the ear doesn't always prevent infections or mite infestation, and a drug is needed to kill the mites. If your dog constantly works on his ears, consult a veterinarian.

Fleas and Ticks: Fleas and ticks are parasites that cannot be ignored. Fortunately, effective medications are available.

All About Dogs

The average dog owner spends more money each year on dog food than is spent to feed a prisoner in jail in the United States.

★

A Great Dane or Irish wolfhound eats about $800 in dog food each year, toy poodles about $120.

★

Perhaps the rarest dog in the world is the lowchen, or lion dog, of which only 52 were known to be alive some years ago. The breed was a famous lapdog of the nobility in southern Europe during the Renaissance.

★

The Canary Islands were not named after the popular little yellow birds, but after a large breed of dogs. The Latin name was *Insularia Canaria*—"island of dogs."

★

The Pilgrims brought two dogs on the *Mayflower*; a mastiff and a spaniel.

★

Dogs' teeth were used as money by Solomon Islands natives until the twentieth century.

★

Dogs were religious symbols at one time. Anubis, god of the Egyptians 25 centuries ago, and Tien Ken, heavenly dog of the Chinese, are two examples.

★

In cold climates, dogs such as the Chihuahua were used regularly as heating pads.

★

Ladies of fashion once "wore" dogs as important items of costume. Toy poodles, Pekingese, and other small breeds were especially popular.

★

Dogs often have been used as political party mascots. For example, the keeshond symbolized the Patriots Party in eighteenth-century Holland.

★

For centuries it was traditional for the Dalai Lama of Tibet to honor members of the Manchu Dynasty by giving them Lhasa apso terriers.

Dequilling a Dog

Anyone who spends much time with a dog in the outdoors will sooner or later face the problem of pulling porcupine quills from its nose and mouth.

Removing them with pliers is extremely painful to the dog because the quills are embedded, like fishhooks.

A much better way is to make a solution of one cup of vinegar and two teaspoons of baking soda. Shake the solution well, then apply it gently on the protruding quills. Wait several minutes and repeat the application. Quills are composed of lime and calcium, and the solution softens and shrinks them. They can then be removed without pain to the dog.

The keenest-scenting animals can detect odors diluted to one molecule in 10 trillion parts of air.

POOCH FLOTATION DEVICE

There's no doubt that a good-quality PFD—personal flotation device—is a vital piece of boating gear. Yet, not even in the Coast Guard's "Federal Regulations Requiring Personal Flotation Devices" will you find the Pooch Flotation Device. It was designed for dogs that accompany their masters on boats, particularly on rafts bound for white water—even though water dogs such as Labradors and spaniels can't swim through big waves and suckholes.

To make a PFD for your dog, take an ordinary Type II kapok life vest and reverse it over the

dog's body, so that the flotation is on the back side. This way, the vest won't interfere with the traditional dog paddle, yet it will provide the additional flotation a dog may need in heavy waters.

Does it work? A Lab survived a tumble overboard into the Devil's Staircase Rapid, a wild stretch of the Rogue River, thanks to the Pooch Flotation Device. Incidentally, having a dog wear his own PFD provides a fine example to children who may be unhappy about having to wear their own.

PROTECTED PORCUPINE

One of the earliest examples of conservation in this country involved the porcupine.

Since the animal could easily by killed with a stick or a rock, American Indians and pioneer woodsmen avoided killing the prickly varmints except when in extreme need, letting them thrive and multiply as a readily available emergency food supply on the hoof.

Antifreeze Poisoning

Ethylene glycol, used in automobile antifreeze, is a deadly poison not only to humans but also to pets. Even a small amount will result in agonizing death. As little as 1½ to 2 teaspoons will kill a cat, and one-third to one-half cup is all that is needed to kill a 40-pound pointer.

Its pleasant odor and sweet taste actually draw animals to it. When ethylene glycol is ingested, its toxic compounds attack the animal's bloodstream and kidneys, causing vomiting, kidney pains and mouth sores, before death comes. Take victims to the vet at once.

When flushing a car radiator, take precautions to prevent animals from coming into contact with the fluid. Do not simply open the cock valve and let the old antifreeze run down the driveway. Flush it away immediately.

PREP YOUR VEHICLE

Camping in a Mini Pickup

Camping in a mini pickup has some disadvantages over camping in a full-sized truck. A little preplanning can help ameliorate those inconveniences, though.

The first thing to consider is the length of the box. I spent extra dollars for a seven-foot bed. Not only does the extra foot allow me to stretch out to sleep, it also increases storage space and allows for convenient transportation of long fishing rods.

A custom-built topper is the next thing to think about. I ordered mine with a door and an awning window on each side. The doors make it easy to reach equipment in the front of the box. They are especially convenient when canoe or boat tie-downs prevent opening the tailgate door. I prefer awning windows to sliding windows because they can be left open for ventilation during a rain. Screen can be taped over the window with duct tape.

Two campers cannot sleep comfortably between the wheel wells of a mini pickup unless they are extremely friendly. To solve this problem I cut a one-half-inch sheet of 4 × 8-foot plywood to the length of my pickup box. When off camping, I place a snow tire in the front of the box and the spare tire in the back. The plywood then spans the wheel wells and the tires, providing plenty of room for two adults to sleep comforta-

bly. Since the plywood is four feet wide and the truck bed is five feet wide, there is ample room on each side to allow for access to the gear stored under the plywood.

I recommend purchasing a topper that is at least 40 inches high from the bed of the box. That allows enough headroom for sleeping and changing clothes. Some fiberglass toppers are produced in a tapered design, which decreases wind resistance and increases passenger headroom.

There are other options available for a topper. A built-in boat carrier is well worth the added expense. One item I decided to do without was a sliding rear window. The cost of replacing the rear window in the truck was not worth the added cost.

You may experience problems with condensation dripping from the ceiling of an aluminum topper whenever the outside temperature drops into the 30s. I suspect that a fiberglass topper would be less susceptible to condensation. In any case, insulation could eliminate the problem.

WATCH THOSE TIRES

Nothing is quite as terrifying as trying to maintain control of a big RV or trailer when a tire explodes at highway speed. Nevertheless, most tire blowouts are preventable.

It only takes a few minutes to inflate tires to the proper pressure. The only problem is that nobody can seem to remember just what the proper inflation pressure is. The answer is found right on the tire itself: Printed on the sidewall, in small type near the rim, are the manufacturer's specifications. You will find the maximum inflation pressure listed there. All you have to do is pump up the tires to the recommended pressure.

As an example, the small tires on a pop-up trailer may be 80 pounds per square inch (psi), a big motor home can be up to 125 psi, and a car or light truck is usually about 35 psi.

The benefits of using correct tire pressures are many. For example, a "hard" tire undergoes less flexing, which causes friction that generates heat and literally cooks a tire. The load-carrying capacity is also increased, and, as a bonus, you get better gas mileage and longer tire life (less flexing again) with the appropriate air pressure in your tires.

While you're down there checking your tires, take out the wrench and check those lug nuts. As bad as a blowout is, it's even worse to see one of your tires pass you by on the highway.

BUG CURTAINS

If your RV is without screen doors and windows and you're in hot insect country, don't resign yourself to sweltering inside a closed camper. An effective bug screen can be made by cutting plastic sheeting (or other very thin fabric) into strips an inch or two wide. Hang the strips close together to form a kind of shredded curtain over the opening. The faintest breeze will stir and flutter the strips. It seems to frighten insects off while also admitting cool air into the RV.

Roll out the Carpet

If you do much off-road driving, buy an old rug and cut two 10-foot strips 18 inches wide from its unworn edges. Roll these strips up and stow them with your gear. When you have trouble negotiating a stretch of soft dirt, sand, or ice, push the strips under the rear wheels to provide traction.

Protection from Floor Rust

Moisture trapped under the floor mats of vehicles leads to premature floor rusting.

To overcome this, take the floor mats out and remove all rust from the floor. Apply several coats of primer, then a coat or two of metal paint.

After the paint has dried, put down either carpet-top rubber link or fabric-tire doormats (available at most hardware stores). These mats allow any moisture on the floor to evaporate quickly and are easy to remove for cleaning.

RULES OF THE ROAD

As sporting people travel across the country in search of fish or game, they are confronted with a host of rules and regulations: a 55-mph speed limit, a No Smoking sign, the seat belt law. A hundred years ago, however, the rules were considerably different. Here is how Wells Fargo asked passengers to conduct themselves in its stagecoaches:

Adherence to the following rules will ensure a pleasant trip for all.

1. Abstinence from liquor is requested, but if you must drink, share the bottle. To do otherwise makes you appear selfish and unneighborly.

2. If ladies are present, gentlemen are urged to forgo smoking cigars and pipes as the odor of same is repugnant to the Gentle Sex. Chewing tobacco is permitted, but spit with the wind, not against it.

3. Gentlemen must refrain from the use of rough language in the presence of ladies and children.

4. Buffalo robes are provided for your comfort during cold weather. Hogging the robes will not be tolerated and the offender will be made to ride with the driver.

5. Don't snore loudly while sleeping or use your fellow passenger's shoulder for a pillow; he (or she) may not understand and friction may result.

6. Firearms may be kept on your person for use in emergencies. Do not fire them for pleasure or shoot at wild animals as the sound riles the horses.

7. In the event of runaway horses, remain calm. Leaping from the coach in panic will leave you injured, at the mercy of the elements, hostile Indians, and hungry coyotes.

8. Forbidden topics of discussion are stagecoach robberies and Indian uprisings.

9. Gents guilty of unchivalrous behavior toward lady passengers will be put off the stage. It's a long walk back. A word to the wise is sufficient.

TRAILER TIP

Just as it's important to carry a spare tire for your boat trailer, it's equally important to have an extra set of trailer bearings tucked away in the trunk of your car. Chances are you may never need them, but it's comforting to know that, should the unlikely happen, you won't have to suffer the time and expense of looking for parts.

Also, to lessen the chance of a bearing breakdown, it's good policy to clean and regrease your trailer bearings and wheels before storing the boat for the winter. This removes any water accumulation that might otherwise rust or corrode the bearings.

Securing Trailer Safety Chains

There is an easy way to prevent the safety chains on a trailer tongue from dragging on the road and possibly coming unhooked: Get two long rubber canvas stretching straps. Hook one end of a strap to the center of each safety chain. Pull the other back under the trailer body and fasten to convenient frame members. Chains snubbed in this manner are still free to move, yet they do not rattle, drag, or come unhooked.

Bumper Jack Hoist

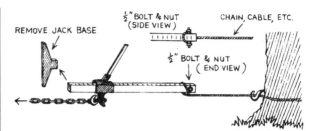

REMOVE JACK BASE ½" BOLT & NUT (SIDE VIEW) CHAIN, CABLE, ETC.

½" BOLT & NUT (END VIEW)

ROPE, CHAIN, OR CABLE TO LOG, GAME ANIMAL, VEHICLE, OR OTHER DEAD WEIGHT.

As an emergency or do-it-yourself hoist, an old-fashioned car bumper jack works great. Remove the jack base, drill the upper end of the jack shaft, and insert a large nut and bolt. With a tow chain or strap wrapped and hooked around this bolt and another looped over the main jack hook, you've got a horizontal or vertical hoist that can easily lift or drag 1000 pounds or more of dead weight in 30-inch surges.

These old jacks are great in a pinch for a variety of jobs, including unsticking bogged vehicles, moving heavy firewood logs, hoisting engines, and—you guessed it—changing flat tires.

How Not to Get Your Gear Stolen

Leaving a car or truck parked on a remote country road while you're off hunting or fishing is an invitation that many thieves cannot pass up. While there is a certain amount of risk in leaving a vehicle unattended *anywhere*, there are a few precautions a sporting person should take:

• Be careful where you store the empty case from camera, fishing rod, or binoculars you're using—a passerby cannot tell that the case is empty without breaking in. Take some extra time to ensure that everything of value, or that even *looks* valuable, is stowed out of sight.

• A locking gas cap seems an obvious idea, but few people take the trouble to use one.

• Use a removable license plate on a boat trailer. A thief will have to plan ahead and bring a plate if he's going to drive off with your rig. That's usually enough to discourage all but the most truly dedicated miscreant.

• There's a school of thought that says a Ferrari will be stolen faster than a Volkswagen. Along the same line, for years I've used an old beat-up suitcase for my spare gear, a home-delivery milk box for a cooler. All are left in the back of my open pickup. They've never been stolen because they look like items I'm taking to the dump.

• Take your keys with you. The safest place for them is deep in your pants pocket.

PRUDENT FORESIGHT

The sun shows no mercy when it comes to some plastics. The ventilating skylight on the roof of a camper is a prime target. In due time, these plastic bubbles literally crumble after being exposed to sunlight. In order to save yourself some money and inconvenience, make some sort of a shading cover—anything to deflect that solar power as your camper stands idle.

If you've had a camper for a while and not checked the skylight, do so. Look for possible fading or a milky color. If you see some, line up a standby. Often replacements are quite difficult to find.

Epizoites are any animals that attach to and live on the exteriors of other animals.

The poppy, buttercup, and
nightshade contain
poisonous alkaloids.

Got a Screw Loose?

If the screws in your camper or recreation vehicle become loose, an emergency remedy is to remove the screw and pack the hole with steel wool. Use a nail to force the steel wool into the hole, then reset the screw.

Recycle Trailer Tires

A good way to shelter an expensive boat or camper trailer lock from rain, snow, and dirt is with a section of worn-out trailer tire.

Use a hacksaw to cut a section to fit—for most needs, a quarter or fifth of a tire is plenty.

The tire's natural shape will keep it securely in place over the trailer coupler.

TAILGATE SEAL

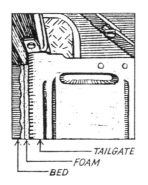

TAILGATE
FOAM
BED

Pickup owners who have a cap over the truck bed know how easy it is for road dirt to find its way into the compartment and coat the bed of the truck and its contents with fine dust. The grime usually enters through the space between the bottom of the tailgate and the truck bed. Here is an easy and inexpensive way to correct the problem:

Lower the tailgate and measure the gap between the bottom and the edge of the bed. Next, remove the tailgate.

Obtain a piece of foam weather stripping, or similar material, at least one-half-inch wide and just a little thicker than the gap measurement. Cut it to the width of the truck bed. Then apply a coat of contact cement just below the back edge of the bed.

Carefully fit the weather stripping over the cement so that the top of it is even with the bottom of the truck bed. Press firmly into place and allow to dry.

Reinstall the tailgate and close it. The bottom of the tailgate will compress the stripping and form a tight seal.

TRY A TOOTHPICK

One frosty spring morning a logger friend discovered a small pool of gasoline under his pickup truck. On checking, he found two pinhole leaks in the gas tank. There is a time-tested way of plugging gas leaks, but my friend was in a hurry to beat muddy roads. He inserted wooden toothpicks into the holes. Within minutes, they swelled and stopped the leaks.

The question that comes to mind is, how long do toothpicks function as gas-leak stoppers? Two months after the incident, my friend said he hadn't gotten around to fixing the leaks permanently but "the toothpicks were still holding up fine."

BOATS, RAFTS, AND CANOES

Inspecting Wooden Boats

Fiberglass reinforced plastic boats proliferated throughout the past decades, leaving wooden boats virtually obsolete. But the prices of synthetic plastics are rising and the idea of buying a used wooden boat may seem more attractive.

But before buying such a boat, it makes good sense to check it out carefully. If it is to be trailered, make sure that rollers are located so that they press on parts that are supported by the frames. Otherwise, the hull can be overstressed and may crack. Ask if the boat has been kept covered—rainwater in the bottom is sure to start an attack of dry rot. Small skiffs should be stored upside down.

Look for dry rot, worm damage (small holes), fatigue or flexing (seemingly unsound areas), and rust spots or green areas in vertical rows on the outside of the hull—especially along the chine or around the stern. Remove a few screws to check whether they have become too small for their holes as a result of rust or corrosion. Look for split or cracked planks and soft spots or darker colored wood along the frames and deep inside the hull.

Test for rot by careful probing with an ice pick or the sharp point of a small-bladed knife. Tapping or sounding for dull spots with a small hammer also is effective. If the boat is made of plywood, look for places where the layers may have begun to separate. If this has begun, the only remedy is to replace the plywood that has failed.

When maintenance such as painting, puttying, patching, and refastening has been done as needed, a wooden boat can have a long, useful, and reliable life.

CANOE EMERGENCY KIT

The first time I went river canoeing my plans included a noon fire and tea for lunch. The first rapid I hit tossed me, and tossed my chances for that hot fire because my matches got wet. Without a fire, my clothes stayed wet till the sun baked them out.

The next time I went canoeing, I took a small emergency kit. I tucked half a dozen heavy paper towels into a two-quart Ziploc™ freezer bag, adding a box of windproof matches, a small can of lighter fluid, and a substantial roll of duct tape for repairs to the canoe itself. Then I zipped the bag closed and taped it under a seat of the boat, again with duct tape.

The paper towels can be used to dry my hands and offer quick kindling. There are probably more benign products than the lighter fluid, but after a spill, especially in winter, I want to *know* something is going to happen when I strike my match.

RAFT CRAFT

The best rafts are constructed of Hypalon™ or neoprene-coated nylon. Don't bother with the flimsy little department-store vinyl "rubber duckies." Get a good-sized raft, 10 to 14 feet long. Look for multiple air chambers (four to six) so that you won't sink if you blow a tube or two.

Get good-quality oars, not paddles or those cheap oars designed to row from built-in plastic oarlocks.

Because it's harder to row from the floor or tubes of a raft—besides being unsafe and uncomfortable and making it nearly impossible to fish—build or buy a rowing frame with an oarsperson's seat plus passenger seats. A frame permits easier and more efficient rowing for precise raft control and gives the oarsperson a better view of what's ahead. It also provides a foot brace, essential for powerful stroking in turbulent waters.

Get your raft first, then measure for a frame. Custom metal frames are a nice luxury. A quick, quality alternative is a wood frame constructed of four 2 × 8s bolted together and strapped to the raft's D-rings. Be sure all bolts are recessed, top and bottom, to avoid poking people or rubber. Carpet scraps or Ensolite foam coverings provide extra protection. Any gear, such as coolers, should be loaded off the floor

(to avoid pinching the floor between the load and a midstream rock). Be sure to secure all gear.

Attach sturdy oarstands and a set of bronze oarlocks (with keeper rings through the holes) to your frame, and you're ready to row.

For better fishing—especially on rivers—try an anchor platform. Build a triangular frame of wood that fits behind the rowing frame over

the stern tubes. Mount a pulley at the tip of the triangle. Use a soft rope for anchoring, so you won't injure your hands hoisting and lowering.

With your raft properly rigged and some basic rowing skills under your belt, you're ready to explore new waters.

Tag-Along Safety Chocks

Whether you are launching a 28-foot cruiser or a 14-foot dinghy, there is something to ensure that the towing rig and trailer stay high and dry: a pair of wheel chocks. They add a great safety margin to both launching and pulling out of the water, and they are easier on your vehicle.

The operating procedure is straightforward enough. After the trailer is in position, the helper places the chocks up tight against the rear wheels of the towing vehicle. The driver then lets off on the brakes just enough to seat the tires firmly against the chocks. The rig is put in first gear, or park for an automatic, the engine is shut off, and then the boat is safely launched.

The real beauty of the tag-along chock system comes into play when pulling the trailer

off the boat ramp. Because the chocks hold the vehicle firmly, there is no mad revving of motors and fancy brake and clutch work, or the loud *clunk* of an abused transmission getting out of the park position. The attached nylon cords tow the chocks right along with the trailer, ready to be put away in the loading area.

You can build a pair of chocks from a 10-inch-long 4 × 6. A diagonal cut is made two inches in from each end. The rough edges are filed smooth and a screw eye mounted in the flat ends of the chocks. The nylon cord attached to the screw eye should be long enough to reach from the chock position behind the towing vehicle's rear tire to the attachment point on either the boat trailer or rear of the towing rig.

Planning a River Trip

Planning a first-time river trip can be a daunting experience. The amount of gear needed for even an overnight excursion is significant, and forgetting just one item, such as a life preserver, can ruin your day in the event of a mishap. The following safety checklist can help.

• Flotation device: When you start to run rivers, you may want to upgrade from a "life preserver" to a "personal flotation device." PFDs are cut to give your arms greater freedom of movement. They also have a back and storage pockets.

• Extra paddle: Bungee-cord it atop or alongside your gear, not underneath duffels, where it will be anything but handy as you drift toward a big hole. And don't buy a beater paddle for your extra. If you do, and you lose one of your good paddles the first day of a week-long trip, it can mean six days of inefficient paddling.

• Painters: Make your bow and stern painters from waterproof cordage, such as Polypro.™ Keep them neatly coiled and tied down; if you turn over, they won't snake out and entrap you.

• Throw line: You may never use this 50-odd feet of line coiled in a throw bag, but if your partner is swept away or stranded on a rock or log, it could save his life.

• Bailer: Simple and easy to forget. A functional bailer can be made from a gallon Blazo™ can.

• Repair kit: Buy a repair kit when you purchase your canoe or raft; this way you have the right patching materials and glue right from the start.

• Lashing: Use a couple of octopus bungee cords for the gear located in the center of your canoe or raft and an assortment of single bungee cords to strap down stray gear such as paddles, guncases, and photo bags. If you're going through heavy water, use nonstretching flat webbing equipped with toothed buckles to lash gear. Don't use rope; knots are difficult to untie when your canoe or raft is underwater.

Camping

Many rivers have become so popular that special regulations regarding fire building and sanitation have been put into effect. Fires must be built in a pan and the ashes carried out. Likewise, human waste must be deposited either in a portable chemical toilet or a jerry-rigged one. A functional latrine can be made from a large army/navy ammo box. Line it with stout, double plastic bags. Place a toilet seat on top if you wish. Defecate in the bag, urinate on the ground. Pour some Chlorox into the bag to keep odor to a minimum and retard the production of methane, which could burst the bag. Carry out the solid waste and dispose of it in your own toilet or at a waste treatment center.

NAVIGATION

Learn something about the river you intend to run. Mile-by-mile guides are published for popular rivers, showing locations of rapids and the best routes through them at different water levels. Topographic maps should be used in conjunction with such guides. Just keep in mind that one author's "big water" may be a piece of cake for you, and another's "moderate difficulty" could mean a swim.

WATERPROOFING

If you're on a tight budget, triple plastic trash sacks will work. However, they will eventually leak. Clothing, food, and camping equipment can be kept perfectly dry in vinyl waterproof bags. Vinyl waterproof guncases are also helpful. Maps do little good when they are buried away. Get a clear waterproof map box that you can put between your knees.

• Clothing: Three items above and beyond the usual outdoor clothing for the season should be considered: a pair of nylon running shorts that will dry out quickly in sunshine or by a fire; flip-flops or river sandals; and for colder climates, a pair of insulated hip boots. All three let you get into and out of the boat often without having to maneuver to shore.

• Photography: Waterproof bags can be bought for single-lens reflex 35mm cameras. Fuji and Minolta make waterproof point-and-shoot cameras, which many people find adequate. I keep my SLRs in a couple of waterproof Bill's Bags (Northwest River Supply) and, depending on the demands of the white water, use them with varying degrees of discretion and bravado. When the water gets big, I use a Nikonos, Nikon's excellent, completely waterproof and fairly expensive ($500) 35mm underwater camera.

SHUTTLING

Rivers unfortunately don't flow in loops. This means that you can't get back to where you started without auxiliary help. Most of the time driving two cars to the takeout, leaving one there, and then driving back to the put-in to start the trip solves the problem. For some rivers in Idaho, Utah, Arizona, Canada, and Alaska, however, shuttles can take days to complete. Hiring a shuttle company to drive your car to the takeout saves gasoline and time. The Bureau of Land Management (BLM) can supply a list of reliable shuttle companies.

RIVER READINGS

Path of the Paddle and *Song of the Paddle* (canoeing and wilderness river camping techniques) by Bill Mason, Northword. *The Complete Wilderness Paddler* (planning and conducting remote canoe trips) by James West Davidson and John Rugge, Vintage Books. *Wildwater* (kayaking and whitewater boating) by Lito Tejada-Flores, Sierra Club Books.

Knots for Boaters

Every boater should know these few simple knots:

Perhaps the most important is the bowline, which can be used to tie a rope to a pole or to join ropes. To tie a bowline, place the end of the rope on the standing part (see illustration). Then, with a twist of the hand, carry the end around through the loop. Bring the end around the standing part and down through the loop to complete the knot.

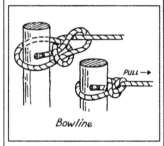

Bowline

This is one knot you should be able to tie blindfolded, with your left hand only. Practice until you can tie it quickly.

The clove hitch is another handy knot aboard a boat, but few boaters know how to use it properly. When used to make fast to a piling, it never slips, no matter how great the strain. To make this hitch, hold the boat end of your line in your left hand, the free end in your right, and toss or drop it over the top of the piling so it falls in the shape shown in

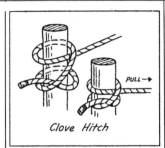

Clove Hitch

the illustration. Then, with plenty of slack in your hands, take a second and similar turn and drop it over the first one.

Practice this by tossing a length of heavy twine over anything that will represent a piling. The two ends should both lead from inside the formation and come out of it in opposite directions.

When a clove hitch is used to moor a boat that's to be left for some time, it's a good idea to make a slippery knot of the free end of the line. A pull on the free end will undo it, then you can yank the final tuck loose, after which you can free the hitch by shoving on the ends of the lines where they enter it.

The clove hitch will not jam tight from wetness or strain.

Slippery Hitch

ROPE RESEARCH

Though boating is becoming increasingly sophisticated, one ancient piece of equipment is still absolutely necessary on every craft from dinghy to huge oil barge—rope. But modern ropes can cause trouble when deterioration remains undetected.

When a rope made of synthetic fiber snaps unexpectedly, it can move at a speed of some 700 feet per second (slightly slower than a 45-caliber bullet), seriously injuring or killing boaters.

SHIM WORN OARLOCKS

Boat oarlocks that have enlarged from use will cause oars to wobble and slip out. Locks can be snugged with shims cut from necks of long-stemmed plastic bottles, the type that come filled with gas additives. The plastic cylinders make rowing a lot easier, and as a bonus, the waxy lubricant in the plastic has a quieting effect on squeaky oars.

If the diameter of the bottle neck is a bit too large to fit the oar horn, cut pieces from elsewhere on the bottle (sides are usually thinner plastic) and insert into the oarlock.

CANOE INNOVATIONS

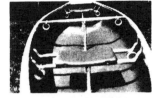

Here are two innovations that are inexpensive: rodholders and rope handles. They can be adapted to most other canoes.

The rope handles consist of two pieces of three-eighths-inch plastic rope approximately 18 to 24 inches long tied to the bow and stern. Before tying a closed loop, I thread a piece of old rubber or plastic garden hose approximately eight inches long on each piece of rope. This prevents the rope from cutting into the hands.

The holders consist of six 6½-inch-long plastic electrical wire straps and six two-inch-diameter PVC pipe couplings. Installation is simple.

First position the pipe couplings underneath the seat supports and center thwart of the canoe or attach in positions that best suit the tackle that you use. Take the electrical wire straps and place them through the couplings and around the tubular section of the seat supports and center thwart. Pull the straps snug and trim the excess strap material with wire snips. The entire installation takes less than 15 minutes. Smaller-diameter couplings may be used, though I have found the two-inch couplings will accommodate cork or rubber spinning rod handles and pistol-grip baitcasting handles better.

Extending Oar Life

Wrapping a small strip of cotton cloth between an oar and a grip-style oar horn can greatly prolong the oar's life. Cut the cloth the width of the oar horn and the length of the oar's circumference. The cloth ensures a firm grip and protects the oar from wear.

Cushioned Oar Grips

Oar handles become rough and hard on the hands after being exposed to the elements for several seasons. To avoid this problem, cut lengths from a discarded bicycle inner tube and slip them over the oar handles. This not only provides a smooth surface but also cushions the grips. If an old bicycle inner tube isn't readily available to you, stop in at a local bike shop. It discards old inner tubes all the time.

FUEL TANK PROTECTOR

To help keep an outboard motor fuel tank from rusting on the bottom, and also to prevent it from rattling on the bottom of your boat while underway, slit a piece of discarded garden hose along its length, fit it around the bottom lip of the tank, and trim the ends for a neat job.

A Simplified Propeller Guard

An engineer by training and a fishing guide by preference, Tom Goodspeed of Turkey Point, Maryland, has invented a reliable, simplified guard for outboard propellers used in shallow, rocky water. Tom shaped a three-inch-wide strip of one-eighth-inch aluminum into an inwardly tailed U and reinforced one side with two rounded one-inch strips of one-eighth-inch aluminum. He bolted the result, which resembles a goalie's mask, by the U tails to the anti-cavitation plate. Safer and stronger than pitchfork shields and the more complicated cages, Goodspeed's guard is removable and requires no welding or adjustments to the motor frame— just two harmless bolt holes on either side of the anti-cavitation plate. Anyone with enough know-how to bend heavy-gauge aluminum and drill holes in metal can make one in an hour.

CARPET FOR BOATS

Carpet samples and swatches made of synthetic fibers, like those left over from recarpeting your home or purchased from carpet stores for nominal cost, are ideal for boating use. They serve well under tackleboxes and gas cans to reduce noise and protect the boat bottom. Shag or other fluffy carpeting helps flyrodders since it will hold flyline stripped onto a deck and prevent them from blowing around.

Carpet swatches can also serve canoeists as knee pads and they help deaden noise from stowed anchors or in the bow of the boat.

Outboard Handle Extension

When running a light boat and outboard motor by yourself, improper weight distribution can be a problem. With the prop powering from the rear and you sitting in the back, it's necessary to shift as much weight forward as possible. A vacuum cleaner extension tube slipped onto the motor handle allows you to move forward a little for better balance. If your vacuum tube doesn't have the right diameter, a used vacuum/repair shop should have one at minimal cost. The tubes have plastic or rubber sleeves already fitted for easy on-off attachment.

BATTERY CHECKER

In order to monitor the charge on a trolling motor battery use a mini-sized battery tester. It works like a small hydrometer, but instead of a floating glass bulb inside, there are five beads. Here's how to use it:

Press the plastic bulb and insert the tip into the battery cell. Allow enough liquid to enter to more than cover the beads. If no beads float to the top, the cell is in a total state of discharge. If one bead floats, the cell is 25 percent charged. Two floating beads means a 50 percent charge; three beads, 75 percent; four beads, 100 percent.

If five beads float to the top, the cell is overcharged, a condition that leads to deterioration of the cell and shorter battery life. Try to avoid this state when charging.

A protective plastic case with directions printed on it is included with the mini battery tester. I fastened the case to the side of a deep-cycle trolling motor battery with electrical tape, so the tester is at hand when needed. (A friend keeps his in his tacklebox.)

Available in discount and automotive stores, it is a very cheap insurance policy against a dead trolling battery.

Put a Leash on Your Outboard

Fastening a safety chain to your outboard or electric motor is sure a lot easier than diving for it should it happen to break loose from the boat. It doesn't even have to be a chain—a short piece of rope can do the job and save a lot of hard work and misery.

Having Good Connections

Any boating angler who gets a lot of use out of an electric trolling motor has probably discovered the need to periodically replace the spring-loaded clips that attach to the battery terminals. After prolonged use, these wear out and fail to provide enough bite for good electrical contact. Sometimes nothing happens when you flip your motor on, or upon arriving at the lake, you may discover that your battery didn't take a proper charge.

To prevent either of these things from happening, simply wrap a heavy-duty rubber band round and round the front portion of each clip on both motor and charger. This works, and replacing the rubber bands once a season is far more economical than buying new clips.

Anchor Rope Depth Indicator

This depthfinder is far from sophisticated, but it gets the job done and is very inexpensive.

With the aid of two felt-tipped markers (red and black), mark your anchor rope as follows: A single red mark around the rope at 5 feet, a red and black mark at 10 feet, a single red mark at 15 feet, two black marks at 20 feet, a single red and two black marks at 25 feet, and three black marks at 30. Use the color code red for every 5 feet and multiples of black for 10 feet.

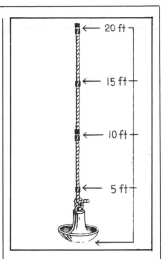

You can feel the anchor touch bottom, and while the line is taut you can get a relatively accurate depth reading.

Featherlight Pack-Along Anchor

Half the fun of a small inflatable raft or a float tube is its light weight. In lieu of the conventional heavy anchor, a length of nylon cord and a two-foot square of nylon mesh, fiberglass window screen material, or a mesh vegetable bag can be used for an anchor. At the launching site, waterside rocks are collected and wrapped in the mesh with the cord. The rest of the cord becomes your anchor line.

POTTED ANCHOR

An anchor in a boat is a necessity, but it can also become a nuisance by banging into the sides of the boat and stowed gear. A simple and inexpensive answer is a large plastic flowerpot. This is both flexible and durable enough to hold a heavy cast-iron or lead anchor. If the pot can't be wedged into a convenient anchor-storing corner, it can be fastened with bolts or screws. As a bonus, the pots are already equipped with drainage slots.

QUIET ANCHOR

A plastic antifreeze jug filled with rocks makes a quiet and inexpensive anchor. The cap can be wired on to keep it from falling off, and the handle is convenient for tying on the anchor rope.

Inflatable Boat Anchor

A common problem faced by anglers in an inflatable boat is that of wind drift. To maintain a stationary position, the boat must be anchored from either end. However, most commercial anchors are not built with the inflatable in mind—their design and sharp edges make them difficult to handle and capable of puncturing the craft.

The answer is an empty one-gallon jug, such as a plastic detergent container.

Fill the jug to the top with pea-gravel, then add water for extra weight. Replace the cap and tie on the desired length of anchor rope. Presto: You have a safe, inexpensive anchor for an inflatable boat. The shape of the jug prevents punctures and it rarely drags weeds up from the bottom of the pond. The approximate weight of the anchor when it is filled is 15 pounds.

Instant Cartop Carrier

Not many mount a cartop boat carrier permanently on a passenger car, but most of us want to haul a canoe or small boat at one time or another.

The simplest solution is a blanket, folded so that it just exceeds the width of your boat and placed on top of the car so it catches the length of each gunwale. Not only will this soft padding protect the paint, it will also protect the boat.

The boat should be tied down firmly at bow and stern. Ropes should come from both corners of each bumper to prevent the boat from shifting.

For Easy Launching

If you're sick and tired of wrestling a recalcitrant boat onto and off a bunk-type trailer, substitute a quick spritz of silicone for sweat and sore muscles. Aerosol cans of pure silicone are available at most hardware stores and auto part dealers. A 14-ounce can is enough to treat two average-sized trailers. Spray a generous coat along the entire length of the bunks' bearing surfaces. No drying time is necessary, so the boat can be loaded immediately. Even the heaviest craft will easily glide on and off.

Silicone won't harm fiberglass, aluminum, wood, steel, chrome, rubber, plastics, and paint, so it can't damage either boat or trailer. Since it's extremely water-resistant, capable of withstanding temperatures from −60° to 500°F, and lasts about 25 times longer than oil-based lubricants, a single application will survive an entire season in fresh or salt water.

Guard Your Boat

Federal crime statistics show that over 12,000 boats are stolen annually. A little extra care on the part of boat owners could reduce this rate considerably. Check out these precautions:

• Every boat made after 1971 is required to have an identification number permanently affixed to the hull. Be sure to put this number in your home records since it is often the only positive identification that police can use to determine ownership of a stolen boat. It's also a good idea to inscribe this number on the hull in an inconspicuous spot.

• Note all pertinent data about the boat. This would include year of manufacture, length, beam, color, identifying scratches and dents, and other information. Also, take some photos of the boat that clearly identify these features.

• Outboard engines should be locked securely to boats at all times. If possible, remove the outboard and store it in a safe place when not in use.

• Use a steel chain or cable and a lock to tie up your boat. Don't leave it at unattended docks—especially at night. Don't leave small boats or canoes unlocked on docks or on the shore.

• When parking a trailered boat, remove a wheel or attach a lock to the trailer hitch. If you store the boat in a garage, keep the garage locked.

• Install an alarm on the ignition of the boat and have a second hidden switch installed, in case a thief bypasses the first alarm.

• Always remove the key from the ignition when the boat is not in use.

TUMBLE HOME

This will make you look brilliant in your next game of Trivial Pursuit. The term *tumble home* refers to the curve of a boat's sides. If the side of a boat is straight up and down, that's *straight*. If the side curves up and outward, that's *flare*. The bows of most boats have a lot of *flare* so they won't nose into waves. If the sides curve back inward, so the gunwale is inward of the side at its greatest bulge, that's *tumble home*. You see it on some canoes and kayaks and larger sailboats.

Preventing Tackle Thefts

If you fear that your tackle may get ripped off at the airport, here are a few tips that have paid off for me.

Nothing looks more attractive than a new jumbo rod case stuffed full of graphite goodies. My trick is to tape onto the tube a bright-colored label reading LAND PLAT MAPS. No hood in his right mind would bother stealing a tube full of useless maps. I also scuff up the case to make it look well worn. If the tube is black, wrap a few strips of red and yellow tape around it. This will help handlers spot the case in the deeper recesses of an airplane baggage compartment and not leave it aboard as you get off. Also be sure the tube is securely locked.

I generally carry my tacklebox aboard as hand luggage, but if it must be checked, I put lures and expensive reels in the oldest, crummiest, most beat-up tacklebox I can find and check it through. Such a box will draw less scrutiny.

Choosing a cheap-looking box and rod case is wise for all kinds of travel. Thieves also frequent hotels, motels, and resorts, and often make curbside luggage switches. A shiny tacklebox and rod case in a vehicle also tempt thieves, who would ignore junky-looking equipment.

CHAPTER TWO

IN THE FIELD

Whether you plan to seek out the roughest possible terrain around for a full-scale wilderness adventure, or simply want to take your children camping in the backyard; if you are going fishing in the neighborhood trout stream or heading out on a whitewater rafting expedition, you'll find plenty of useful tips and good ideas here.

Arranged by situation (at the campsite, on the trail, and on the water), this chapter addresses life in the field. Campers will discover ideas for shelters—new and ancient—for every environment; fire-building strategies for any number of situations, solutions to the problem of how to stay warm; a variety of campsite projects; tips on how to improve your photography in the wild; weather forecasting hints; and much more. Hikers are offered a brush-up course in basic navigation, health and safety tips, and other useful suggestions. Boaters—whether traveling by raft, canoe, or other craft—are treated to a review of boating skills and safety practices, repair techniques, and more. Anglers can learn from the secrets of professionals about their sport.

AT THE CAMPSITE

WILDERNESS TIPS

• Don't break off dry branches to build a fire. Whenever possible, clean up the forest floor for firewood. Leave those dry branches on the trees until they must be snapped off because all other wood is too wet to burn.

• Gather enough wood to get you through the night. Leaving the campsite to find wood at night can be hazardous, and even with a light you could fall or get a branch in your eye.

• Even if you don't need eyeglasses, think about buying a good pair for camp use. If you need no correction in the lenses, get the best tempered clear glass lenses. In the far reaches of a wilderness camp, a hurt eye is big trouble, and an eye can become injured from a twig, from splashed grease, from a spark out of the fire, and countless other ways.

• Don't cut your firewood by a streambank. This wood is often moist and may pop and explode all evening.

• If you camp in snowy country, never make your fire beneath a snow-laden tree. The heat will melt the snow above and cause it to fall, perhaps into the center of your fire.

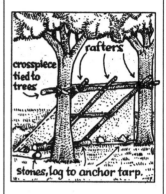

A TENT FOR LESS

An efficient, inexpensive shelter can be made from a 9 × 12-foot tarp, available in most hardware stores. A waterproof plastic coating and brass grommets make it ideal for the occasional camper.

The tarp is easily fixed to a crosspiece tied horizontally to two trees about five feet apart. Three poles angling from the crosspiece to the ground provide support. Stones and logs anchor the sides of the tarp to the ground.

The result is a light (less than two pounds), portable shelter costing under $10.

MOUNTAIN CAMPING

Almost by instinct, first-time mountain hunters or campers put the entrances of their alpine tents downwind. It seems to be the right thing to do. It isn't. You'll spend the night in a noisy flapping tent, with the fabric alternately billowing and collapsing down on you.

When the wind is blowing consistently, an experienced mountaineer faces the tent entrance into the wind and adjusts the opening to allow a slight ballooning effect. The

wind blowing into the entrance pressurizes the tent slightly, distending the tent walls. Flapping is minimized.

Tricks with a Tarp

A tarpaulin—a rectangle or square of waterproof material equipped with eyelets on all sides—provides the simplest form of shelter when you are outdoors. Here are four you may find useful:

TEPEE: Rig four poles to a peak so that lines drawn from base to base make a square. Wrap your tarp around it, and tie it down with thongs to the eyelets.

LEAN-TO: Cut two crotched poles six feet high and two three feet high, as well as two long straight poles to lay across both sets—six poles in all. Set up both sets parallel, six feet apart. Run your tarp from the high ridge back and down over the low ridge to the ground. Guy all four crotched corners so they will pull the tarp tight.

FORESTER'S TENT: Cut a pair of sheer poles, tie to-

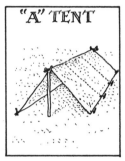

gether at the top, and spread so the crotch will be about six feet above the ground. Run a long pole from the point where it rests in the crotch down to the ground at the rear. Sling your tarp over this, and weight, stake, or tie down the sides, folding them under

near the back end of the tent.

A-TENT: Finally, of course, there is the open-ended A-tent, which is so simple it requires no explanation.

Bivouacs of this type are not as permanent or comfortable as a tent, but they are lighter and easier to set up.

Makeshift Pillow

If you camp out often, try this simple remedy for the camper's pillow syndrome: Pack the extra clothes you are taking along with a standard pillowcase. When you retire, just fold the clothes you are not wearing and put them into the pillowcase, where they will both stay put and give your head a softer resting place.

CAMPING CARPETS

In wet weather, a little scrap of rug can turn muddy shoes from a nightmare into just a nuisance. Place a small square of carpet in front of and behind the tent door flap to reduce wear on the floor and keep grit and dampness in

their proper place. Samples with seamed edges can be obtained for next to nothing from carpet stores. These are also useful for people to sit on in the backs of station wagons and on wet picnic benches, when they have to.

HOW TO BE SAFE INSTEAD OF SORRY

Once you have achieved a campsite layout that is efficient and comfortable, stick with it. Make all camps similar, with everything in relatively the same place so the routine of daily camp life becomes automatic. Changing the mechanics of camp layout can be dangerous.

Since the grizzlies in and near our western national parks have decided to fight for their rights occasionally, there's been a plethora of advice to campers on the bear problem. A lot of it is good and a lot of it is poor. In bear country, even black bear country, *never ever* have the sleeping tent smelling of food. *Any* food. The sleeping bag particularly should not reek of chocolate bars, pepperoni, or cheese crackers surreptitiously sequestered therein for a comforting midnight snack. If you'd eyeball a dissected grizzly, you'd see that his enormous olfactory nerves allow him to home in on the merest wisp of scent.

Look at it from the bear's view. A heady, tantalizing fragrance of some exotic goody sets his jaws to slavering with comestible lust. He decides to go get it. So, set the camp kitchen away from the sleeping tent at all times. Scrupulously wash all utensils. Seal foodstuffs in hermetic containers. A grizzly might noodle out the contents if he stumbles over the containers, but food cared for this way will not lure him out of the forest into your lap.

We mention bears as they're more colorful, but keeping a camp free of food odors, discourages mice, rats, polecats, raccoons—any hungry critter.

A distinct hazard in camp that many overlook is the plethora of lines (ropes). In most worthwhile working camps they abound. Take clotheslines. A camp clothesline should never be strung unless it is supporting drying or bleaching clothing or other fabric. When clothes are dry the line should be taken down, for some simply ghastly accidents can ensue. A running person can garrote himself. Injured Adam's apples and even broken necks occur.

Those tents that have guy ropes and stakes abounding can (but need not) cause all manner of broken toes, horridly scraped shins, and embarrassing falls. The worst skinned-up and busted nose I ever saw came from a pal of mine running into a tent line at night, chasing a hyena. It's prudent to festoon all these dratted support ropes with something white. I have seen stakes dabbed with luminous paint.

The heart of any happy camp is the fire. It's cozy, flickering tongues of flame and the subsequent shimmering, glowing coals—while the black, ominous forest closes in and the stars glitter overhead—are among man's chief delights.

But a campfire should never be near or even downwind of, if possible, tents, flies, or bedrolls. Both heat and errant sparks can cause damage. For open-fire cooking bring a shovel for manipulating coals, long picnic forks and spoons, plenty of kitchen mittens, and pliers for handling hot pots and lids.

A disagreeable thought, but one we surely should mention, is the danger of getting a bad cut. This can just about be eliminated if the camper will see that all of his cutting tools are exceedingly sharp. *Razor* sharp. It may be hard to believe but a sharp tool is a safe tool. All knives, axes, and hatchets should be uncompromisingly keen, and a good hone should be handy for the purpose. Dull edges slip and ricochet off the work at hand. A knot in the wood can turn a dull ax into your ankle or foot. A dull knife can slip into your arm or hand like rapier into a goatskin of wine.

Thousands of gouts of precious blood have been shed due to incautious campers rummaging among the utensils for a knife. All camp kitchen knives and axes should be in sheaths when not in use. Suitable leather scabbards are the most common forms of protection among camping cognoscenti.

As for garbage, the same rules that apply to food should be followed. It attracts beasts and insects if not disposed of properly. In conventional campgrounds it goes into a garbage bag and then into a can. In the wilderness, garbage should be thoroughly burned, and the charred cans packed out.

And about insects, while it is fashionable to disparage insecticides, a short burst or two *inside* the sleeping tent will protect campers from virulent spiders, ticks, scorpions, and other tiny malefactors. Don't pitch camp too near underbrush because it harbors insects. Or to a tree taller than its neighbors. Under a big tree is not wise, either, or where an old (and maybe rotten) tree can topple on you in a high wind.

The above applies to cliffs, too. The shelter at the bottom may look secure, but the heat of day and cold of night can loosen a big chunk of rock. And never camp in a dry riverbed in the West, as rampaging floods are common, out of a clear blue sky, from the mountains far away. Always camp well above the highest high-water mark at stream, lake, or oceanside. If it's not against the law, dig a little trench for runoff around your tent. Some newcomers to the game say this isn't necessary. Don't believe them.

Any parent will tell you it is impossible to watch toddlers every second, so if you have little ones, do not camp near frothing rivers, severe tides, cliffs, and so on. Your camp is probably the safest place on earth. But remember you are venturing into an unfamiliar environment. That is why astute campers set up camp the same way every time—and get into a routine, just like at home.

THE ESKIGAN

The Cree Indians inhabiting the James Bay lowlands of northern Canada need a simple, warm shelter, and the eskigan serves this purpose well.

The eskigan looks like a tepee and is made of hand-hewn logs that are set in conical tepee fashion, then sealed with earth, moss, or bark. An opening is left in the roof to let smoke out. The door of canvas or hide is often removed after the hunting and trapping season is over, so roaming bears or wolverines sniff around without tearing it to shreds.

The floor of this shelter is lined with spruce boughs, and a small fireplace keeps the occupants warm, even in the −50°F temperatures typical of northern Canada.

One eskigan I saw at Kesagami Lake in northern Ontario had small spruce trees growing out of its walls. One of the Native American guides told me this particular sod tepee had been used continuously for 30 years.

Although in most parts of the world modernization has drastically changed the lives of native peoples, the eskigan is not a relic of the past but a functional camp for Native Americans who still depend on hunting and trapping as sources of income.

Tent in a Flap

Nothing is worse than trying to get some much needed rest while your tent performs an impersonation of a tom-tom. The tent-flap problem has been aggravated recently by the development of rain flies and vestibules (the more material, the more noise).

While it's impossible to deaden the noise totally, you can do something to muffle it. The next time you drive the stakes, don't tie the rain fly or roof directly to them. Place a short bungee (or heavy-duty elastic) cord well between the two. Not only will it absorb the wind's shock and noise, but it will also increase the amount of wind stress the tent can safely take. The floor, of course, should still be staked directly to the ground.

This system has another hidden advantage. If someone accidentally trips on the guy lines, odds are the bungee will stretch without tearing the tent—an attractive advantage when kids are running around.

FOILING THIEVES

Cars parked by outdoors people are often sitting ducks for vandals. Station wagons and lift-back models are particularly vulnerable. It helps if cases are left unzipped and rod cases uncapped in a way that clearly shows they are empty. For smaller items, such as cameras and spare reels, a cooler is an ideal storage place. Few thieves will bother to break into a car for refreshment, and most coolers are large enough to accommodate a few valuables even if they are used for food and beverages.

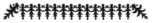

An oometer is an instrument that measures the size of birds' eggs.

Wet-weather Camp Tip

I often camp in national forests, and several times I've carried out pieces of soggy, dirty carpeting that a thoughtless camper left behind.

A better flooring for those camping when it's likely to rain or snow, or for anybody who camps off the beaten track, is fresh straw. A bale of straw will cost only about a couple of dollars, and it's money well spent.

Simply spread the straw over the ground before you pitch your tent. Be sure to keep it away from the campfire. The straw will keep your tent floor dry and clean, offer some padding, and act as a dirt catcher at the door.

When you pack up to leave, scatter the straw and let nature do the rest. In a few months most of the straw will have disintegrated and provided the forest floor with a little extra duff. It's nature's way of both preventing erosion and slowing down runoff.

Pole Frame Clothes Hanger

In practically any type of tenting, one of the difficulties encountered is finding enough room to hang clothes. It is especially a problem during fall hunting trips, when wet weather often prevails and drying out clothes is a necessity.

The solution is to construct a pole frame at the back of the tent. The poles can be driven into the ground and wired or nailed to the ridgepole to pro-

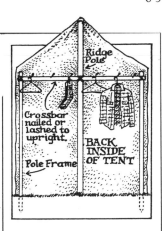

vide a sturdy clothing rack. Nails at intervals along the poles provide hanging spaces for wet socks, shirts, etc.

Give Nature a Chance

Few of us can resist the urge to hold, cuddle, and pet the young of some wild creatures. But this can be unfortunate for the animal and the human involved.

Don't assume that a baby animal left alone is an orphan—this is rarely the case. Most wild animals flee when man comes snooping around, and they normally leave their young alone and hidden, visiting them only for brief feeding periods. This protects the scentless and camouflaged youngsters from predators.

Orphaned wild animals taken into captivity rarely live long and most make poor pets. Wild animals often turn vicious when they mature, sometimes biting, clawing, or occasionally killing their owners. They can also be the transmitters of diseases such as rabies, distemper, and tuberculosis, or carriers of parasites such as tapeworms, mites, and lice.

People realize too late that they should have left a young animal alone. They attempt to return it to the wild where it cannot fend for itself, or take it to a zoo, which probably won't have room for wild pets that are unmanageable.

When you discover young animals in the wild, the best thing you can do is quickly and quietly leave the area. The mother will return, probably at night, and all will be well again. So give nature a chance—she's been raising young for millions of years!

PRACTICAL FIRE-MAKING

A "woodsman's fire" is more than just a heaped-up blaze. It's a controlled, practical flame that 1) can be built in minutes, regardless of where or when, in rain, snow, or wind, and 2) takes only a single match to light. These are tough standards, but they're attainable with practice and an understanding of fire-building theory.

The key is this: A good fire is built in stages, small fires progressing into a single large one. First the match—the tiniest fire—ignites the tinder. Tinder must catch quickly, creating the "second" fire of the progression. This in turn lights the kindling, which is laid lightly over the tinder in a way that does not suffocate it. Kindling should be thin and very flammable—small dry twigs being the most common form. When the kindling ignites, it starts the fuel (the larger branches, for instance), which, when fully caught, creates the main fire.

Good tinder is crucial to fire starting. In evergreen country, dry needles and tiny dead twigs make excellent tinder. These are found at the base of a tree, under the lowest live boughs—where they'll be dry even in a pouring rain or heavy snow. Pitch is another wonderful tinder; this gumlike substance appears as yellow, white, or clear oozings on conifer trunks, especially next to wounds or boils in the bark. Bark itself, when dry, can be good tinder, best of all when pitch-ridden or taken from deadfall birch or juniper. Other natural tinders include dry grasses, weed stalks, and thin shavings from dry softwood branches.

Kindling is really only a larger form of tinder—or a smaller form of fuel. The idea here is to find small, dry, and flammable twigs, stalks, and split branches that will ignite easily.

Gather an abundant supply of tinder, kindling, and fuel before you begin the fire-building process. Then find a dry, level surface on which to build. (On snow or wet ground, start by laying a base of dry sticks or logs.) Now arrange your tinder in a loose heap. Over this, in tepee fashion, lean the kindling. Leave sufficient room for air circulation, since good oxygen flow is crucial to a fire. Experienced campers often go ahead and overlay the main fuel at this point, either leaning it tepee fashion over the kindling or arranging it on a basically horizontal crosshatch pattern. Beginners are better advised to light the tinder now, putting the match to the windward side (allowing the moving air to push the flame deeper into the tinder pile rather than away from it). Good tinder will catch immediately; the kindling should also ignite soon (it may need some rearranging or careful feeding of incrementally larger bits to raise the intensity of the flame). Once the kindling is lit, add the smaller pieces of fuel, always remembering to lay it in lightly enough to allow for air circulation.

MATCHLESS FIRES

Everyone should carry an emergency fire-starting kit consisting of a carbonium spark stick (Metal Match™), and a waterproof container of steel wool.

When struck or scraped with a knife, the carbonium stick produces a shower of sparks that will catch and ignite in a base of fluffed-out steel wool. This little fire kit provides a reliable backup should you run out of matches.

FIRE DO'S AND DON'TS

Don't build excessively large fires; they're difficult to work with and waste fuel. They are also more likely to spread out of control faster than you can react.

In high-impact areas, fires should be forgone altogether. The heavy toll on vegetation can be appalling. Avoid making fires in ecologically fragile areas, such as alpine terrain, where "fuel" takes decades to grow and where fire scars take years to disappear.

Completely extinguish all fires before you leave them. They should be watered down, stirred, reduced to cold ashes, then scattered and "erased" as much as possible to minimize both physical and esthetic impact for the next passersby—human or animal.

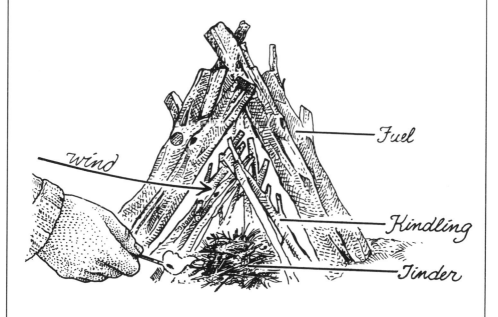

Contain That Fire

What marks a conscientious woodsman is *how* he builds a blaze. (Many prefer to cook on stoves these days, avoiding the hassles of blackened pots, irregular heat, and scarce or nonexistent wood.) Where fires are not yet illegal, they have their many traditional uses, including warming up campers and drying clothing.

One excellent way to minimize the impact of fire building on fragile environments is to employ a metal fire pan to contain the coals.

Fire pans are especially popular—and sometimes required—when river camping. Fires built on sandy riverbanks leave behind charcoal and ashes or ugly, blackened rocks that last forever.

A simple fire pan can be nothing more than a metal container with sides high enough to keep ashes and charcoal bits from spilling out. Garbage can lids or oil drain pans make good, quick fire pans. A fold-down grille for cooking is a nice addition.

It's a good idea to fill your pan with a layer of sand before lighting a fire. This insulates the metal from intense heat, which can warp the pan. Let the fire burn down as much as possible, and use only paper refuse, to lessen residue. After the fire has died, sift out the sand and fine ash, then pick out all charcoal bits. Use these on the bottom of the pan for your next fire (carry them inside an army surplus ammunition box).

One advantage of fire pans: If you want to move the fire, all it takes is a thick pair of gloves to lift the pan. And if the rest of your campsite is clean, nobody will ever be able to detect that you were there.

WOOD HUNT

When afield you can usually find dry campfire kindling around the trunks of spruce trees and scrub pine. Dead twigs and small branches near the bases of these trees are protected from rain by the heavier branches overhead. Broken into pieces, such material makes efficient fire starters.

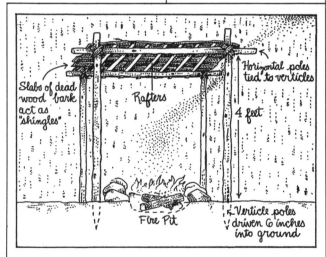

Slabs of dead wood bark act as "shingles"

Rafters

Horizontal poles tied to verticles

4 feet

Verticle poles driven 6 inches into ground

Fire Pit

Building a Fire Shelter

Keeping an open campfire going in wet weather can be a real challenge. An easy solution is to erect a simple-to-make shelter over the fire. Drive four poles 4½ feet long into the ground about four to six inches beyond the fire circle. Connect these at their tops with horizontal crosspieces attached to the verticals with string, twine, or wire. Lay one-inch-wide rafters over the crosspieces to form a roof frame. With an ax, strip slabs of dried wood or bark from fallen, partially decayed pine trees. Place these shingles over the rafter poles to form a protective cover. It will shield your fire from even a moderate rainfall.

When Smoke Gets in Your Eyes

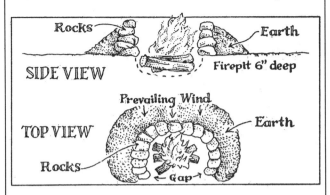

Rocks — Earth

SIDE VIEW   Firepit 6" deep

Prevailing Wind

TOP VIEW   Earth

Rocks   Gap →

CAMPFIRE STARTER

It's quite a job to start a camp-fire on a windy day. Nothing is more frustrating than going through match after match without success. Solving this problem is really very simple: Arrange dry kindling and pieces of dry paper inside a paper bag. Place the bag with its mouth away from the wind, then light a match inside the bag. Presto!

Drifting smoke from a fire is one of the unpleasant aspects of camping out. The smoke can never be completely controlled, but it can be managed.

Often the gaps between rocks in a fire circle allow wind to fan the flames, driving smoke into your face.

To beat this problem, dig a fire pit six inches deep (see diagram). Construct a circle of rocks about 12 inches high around the pit, but leave a gap at ground level on the side away from the prevailing wind. This will create a good draft for the sunken fire. Last, pile dirt on the outside of the rock circle, sealing any gaps.

Emergency Fire Starters

When your matches are wet or lost, there are two possibilities for getting a fire started.

A six-volt lantern battery is one. Attach a couple of short leads to the terminals, then check to see if you can strike a spark hot enough to ignite a bit of rag or cotton doused with stove fuel. If the spark is too weak, put a pinch of steel wool between the wire ends. The wool will heat up quickly and burn, setting the fueled rag ablaze.

You have another easy shot at a fire if you have a sparky lighter on your liquid fuel lantern. Simply light the lantern, then wet the end of a dry stick or cotton swab with fuel carefully and then insert it into the match hole.

In a true emergency, get your fire for the fuel-wet bit of rag from the ends of jumper cables hooked up to your vehicle. Caution: Do not create sparks near the battery; they have been known to create an explosion from leaking hydrogen. Also, electronic gear can be knocked out of whack by battery shorting.

CAMPFIRE TIPS

A pair of heavy canvas gloves are handy for working around the fire. Soaked in water, they're almost as good as asbestos to prevent hand burns.

To roast smaller pieces of meat or fish safely, take along a few extra paper plates and impale them on roasting forks close to the handles to protect your hands from the heat. Remember, though: They are paper, so make sure that they don't get too close to the heat.

Palm trees have no bark.

BEAVER WOOD

Dry sticks and limbs on the tops of beaver dams have most of the resin washed out of them and are stripped of all bark. Consequently, this wood burns without producing an appreciable amount of smoke or affecting the flavor of food cooked over it.

Since dam wood is normally wrist sized or smaller, it doesn't need to be split. Therefore, beaver country wanderers can leave their axes at home and carry a lightweight saw for cutting these handy limbs to the appropriate length.

While fishing, hiking, or paddling through wilderness waterways, keep an eye open for beaver dams and houses along the shorelines of lakes, creeks, and rivers. Pick only the uppermost dry branches and leave the rest. The beaver will never miss them.

Simple Radiant Heat

You can turn a campstove or trailer stove into a heater: Just place a clay flowerpot upside down over the burner and turn the burner on low. (The pot should be about six inches in diameter.) Remember to open a roof vent. The pot radiates heat nicely and will remain hot for some time.

A Cord of Wood and More

Outdoor buffs know that a cord of wood measures 4×4×8 feet and is used to make cheery fires. Aside from the myriad of wood products made for the building trades, and depending upon the particular tree species and how it is reduced, a cord of wood is also capable of producing any one of the following: 7,500,000 toothpicks; 280,000 tent pegs; 310,000 duck or goose calls; 2,700 copies of the average daily newspaper; 942 one-pound books; 1,100 hunting bows; 96,000 cedar arrows; 4,500,000 postage stamps; 460,000 personal checks; 480 pairs of cross-country skis; 880 pairs of snowshoes; 330,000 bass plugs; 210 gunstocks; 90,000 sheets of typing paper; 61,000 envelopes; 250 copies of the Sunday *New York Times*; 740 canoe paddles; 300 pairs of oars; or approximately 1,200 monthly copies of *Sports Afield* magazine.

The Value of a Tree

What is a tree worth? It could be $196,250.

This startling estimate comes from the Agricultural University of Calcutta, India, where Professor T. M. Das figures that an average tree living for 50 years would generate nearly $31,250 in oxygen alone. Its air-pollution control is worth another $62,500. A tree also helps control soil erosion and adds to soil fertility, and this vital function is worth an additional $31,250. By recycling water and controlling humidity this average tree climbs $37,500 in price. Final dollar values of $31,250 for sheltering animals and $2,500 for protein production bring the total to just over $196,000. And that doesn't include lumber or the beauty.

The professor claims that trees sold commercially reap less than 0.3 percent of their real value.

Match Extender

Getting flame to the tinder deep inside a cold cabin woodstove can be a sooty and maddening process if you are shivering barefoot in long johns before daylight. A simple stoveside device for quicker fires can be rigged in minutes.

Pick up a tiny spring-jawed alligator clip at any hardware store. Clamp its base to a two-foot piece of stiff wire and bend a loop or hook into the other end for hanging handily near your stove. By inserting a lit match in the alligator jaws, you can easily reach through stacked kindling and well into the sooty innards of the old cabin warmer for faster fires.

COB FIRES

If you camp outdoors, next time you're near a cornfield ask the farmer if you can have a couple of dozen picked cobs. Take them home and let them dry out thoroughly. Bag them in plastic and use as quick and easy fire-starters.

You may also elect to dip them in some melted wax and again let them dry. Waxed cob fire-starters are even better.

FIRE ENGINE

Long before Rudolf Diesel invented the engine that bears his name, tribes in southeastern Asia were using the same principle of compression ignition to light their campfires. By hollowing out a bamboo cylinder and fitting it with a wooden piston, they created an ingenious fire-starting device.

Wood shavings were placed in the bottom of the cylinder, and the piston was inserted into the top. Striking the piston a sharp blow compressed and heated the air inside the cylinder enough to ignite the shavings, which were then deposited in a tinder bundle and blown into a flame.

Exactly how they came up with such a revolutionary device remains a mystery.

Campground Shower Tip

How annoying it is to step out of a refreshing campground shower onto a floor full of sand! It sticks to absolutely everything. That situation goaded me to devise a bathmat solution for public showers. I found that a large paper grocery bag, placed printed side down, is ideal. It's thick enough to absorb most of the water and also keep cement floor chills away from the feet. It's disposable and sometimes reusable, and it's clean, sanitary, and free.

FRESH FEET

One of the hardest things to do in camp is to pull on a pair of cold, clammy boots in the morning. Changing socks at midday will help alleviate this problem.

Start out with a pair of socks in a pocket or pack, and change when you break for lunch. If your feet sweat a lot, dust the socks with powder before you leave camp.

Having another pair of boots or shoes to wear around camp also allows more drying time for your working boots.

Your boots may still be cold in the morning, but you can keep them from becoming clammy.

VAPOR BARRIERS TO KEEP YOU WARM

What are these magical envelopes called vapor barriers and how can they keep you warmer this winter? Let's start with a few fundamentals about how our bodies lose heat. Whenever the air temperature is less than your body's (98.6°F), you give off heat to the surrounding environment. This happens in four distinct ways: 1) conduction, or direct contact with colder objects—for example, you sit on a rock; 2) convection, or the movement of warm air away from your body—a cold wind blows over your skin; 3) radiation, or what might be termed "emission without contact"— you stand around without a hat on; and 4) evaporation, or the loss of body heat through the moisture you exhale in your breath and in the sweat that evaporates from your skin.

We prevent the first three types of heat loss every time we go camping. A foam pad under our sleeping bag stops heat loss by conduction. A wind shell prevents heat loss by convection, and placing a hat on one's head cuts out loss through radiation. Vapor barriers, on the other hand, are less commonly used. They are coated fabrics, and their impermeability prevents the cooling effects of evaporated perspiration.

To understand how these fabrics work, you must visualize the two sorts of perspiration that we emit. The first is called sensible—the stuff that appears on your brow after running half a mile. The second, named insensible, is produced every second of everyone's life and is continually evaporating. It's what keeps our skin moist, so that we don't shrivel into prunes. When both temperature and humidity fall, the sweat glands produce more insensible perspiration until a moisture level of 70 to 100 percent humidity is created close to the skin. As the production of insensible perspiration continues, evaporation, unless prevented by something such as a vapor barrier liner, also increases and the body loses heat. In hot weather, this heat loss is exactly what we need. In cold weather, we get chilled.

To make matters worse, this water vapor has to go someplace—namely, through the down or synthetic insulation of your sleeping bag. It then condenses on the inside of the shell of your bag and possibly freezes, sealing the pores. More water vapor hitting this frozen layer will also freeze, decreasing your insulation night by night.

A vapor barrier liner (VBL) immediately does two things. Since you're contained in a miniature greenhouse, the humidity around your body rises. When it reaches nearly 100 percent, your insensible perspiration stops and thus heat loss also stops. Since you, the moisture producer, are now separated from your sleeping bag's insulation by the VBL, your down or fiberfill doesn't get wet. Champions of this system claim that, when used properly (shut tight around the neck), a VBL will increase the temperature rating of a sleeping bag by 20°F.

Two points should be emphasized about the use of VBLs. First, you won't get drenched in your own sweat. When the humidity inside the VBL becomes high enough, insensible perspiration stops. In the morning, you're only slightly damp.

Vapor barrier sleeping bag liners cost about $25 and are a worthwhile investment for winter campers. VBL boots, originally designed for arctic troops, and the newer vapor barrier clothing have an even wider range of applications, particularly for people who move slowly or actually sit in cold weather.

Let's look at the clothing first. It works in the same way as a vapor barrier sleeping bag liner—by trapping insensible perspiration close to your skin and stopping evaporative heat loss. VBL shirts and pants have one catch, though. If you start to move quickly, you'll heat up quickly. Then it's important to shed clothes and vent the shirt and/or pants through the neck and cuffs, or armpit and hip vents if they've been provided. Ideally the shirt and pants should be worn against your skin. However, they can also be worn with polypro underwear for greater comfort.

The nature of your outing will indicate whether to use VBL clothing. If you're going to be sitting or walking slowly, try it. If you're planning to hike quickly, snowshoe at a good pace, or do some cross-country skiing, regular winter clothing would probably be a better choice.

VBL boots, on the other hand, can be used when you're moving rapidly. After all, who hasn't experienced cold feet (even while running) in cold temperatures? Vapor barrier boots can help cure this condition. Perhaps the finest of the genre are Bata's Zero Guards. Sometimes called Mouse Boots, the Zero Guard's insulation consists of wool and felt layers permanently sealed between rubber outers and inners. You wear the boots with one pair of wool or pile socks and, as might be expected, your feet sweat moderately. But since evaporative heat loss is prevented and the sealed insulation can't be wet, your feet stay warm. The Zero Guard, used regularly in the arctic, is designed to keep toes safe from frostbite in temperatures as low as −70°F. The boot works well on snowshoes and in certain ski bindings. If you have perennially cold feet on a deer stand or in a blind, this boot's for you.

Wearing the Zero Guard, which weighs seven pounds for a pair of No. 8s, can often be overkill. But there are ways to incorporate VBLs into your regular boots. First put on a thin polypro liner sock, and then pull the VBL sock over it. You next put on a wool or pile sock, and finally stick your foot into your boot.

Another way of using VBLs on your feet is to dispense with the plastic bags altogether and go to neoprene socks, much like the wetsuit booties that scuba divers wear. These thin socks, designed for use in hiking boots, can be ordered from Rooster Mountaineering.

Portable Shower

For a portable shower that's easily assembled in five minutes, folds into any small space, and is inexpensive to construct, you'll need a screwdriver, knife and bootlace, plus a water bag, faucet hose with shower head, hose clamp, an S hook.

To assemble, cut the faucet attachment off the hose, push exposed end over water bag's spout, and secure snugly with hose clamp. Test the clamped hose for ease in pulling the spout on and off so you'll be able to easily take apart the shower for decamping and storage without having to use the screwdriver again.

To hang it up, thread a bootlace through the hole in the water bag's tab and knot the ends. For good gravity flow, loop the lace over a branch or nail about eight feet off the ground and secure the lace back to the tab's hole with the S hook.

Hang it in a sunny spot when you're out in the woods, and you'll have a warm shower waiting when you return.

Avoid Chapped Lips

Chapped or sunburned lips are an annoyance, and people have tried everything from dishwashing liquid to boot grease to protect themselves. Items such as these may work, but the taste can be awful, and some should not be ingested.

A good lip balm is butter. If your lips are already cracked, it may sting a little, but it will prevent drying and splitting.

Catsup (if thick enough) and mayonnaise can also be used, but they might sting because of their acids.

Block Those Mosquitoes

A very convenient combination sunblock and mosquito repellent can be made by enriching your sunblock. Our ancestors used a very efficient bug repellent made from oil of pennyroyal and oil of thyme in a lard or olive oil base. Add 10 drops of oil of thyme and 20 drops of pennyroyal to the jar of sunblock. Shake well. Apply to exposed parts of the body, and you'll neither sunburn nor get eaten by bugs. A bonus is that you will smell more like herbs than like insect repellent!

TOASTY WARM

Expensive sleeping bags have vast amounts of dead-air space that works as insulation to keep you warm even on the coldest nights.

If your bag has space to spare, you could stuff more insulation inside.

Why not put tomorrow's change of clothes in the bag with you? They'll provide more comfort—and be warmer the next morning.

How to Make Your Ears Bigger

Most animals hear a lot better than we do. There are several reasons, but one is because their outer ear, or pinna, is much larger than ours, as well as more directional. We can improve our hearing in the field by simply cupping hands around our ears.

This is easy to prove: Simply turn your head toward a sound, preferably a faint one such as a distant stream. Cup your hands around your ears and turn toward the sound. It will become much louder.

Wind is identified by the direction *from* which it is coming. For example, southeasterly winds are coming *from* the southeast. Remember weathervanes point *to* the direction from which the wind is coming— in this case the vane would be pointing to the southeast.

HOT WASH

When camping, fill a vacuum bottle with very hot water before you retire in the evening. When you get up in the morning there is nothing nicer than a hot washcloth as an eye-opener—unless it is coming back to camp and having that same hot vacuum bottle full of water ready for a wash-up.

SLEEPING WARM

Sleeping warm can make the difference between a dream trip and a miserable one. The location and the position of your sleeping bag go a long way in deciding how warm or how cold you'll sleep.

Winds generally blow up-slope during the day and downslope at night. Place your sleeping bag on level ground, With the head facing downslope, to keep the wind blowing around rather than in your sleeping bag.

Avoid making camp in meadows or low-lying open areas. Cold, dense air settles in these coverless spots during the night; so does moisture. Move to higher ground, even if it's just a few feet higher, with some trees or some other cover.

Last, make sure to keep your sleeping bag and clothing dry, layer clothing for comfort, and use a foam roll sleeping pad to insulate your body from the cold ground.

Red Light For Night

Sporting people who pursue outdoor activities at night can take a tip from astronomers, who know that red lighting doesn't hurt your night vision. Covering the lens of a flashlight with a piece of red plastic will provide illumination without spooking game or surface-feeding fish.

There is also a definite safety factor involved with using red light at night. The inner structure of the human eye is made up of rods and cones. The cones, used in bright daytime light, give us color vision, while the rods are used in low-light levels to provide sensitive night vision.

Once the eye is darkness-adapted, the iris expands to approximately 7mm to let in the maximum amount of light the eye can detect. If you switch on a white light, the eye reacts by contracting the iris. After the light is switched off, it takes several minutes for your eyes to regain their night vision. The cones of the eye are not as sensitive to red light as they are to white light. So red light helps to overcome this problem, making night fishing or hunting much safer.

READING THE SKY

Theophrastus of Eresus, a pupil of Aristotle, is said to have been the first to make a common observation: "Red sky in the morning, sailor take warning/Red sky at night, sailor's delight." Jesus Christ, admonishing the Pharisees, repeated the proverb (Matthew 16:2–3), as did my grandfather and my father, and, I guess, as I will.

Here, I hope I can offer a bit more specific weather lore, for being able to read snow in the clouds and taste rain in the wind is both a handy skill to possess and a testament to one's intimacy with the wiles of nature.

CLOUDS

Masses of visible water droplets or ice particles, clouds enact the current weather and presage what will come. Cloud shapes, of which there are hundreds, belong to 11 basic categories that are divided into four groups: high-, middle-, and low-altitude formations, as well as a towering variety.

• High-altitude formations: Less than 100 feet thick and found from three to eight miles high, cirrus, cirrostratus, and cirrocumulus clouds consist almost entirely of ice crystals. They can be identified by their white, sheer filaments, appearing to be blown before the wind. Very high, very thin cirrus clouds can be either an indica-

tion of fair weather (if they're not followed by cirrostratus) or a warning that a front is approaching within 18 to 36 hours. If you see lower cirrus arranged like zebra stripes or mare's tails, be sure to prepare for possible bad weather. When such clouds are followed by cirrostratus, a transparent gauzelike covering of the sky, the chance of precipitation during the next 24 hours rises to about 80 percent. If these clouds are followed by altostratus within several hours (see below), there's a 90-percent chance you'll get rain or snow within 6 to 12 hours. Both cirrus and cirrostratus clouds create a halo around the moon; neither cloud should be confused with cirrocumulus, which often looks like someone blew miniature marshmallows or foam packaging across the high heaven. Cirrocumulus isn't an indicator of change but rather a signal of fair weather.

CLOUD TYPES

Cumulus

Cirrus

Stratus

Cirro-cumulus

• Middle-altitude formations: Altostratus and altocumulus clouds are heralds. The former looks as if someone spray-painted the sky gray, obscuring the sun. Some light rain or snow is possible but not usual. If, however, altostratus has been preceded by cirrus or cirrostratus, the chance for steady precipitation in the next 6 to 12 hours rises to about 90 percent. Altocumulus often look like flotillas of small sailing ships, white or pale gray in color, arranged in ranks. Rain or snow doesn't normally fall from these clouds, but when low-level, towering cumulus clouds follow, be prepared for rain.

• Low-altitude formations: Stratocumulus, stratus, and nimbostratus clouds can all produce precipitation. The first is often seen in the winter. Big, amorphous mounds group together, often leaving a hole through which opalescent shafts of light ("godrays") lance. Rain or snow from these clouds is often short-lived. Stratocumulus frequently indicates a clearing evening with colder temperatures. Stratus is a homogeneous, low-lying layer that looks like fog but doesn't rest on the ground. Drizzle, not rain, is its gift. Nimbostratus clouds—thick, low, dark gray—drop steady and prolonged rain or snow. They can often be identified by the ragged patches that tear from the main cloud.

• Towering formations: Seen almost exclusively on warm or sunny days, cumulus clouds look like distinct clumps of white cotton candy with gray bottoms. Formed by convection currents, cumulus clouds are born in the morning, flower in midday, and die by sunset. They are the cherubs of summer and give us no more than a brief shower. Cumulus congestus are the cauliflowerlike, disgruntled-looking clouds that form as cumulus clouds glob together. Some rain can fall from congestus. The cloud is an indicator of more severe weather ahead, brought via cumulonimbus—the thunderhead of the sky—with a base several miles wide and an anvil-shaped top that can reach 55,000 feet in height.

ADIABATIC COOLING AND HEATING

Adiabatic means "occurring without loss or gain of heat" and refers to the temperature changes that take place as air currents travel over mountains. As an air mass is forced upward over terrain, it cools due to decreasing pressure at a rate of 5.5°F per 1000 feet. If the air is humid, the adiabatic cooling rate is 3.5°F per 1000 feet. If the dew point is reached, cloud formation and precipitation result. Coming down the lee side of the mountain, the air warms at 5.5°F, since it has lost most of its moisture on the windward side. Having this knowledge helps one choose clothing and strategies with more precision.

Let's say that it's raining and 42°F at your camp and you plan to head 3000 feet up a mountain. You can assume it will be snowing when you arrive and that you'll need appropriate garments. On the other hand, if a front is moving through a mountainous area, you might assume that the windward side will be receiving the brunt of the weather, and expect clear but windy skies on leeward slopes.

Folk Forecasts

To our forefathers, the right weather forecast often meant the difference between life and death. Farmers read almanacs for general climatic trends but kept a close eye on natural signs for local fine-tuning. They were sensitive to the balance and rhythms of nature, to the subtlest changes in plants and creatures, believing that Mother Nature gave inside information. The resulting folklore was sometimes pure superstition, but it often had scientific basis.

The farmers believed that the more the dogwood bloomed in spring, the colder the coming January. If apples bore tough skins, buds wore heavy coats, and if oak boughs sagged with acorns, a hard winter lay ahead. "When the corn wears a heavy coat, so must you." "Onion skins very thin, mild winter coming in; onion skins very tough, winter's going to be very rough."

When bald-faced hornets hung their nests up high, the snows would fall deep that year. In the fall, if squirrels put on heavy coats, chipmunks kept their tails high, and mice came early in the house to nest, it spelled trouble, better look out!

ANIMAL FORECASTS

Animals have long been thought of as nature's meteorologists. Here are some ways in which they are supposed to foretell weather:

• Cows lying in a field signify oncoming rain.
• A thick coat on a woolly bear caterpillar suggests a hard winter.
• Bees stay near their hives if rain is imminent.
• When the groundhog sees his shadow on February 2, it means six weeks more of cold weather yet to come.
• Crickets that chirp quickly are harbingers of warmer days.
• Flies bite more often before a rainstorm.
• Squirrels work more feverishly storing nuts before a harsh winter.

The Outdoor Body as Barometer

The next time you feel irritated enough to ram your fist through the wall of your tent or camper, take a look at the sky. Chances are bad weather is on the way.

Dr. Michael DeSanctis of Minnesota's Buffalo Mental Health Center believes that as much as one-third of the population is abnormally sensitive to weather changes. When it turns from fair to foul they can suffer lethargy, dizziness, headaches, and depression.

Weather-sensitive individuals tend to have short-lived changes in mood, energy levels, and pain tolerance. You can put the blame on ions. Air ions affect the production of serotonin—a hormone that affects sleep cycles, sexual arousal, and emotions.

DeSanctis claims negative ions, which are associated with pollution-free air, high altitudes, and improving weather phases, can reduce stress and anxiety, promote faster reaction times, and increase one's vigor.

What strikes DeSanctis, a clinical psychologist, is how collective weather variables have gone largely unnoticed by traditional psychologists and psychiatrists, e.g., Freud, Rogers, Piaget, and Skinner.

"All I'm saying," DeSanctis says in conclusion, "is that there is a significant amount of variance in behavior associated with weather."

Locating Highs and Lows

Low-pressure areas usually bring unsettled weather conditions, while high-pressure areas generally bring fair weather. Because of the great impact weather has on outdoor activities, it is useful to know whether a high or low front is approaching.

You can determine the location of a high or low front without a barometer or current weather forecast. Stand with your back to the wind and then turn right about 45 degrees. Your back is now to the wind, and the low-pressure area is to your left and the high to the right.

Since highs and lows move in a generally eastward flow, whatever weather condition is to your west will probably move over you.

These rules do not hold true for local breezes, such as sea breezes; and highs and lows may become stationary or dissipate before they reach you. However, these tips can be very valuable in making your personal weather forecasts and planning your future outdoor ventures.

WEATHER PROVERBS

Do you know why that old adage "If a goose flies high, fair weather; if a goose flies low, foul weather" is true? It's because with fair weather the optimum density for flight is higher in the sky than in bad weather, when the best flying condition is closer to the ground. Birds are very sensitive to the aerodynamics of flight and act accordingly.

★

"The squeak of the snow, the temperature will show" is based on the fact that cold air creates high frequencies of sound waves. That's why a boot will squeak on snow in frigid weather.

★

"Ditches and manure piles smell stronger before a rain" because low pressure creates more hydration (wetting) of molecules, which aids the sense of smell, be it of a person or a hunting dog.

★

Fish bite better just before a rain because low air pressure makes fish food on the bottom rise to the top. The fish follow it—right up to the bait you are then using.

Weather Warnings Help

Birds, campfire smoke, and cottonwoods can serve as weather warnings for people outdoors.

When a low-pressure system (falling barometer) begins, small birds and bats will fly at lower elevations. Some believe this is because they are sensitive to low pressure, but more likely it is because the insects they seek are hugging the earth then.

Smoke from a campfire will stay near the ground during the onset of a low-pressure system. So when smoke rises it is an indication of good weather.

Trees in the cottonwood family are also a good indication of fair weather turning foul. As an atmospheric low moves into an area, the alders and cottonwoods will show the undersides of their leaves.

These weather warnings will generally occur 2 to 12 hours in advance, sufficient time to pull your slicker and boots from the closet.

Singing Sands, Humming Waters

Some witnesses say it's the sound of a million fingernails raking across a distant blackboard, others imagine it's something groaning. In about 30 places of the world, the sands of the deserts "sing."

In this country, singing sand may be heard in three spots—Crescent Dune near Tonopah, Nevada; Sand Mountain, ten miles east of Reno, Nevada; and at Kelso Dunes in California.

Scientists at Purdue University say the singing is the result of myriad grains of sand sliding and chafing against each other.

Other natural musical events also appear in nature. Besides the familiar babbling and murmuring brooks, some lakes and oceans are associated with inexplicable hummings, whisperings, and detonations. The Finger Lakes region of New York State has long been the site of mysterious noises that sound like the booming of a distant cannon. Similar noises have been reported along the East Coast from Canada to the Florida Keys. Visitors and rangers at Yellowstone Lake in Wyoming have described hearing a bewitching ringing or harplike sound over the lake.

Smoke Signals

To make one of the best wind-direction gauges available, save some fine, white ash from a defunct campfire or home fireplace or stove. Fill a small porous bag—little cloth tobacco bags are perfect—with the ash. The little pouch can be carried in a plastic sandwich bag to keep it dry and to prevent it from getting its contents on your clothing.

In the field, simply shake the bag and a puff of the white dust will appear. Air currents will carry this smoky dust easily, and you can determine wind direction and see how air currents are moving.

BOUNTIFUL AMERICA

The first visitors to America's shores found fish and game in such quantity that they could scarcely believe it. Sea turtles weighing as much as 90 pounds, oysters as big "as a horse's hoof," and deer were so plentiful that "venison nauseated our appetites."

Wild tom turkeys weighed as much as 50 pounds. As for ducks, "the water was so black with them it seemed, when you looked from the land upon the water, as if it were a mass of filth or turf, and when they flew up there was a rushing and vibration of the air that sounded like a great storm coming through the trees."

MOON MONTHS

January	Winter or Wolf
February	Trapper's or Snow
March	Fish or Worm
April	Planter's
May	Mother's or Flower
June	Stockman's
July	Summer
August	Dog Days or Sturgeon
September	Fall
October	Harvest
November	Hunter's or Beaver
December	Christmas

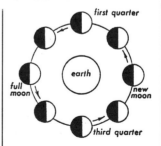

Early Meat Preservation

Pioneer families often had to hunt hard and long to fill their meat larders. Then they faced the dilemma of preserving the bulk of the meat before spoilage. During the long winters, they merely hung the carcass until it froze solid, then hacked off chunks as needed.

During the warmer months, improvised smokehouses were a common sight along the frontier, and families devoted many hours to drying and smoking meat and fish.

Indian groups would often share their age-old meat-processing secrets with neighboring white settlers. The Abnaki tribespeople, who roamed the Adirondack regions and up into Canada, developed an unusual preserving process: They would salt the meat, then coat it liberally with a mixture of wild herbs and maple sap that formed a tough, airtight skin about one-sixteenth of an inch thick. When this plasticlike skin was peeled off, the meat would be beautifully preserved and not unlike the fresh product.

Antarctica has wind gusts that are measured at 200 mph. These intense circumpolar winds never cease.

POT STRINGER

Pots and pans present storage problems when not in use. You can solve the dilemma by carrying along a chain fish stringer, something you probably already have in your tacklebox. Hook the upper safety snap to a tree limb, letting the lower snaps dangle at about chest level. Hook your pots and pans through the holes in

the handles. Not only are they out of the way, but each pan is readily available.

Keeping Track of Camp Tools

Axes, saws, and other tools frequently get left in some distant part of the woods as campers haul armloads of fuel back to the campsite. You go back but can't find them.

Try wrapping the handles of your tools with fluorescent tape. The colorful tape stands out against the forest and makes it easier to find those implements.

TWIG PROJECTS

Twigs are great building materials for projects to keep the kids occupied and provide the family with souvenirs.

You need small cardboard boxes (ideally no bigger than two inches square) with a couple of tiny windows cut out. Collect twigs about as thick as a child's finger. They can be cut lengthwise with a penknife wielded by an older child or adult. Using a bottle of wood glue or Duco cement, the twigs can be stuck to the boxes like house siding. Fold a flat piece of cardboard in two for

the peaked roof and stick it on, covering that with twigs too.

You'll end up with a miniature wood cabin perfect for decorating an electric train village or putting under the Christmas tree. If you have collected these twigs at a memorable campsite, be sure to write the date and location on the inside of the box so the cabins you assemble will become real family treasures.

With a bit of imagination, a few simple tools, and wire or nails, there are endless items crafted from simple twigs.

The Useful Nettle

The stinging nettle grows wild throughout much of North America. Just about everyone who has roamed the fields and woods has learned the hard way to avoid touching it. Some outdoors people, however, realize the potential usefulness of the plant, especially in case of an emergency.

Young, tender shoots and leaves, high in vitamins A and C, may be eaten after boiling. The fiber rendered from the stalks can be used to manufacture twine and rope, which is excellent for lashing, lifting, towing, or making snares.

The nettle can be utilized from spring well into winter, but is most easily harvested in fall and winter when the stalks are fairly dry and ready for immediate use. Should the stalks be green, however, they can be harvested (with a pair of gloves) and allowed to dry over a smoky fire.

To obtain an unbroken segment for twine, the stalk must first be gently crushed and split open. This exposes the pithy center which should be broken into segments of an inch or so and peeled away from the fiber, one by one. A word of caution: If the fiber is peeled from the pith, it will break and come off in short strips. When the pith has been removed, all that remains is a long, wide

strip of raw twine, sometimes more than seven feet in length, as nettles commonly reach this height. Rub the entire length between your palms for a minute or two in order to make the fibers more pliable, then twist the segment until taut. For longer lengths of twine simply braid and twist the ends of several pieces together. A number of these may then be twisted together, side by side, for heavier rope.

How tough is this homemade twine? Certainly not as durable as a piece of good nylon cord, but it is strong. Many Algonquin tribes used nettlestalk fiber almost exclusively in the manufacturing of their bow-strings.

Knife Polisher

Wood ashes make an excellent cleaner for knife blades. To clean a stained or dirty knife blade, put ashes on a soft cloth and rub the stains away. It won't scratch the surface or remove the finish from an expensive knife.

To keep stored knives looking like new for years, lightly rub the blades with ashes and roll the knives up in a soft cloth before packing them away. When you want to use one, the ashes can be removed much easier than polish or an oil preserver.

WILD PLAQUES

Many small, odd-shaped chunks of wood are produced in the process of cutting and trimming logs. Some of these can be used to make decorative knickknacks for home and camp. Flat ones make nice wall plaques to display photos, small trophies, fishing flies, or whatever. Wedge-shaped chunks with flat bases can be used to make fireplace mantelpieces.

Sand rough surfaces where necessary, then glue on the item to be displayed. Varnish the entire plaque. The three raw plaques shown here were found within five minutes at a yarding area near my home where logs were being cut.

Pioneer Home Remedies

Pioneers had to concoct their own medications if they were to survive along the isolated frontiers. To repel insect pests that thrived in the big woods, many cooked up a pungent dope they called Nessmuk Juice. It consisted of three ounces of pine tar, two ounces of castor oil, and one ounce of pennyroyal oil, simmered over a slow fire.

Camphor became a legendary cure-all. Early lumbermen carried some in their pockets to repel the hordes of body lice that invaded the unsanitary bunkrooms. Settlers carried it in bags about their necks to ward off diphtheria.

Common ailments such as flu and colds were treated with a decongestant created by boiling hemlock boughs and buds. You inhaled the fumes. Also popular was the proverbial skunk oil. Fat was removed from carcasses of trapped skunks and rendered over the fire. The resulting liquid was then bottled. When needed it was reheated and rubbed liberally upon the chest and throat of the pa-tient. It had no odor and was indeed an effective decongestant.

Boneset was also used to treat flu and colds. An infusion prepared from the tops and leaves of the plant was taken orally while still hot to reduce fever.

Felling Small Trees

When felling small trees (one-foot diameter or less), consider the following tips:

1. Make sure your blade is sharp and the axhead is firmly affixed to the handle.

2. Wear safety goggles, safety shoes, and a hard hat.

3. Clear out all brush and warn bystanders to stand clear.

4. Decide where to "throw" the tree. Check to see if limb growth is heavier on one side, and fell it that way. It's going in that direction anyway.

5. Holding the ax blade at a 45-degree angle, notch out the tree at waist height on the side opposite the throw direction. Cut about two-thirds

through the trunk, then notch out the other side, leaving a few splinters (see sketch).

6. Place a wedge in the smaller notch and strike it with a hammer or sledge (not the axhead). STAND BACK—the trunk may kick back and injure you.

7. When the tree is safely on the ground, remove the limbs. Chop off each at its base toward the tree crown. This is when most injuries occur. *Watch your legs and feet.*

8. After collecting the limbs, cut trunk into desired lengths, notching as before.

9. To split wood, stand the shorter pieces on end and strike the center perpendicularly with ax or wedge and sledge. With longer pieces, strike top side of the log near one end along the grain. If the piece is stubborn, remove ax, place a wedge in cut, and use the ax on opposite end. Continue alternating wedge and ax until the piece splits open.

THROWAWAY TROUSERS

An ingenious person can find many good uses for worn-out trousers. Old denim, poplin, and corduroy trousers can have new lives.

One of my favorite recycles, especially for dungarees, is to make sandbags out of the legs. I cut the leg off to the size of bag I need, tie one end tightly shut with a double loop of stout twine, fill the leg with dry sand, then tie the other end closed. The denim is woven tightly enough to prevent any sand seepage, and the bags make camera rests for sighting in your rifle. They're also good to use as cushions to kneel on in a canoe.

You can also use shorter leg segments as equipment storage bags. Just cut off a piece one and a half times as long as the

intended item, and stitch one end shut. I have a snap installer, bought at an automotive store, and use a double snap closure on the storage bag. Old dungarees are good because the fine weave of the cloth keeps out the dust.

Cotton corduroy trousers make perfect cleaning cloths. Cut up into small squares, they are perfect for cleaning outdoor equipment; in larger squares they serve as wipes when checking oil.

The legs of corduroy and poplin pants are handy for storing tent or canopy poles. If one leg isn't long enough, sew on the other. Sewn lengthwise, they make excellent fishing-rod storage bags, with individual compartments for each segment of the rod.

Multipurpose Camera Case

A small cooler makes an excellent camera case. It will keep camera, film, and lenses at nearly room temperature for hours, whether on a boat in the broiling hot sun, or in subzero conditions. This is particularly advantageous when you must leave the camera in a locked auto in the sun.

If you attach a lanyard to one handle, or to the hasp that secures the box closed, the cooler can be safely carried on

the car top. Also, if your boat should capsize, the cooler will float and serve as an effective life preserver.

The better-constructed coolers allow you to stand on them so you can photograph difficult shots to get—over people's heads.

The innocent cooler, seen inside your station wagon or truck, gives the thief no clue whatsoever that it contains valuable camera equipment.

Snakeskin Trophies

You don't need an expensive taxidermist to preserve a snakeskin. Simply slit the snake up the belly and pull the skin free with pliers. Then stretch and tack it inside out on a piece of plywood, salting heavily with (noniodized) pickling salt. Allow the skin to dry for several days in a cool, shaded area. When cured, it can be sewed or glued on a flat backing to hang on the den wall, or cut and sewed to make a decorative hatband.

Photography from Your Vehicle

Wildlife photographers quickly learn that even the wariest animals can often be photographed more easily from an automobile window than on foot. Leave the vehicle, and animals and birds will be long gone. Pull over slowly and well off the roadway. And always use a camera rest such as a sandbag, or a special window camera holder. Make sure to use a telephoto lens whenever possible.

It's a Snap

Not many years ago the high cost and the intricacies of a camera best suited for outdoor activities kept many from adding a good 35mm camera to their outdoor equipment.

In the past few years the automatic 35mm single lens reflex camera arrived on the scene. The quality of its pictures and the ease of operation make it ideal for use outdoors.

There are three basic types of automatic SLRs. With one, you set the shutter speed and the camera automatically adjusts the aperture. This SLR is particularly good for stopping action, such as an animal or person in motion or a boat moving. Another type permits you to set the aperture and the camera sets the speed. This camera is particularly fine for scenery—shots in which background is important. The third, the most expensive of the three, has both options.

Some of these automatic cameras now have a programmed option as well, which automatically sets both the speed and the aperture.

A good camera with a quality long zoom lens is perfect for capturing fleeting subjects on film: a bird in flight, a poised deer, or a leaping fish.

Rainy Day Pictures

It is not necessary to leave your camera behind just because it's raining. A medium-size Ziploc plastic food bag and a bit of plastic electrician's tape can waterproof it.

Cut a hole just large enough for the camera shoulder strap to fit through the two seamed corners of the bag. Put the

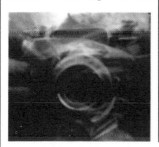

camera into the bag and thread the strap out one of the corner holes, back through the other, and refasten it to the camera inside.

Cut a five-inch strip of the tape. Fold the bag corner tightly around the bottom of the strap and tape, overlapping bag and strap. Repeat on the other corner.

By closing the bag, the camera is locked in the watertight container. With only a quick rip and a flip up over the camera, you can be ready for that special picture no matter where you are going or what the weather may be.

FOUR EASY LENSES

Serious sporting people take along some type of camera to record their adventures. Unfortunately, most of us can't afford the wide assortment of interchangeable lenses we'd like to have. An inexpensive solution is buying what is known as an extension tube, which costs only a fraction of the price of a new lens yet offers superb results.

There are two types of extension tubes. One is designed to reduce the focal length of a standard lens, and the other, called a tele-extender, is used to increase the focal length.

You attach an extension tube to the front of your camera, then attach a lens to it to take dramatic close-ups or telephoto shots of distant subjects. Check the instructions carefully as these nonoptical extenders require exposure compensation.

Since extension tubes commonly come in three-part stages that can be used individually or coupled together in any combination, you get the versatility of having four different lenses at your disposal for the price of one.

The Closer the Better

Anyone with a 35mm SLR can produce fine close-ups. You don't need to pack a lot of extra gear, or spend a great deal of money for lenses.

The lens that comes with a camera with the standard focal length of 50mm is fine. All you do is give it some help.

To get those fine detail shots, though, you must overcome your camera's inability to focus much closer than 15 to 18 inches with the regular

lens. The easiest way to change this is with close-up attachments. These are clear and mounted in metal or plastic filter rings to fit the front mounting threads of the lens. The available diameter sizes are from 46mm to 67mm. If your lens uses 52mm-diameter

filters, this is the size of the screw-on close-up attachment you need.

With the close-up attachment on the lens, the camera's built-in meter sets the exposure and you focus as you normally would.

The lens attachments come in starter sets of Plus 1, 2, and 3 diopters and go as high as 10 diopters. The higher the number, the closer you can focus. You can stack them one on the other, to get a Plus 6. A tiny fly or popper will fill most of an entire negative.

Fast Films

Because outdoor photographers often work in low-light conditions with telephoto lenses, the need for faster films capable of producing quality results has long been recognized. Two films I've recently discovered fulfill this need.

For color, the film I'm now using is Kodak 5293. Developed for use in the motion picture industry, it is, however, available in 20- and 36-exposure rolls for 35mm still photography. The film's normal ASA rating is 400, but when pushed to 800 (daylight), color rendition and acu-

ity only suffer minimally.

For black-and-white, I've adopted a relative newcomer to American photography—Ilford XP1. With a normal ASA rating of 400, this film can be exposed at anywhere from ASA 100 to ASA 1600. What makes it unique is that the ASA setting can be changed at any time in the same roll of film—literally a different ASA for each frame.

The secret of XP1's flexibility lies in the developing, a process that closely resembles C-41 color chemistry. In fact, C-41 can be used for XP1 de-

velopment, though I've found the manufacturer's chemistry produces sharper results.

Another plus to XP1 lies in its limited graininess. When exposed at its normal ASA 400, it grains like other panchromatic films with ASAs of 100 or less. When overexposed by as much as two f-stops, i.e., shot at ASA 100, the result is a virtually grainless negative.

XP1 film is available at many photography shops and may be purchased in 20- and 36-exposure rolls or 100-foot lengths for bulk loading.

Animal Photo Savvy

Ever wonder how outdoor photographers get those dramatic pictures of wildlife? You might be surprised to learn that many are taken not in the wild but under fairly controlled conditions in state parks, wildlife refuges, etc. Knowing this, you can take photos like the pros, if you follow a few basic rules, which will allow you to take equally magical shots.

Even when wild creatures are more curious than frightened, use a telephoto lens. Attempt to fill the entire viewfinder of the camera with your subject. The bird or animal should dominate the scene and not be a secondary factor. A close-up is far more dramatic. Manipulate the background. Don't let anything creep into your photo that doesn't belong there—a telephone pole, for example, will ruin the effect. The background—trees, undergrowth, etc.—should appear as the subject's natural habitat. "Framing" the subject by utilizing trees, branches, and bushes in the foreground also adds to the dramatic effect. A long focal length telephoto "pulls" the scene tightly together to make the habitat seem thicker than it really is.

Finally, film your subject when it is alert rather than bored. A semitame animal, especially, is accustomed to people and is usually relaxed, and this would be obvious in the picture. A deer, for instance, should have its ears cupped alertly rather than lazily folded back. A whistle, such as the type a sports referee uses, will do the trick. Just before pressing the shutter-release button, blow sharply on the whistle. The deer will respond and you'll have a photo you'll be proud to show your friends.

SOCK SIGHT

An old sock, a plastic bag, and a garbage-bag tie can help in shooting your camera.

The sock sight is a variation on the bean bag, a tool often used by photographers for getting stability for long lenses when they do not have access to a tripod. The advantage of the sock device is that the contents need not be lugged into the field.

You do need an old sock that is long and stretched out. White cotton athletic socks seem to work best. Insert a long, narrow plastic bag (like the ones that protect newspapers from rain) inside the sock; leave the mouth of the bag hanging outside the sock.

Once you are in the field, fill the bag with whatever is readily available. Dirt or sand is best for getting a sure rest for sighting, but other materials such as snow or leaves can be used. Tightly seal the plastic bag with the garbage-bag tie. Push the plastic bag down into the sock and then tie the end of the sock into a knot.

To use your sock for sighting purposes, simply place it on a stable surface—a tree trunk or a rock. Lay your telephoto camera lens and fire away.

POCKET CAMERAS

If you recently bought a new high-tech 35mm pocket camera, you will find it a blessing to take afield after lugging an SLR and accessories. The pocket 35 can produce super pictures with little or no hassle. I have owned one for two years, and would be lost without it. By following a few simple rules, you can produce great shots every time.

• Use a medium- or high-speed (200 to 400 ASA/ISO) film indoors or out.
• When photographing people in the morning or evening, put their backs to the sun and use the flash. Most cameras can read the sunlight and determine the amount of flash to fill the shadows on the faces.
• If you want to shoot scenics, especially at first or last light, use a tripod (most cameras have a socket in the bottom). The camera selects the shutter speed, which is often too slow to allow for sharp hand-held pictures.
• Consider one of the new sports models. Most are waterproof or water repellent— great for days spent in the duckblind or bassboat.
• Go to your camera store and buy a belt pouch. It keeps the camera clean and dry and at your fingertips.

PHOTOGRAPHIC MEMORY

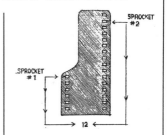

Nothing is more frustrating than pulling a roll of partially exposed film from your camera bag and not being able to remember what number exposure was last taken. If you've tried to mark the film, each attempt you've made probably resulted in smeared, illegible numbers.

Next time you have to remove film at midroll, try this: With the glossy side of the film facing you, break the appropriate sprocket holes. For example, to indicate the number 12, break the first sprocket on the left side and the second on the right side. For numbers less than 10, only break sprocket holes on the right side.

It's been my experience that no matter which two sprocket holes have been broken, the film will always reload quite easily.

Pole-Packed Pictures

You can eliminate picture shakes with a ski pole unipod. Insert a $\frac{1}{4} \times 20$ roundhead stove bolt about $1\frac{1}{2}$ inches along up into and through a ski pole handle and anchor it with a lock washer and nut, leaving approximately one-third inch of the bolt exposed. Complete the project by screwing a ball and socket, which is available in photographic stores, onto the remaining exposed roundhead bolt and against the nut.

ON SCHEDULE

The Canada goose may be the most punctual of all North American waterfowl. Goose watchers living in southern Illinois set their calendars by the first arrivals, each September 21, of honkers migrating from the Hudson Bay-James Bay region of Canada.

This vanguard seldom misses the September date, landing on a three-refuge complex in Union County, Horseshoe Lake and the Crab Orchard National Wildlife Refuge.

From that day through early December more Canada geese arrive, until the birds in the flock are wintering in southern Illinois.

GRAY MATTER

Automatic cameras that adjust shutter and lens are not completely foolproof, and sometimes they underexpose, making your pictures too dark.

The most notorious culprit is backlight, a condition in which the sun is behind your subject. To overcome this, some cameras have backlight buttons. One type works no matter how far you stand from your subject.

The easiest and most accurate method for getting the best color pictures is to use a Kodak 18 percent gray card. Trying to understand how it works will only confuse you, so just deal with the bottom line.

Photo equipment stores sell the 8 × 10-inch gray cards for a dollar or two. I cut one into two 5 × 8-inch sections and a second into four 4 × 5s. I prefer 5 × 8 and have set a three-quarter-inch grommet in one; for a serious bout of picture taking, I sometimes wear it on a parachute cord around my neck. The 4 × 5s go into a shell vest, or camera bag.

To use a gray card, shift your camera to the manual mode. Hold the card in front of your camera, set the shutter and lens as the meter indicates, and shoot.

The gray card works under all light conditions, not just with the backlight. In many cases it will give you more accurate colors than the automation. Use it any time you deal with a change in either the brightness or the direction of the light.

Beating Picture Washout

A polarizing filter and the correct positioning of the camera lens can reduce the possibility of wash out.

The filter reduces reflections and glare, darkens blue skies, cuts atmospheric haze, and intensifies colors.

Get a polarizing filter that matches the diameter of your camera lens. It will have two screens. One screws onto the lens and remains stationary. The second rotates directly in front of the first screen and acts like a valve in adjusting the amount of light that enters the lens. When the notch or handle on the second screen is rotated until it is at a right angle to the sun, less sight will enter the lens, causing a darker picture with reduced reflections and glare.

When first taking pictures with a polarizing filter, experiment with the second screen rotated to different degrees in relation to the sun. This will help you to avoid pictures with a dark sky, aqua-green water, and milk-white shoreline.

Since the polarizing filter reduces the amount of light, you either have to increase the exposure by about 1⅓ f-stops or adjust your shutter speed upward. One way to accomplish this is to make a normal, through-the-lens reading before you attach the filter, and then adjust the aperture or shutter speed after you have added the filter.

While a polarizing filter can reduce reflections and glare, it cannot help a picture that is washed out because of incorrect position with respect to the sun. For best results, keep the sun at your back.

Polarizing filters are inexpensive. Get one with a rotator handle built into the second screen. It is more maneuverable and provides quick response to the varying conditions in the field.

BUG OFF

Cleanliness and a few simple precautions can help keep you from turning into a "bug salad" during camping.

• Choose an open campsite with plenty of breeze, so it will keep the camp cool and the bugs out. Avoid low, marshy spots and standing water.
• Keep your campsite clean. Store food properly, pick up all trash, and clean up spills —especially drinks—immediately.
• Start each day by dosing up with repellent. Spread lotion or cream on skin, clothing, shoes, and socks. For heavy chigger areas, sulfur can be dusted on your pants, shoes, and socks. Avoid spraying directly on tents and eating surfaces. These chemicals are poisonous, and the spray can destroy a tent's waterproofing.
• End each day with a tick check. Cover any you find with petroleum jelly or oil to kill the tick, and then remove with tweezers. Apply hydrogen peroxide, Merthiolate,™ or other disinfectant to kill any germs left behind. Be sure to look for the tick's head. If it doesn't come out, see your doctor. Leaving it embedded will cause an infection.

Keep Bugs at Bay

Campers are eternally plagued by flying critters: flies, wasps, hornets, and yellow jackets in particular. Bugs like to show up when you're preparing meals, and if you decide to clean fish, they swarm.

There's an easy way to keep these nuisances at bay. Simply pour something sweet on a rock or stump away from your living or working quarters. I like a bit of pancake syrup or molasses, but in a pinch you can dissolve several tablespoons of sugar in a cup of water. Dump the sweet concoction no more than 15 feet away from where you're eating or cleaning your catch. The critters will leave you alone.

Dealing with Bug Bites

Biting and stinging bugs can be a real nuisance, but you can ease the pain and irritation with a solution popular with lifeguards in Hawaii, where the mosquito problem is as bad as it is on any backwoods lake. The ingredients are ammonium hydroxide, a common household cleaner, and a few drops of an oil, such as baby oil or mink oil. Mix these and store in a small container.

When applied to affected areas, this solution gives welcome relief from the bites and stings of blackflies, horseflies, deerflies, bees, wasps, chiggers, and mosquitoes.

BAR THOSE BITES

One nearly forgotten mosquito-bite remedy is plain bar soap. Dampen the bite, then rub the bar over it a few times. The thin film left behind takes the sting right out. An added advantage: Bar soap seems to be the easiest thing to find in camp, or in your backpack.

Repelling Ants

A piece of soft white chalk will repel ants. Use it to draw a heavy mark around the edge of your table or eating area. Keeps most crawlers away, too.

BLACKFLY RELIEF

Hungry blackflies torment man and beast alike, but anglers are the most susceptible near fast-flowing streams, a favorite haunt of these insects.

Although numerous commercial and homemade fly repellents are available, none are 100 percent effective. In most cases, the only recourse is to dress in tightly knit pants tucked into high boots, and to wear a headnet, gloves and a tightly knit shirt with long sleeves.

Unfortunately, most shirts have slits at the wrists, and blackflies are most resourceful in finding the tender skin exposed by these openings.

To solve this problem, cut off the feet on a pair of old socks (lightweight nylon is preferred). Then slip the leg sections onto your arms, elastic ends first, much like putting on wristlets. The tubes should cover the slits, and the elastic tops will keep them in place. This also eliminates the need for you to wear a long-sleeved undershirt.

TICK DETECTION

When afield during the spring and summer, ticks can be discouraged from hitching a ride by applying insect repellent to boots and pant legs. However, some ticks seem to ignore this line of defense and attempt to hop a ride anyway.

Ticks that aren't warded off by repellent can be detected if you wear white socks pulled up above boot tops and over lower pant legs. The pests show up well against the light background. This trick also prevents ticks from getting inside pant legs.

FAST TICK REMOVER

I don't believe recent stories that viscous substances are useless in removing woodticks.

I used to pull the loathsome creatures off and dispose of them, the inevitable result being a red welt that itched for days. Last time, weighing some of the scare information about Lyme disease, I plastered the woodtick with a heavy coating of bacon grease. Within a minute or so the tick had raised its hindquarters in the air, and its body language seemed to indicate it was in distress. After five minutes I brushed the tick off with a tissue and crushed it.

The next day only an itchy red mark remained to remind me that I had been bitten.

Porky Repellent

Porcupines can become an expensive nuisance around wilderness hunting and fishing camps, especially during the off-season. These rodents have an appetite for salt and other minerals, and no wooden structure or implement is safe from their busy incisors.

To keep porcupines away from camps and outbuildings, spread mothballs around foundations, hatchways, and any openings where they might try to enter. One application in spring and another in the fall will keep these scavengers away for good.

CAMPING IN BEAR COUNTRY

Once roaming from the Great Plains to the Pacific, and from central Mexico to the Arctic Ocean, the grizzly now numbers fewer than 700 animals in the lower 48 states and is confined to a tiny strip of wild Rocky Mountain country in northeastern Montana, northern Idaho, and northwestern Wyoming. Since this country also encompasses three of our more heavily used national parks—Glacier, Yellowstone, and Teton—there is a fairly good chance that backcountry travelers will see a grizzly. If you plan to camp in a national park or hunt or fish in grizzly country, you'd do well to learn the habits of this creature.

The grizzly is covered with shaggy fur that can be any color from black to cream. He stands about three-and-one-half feet high when on all fours, and has a large hump on his shoulders and a wide, dished-in face. Full-grown male grizzlies average between 350 and 800 pounds.

The grizzly, like his cousin the black bear, has a rolling gait and can outsprint most other animals, including people, over short distances. Unlike the black bear, which has curved claws, the grizzly has straight claws and cannot climb trees when full grown. He is incredibly strong and can break the neck of a moose with one swipe of his paw. He has poor vision, good hearing, and a superb sense of smell.

Despite the grizzly's formidable characteristics, his inclination is to flee human encounters. For this reason millions of people can and do safely travel and camp in bear country.

Grizzlies in national forests, where they are foraging for wild food and are hunted, tend to be wary of humans and will most often run away upon scenting one. However, grizzlies in national parks, where they have learned to feed on garbage and where they have grown accustomed to non-threatening human and vehicular activity, may show unpredictable, aggressive behavior.

The chances of running into one of the latter bears are higher than encountering a wary bear, and the possibility of being attacked by one is approximately 100 times greater than being attacked by a "wild" bear. In fact, there has been only one documented out-of-park death attributable to a grizzly in recent history.

When entering a known grizzly bear area, check with park or forest service personnel to see if there have been any recent bear-people incidents.

Odor attracts bears more than any other stimulus. Therefore, try to use freeze-dried food instead of products such as bacon, sardines, or salami. Use a backpacking stove instead of a wood fire. Don't use deodorant, perfume, or sweet-smelling soap. Avoid sexual activity. Women should stay out of grizzly country when menstruating. (Although there has been no satisfactory study conducted on this issue, two of the deaths in national parks involved women who were menstruating, and thus the Park Service recommends this precaution.)

When making camp, set up a separate sleeping area and a separate cooking area, preferably 100 meters apart. The latter should be downwind of your tarp or tent. Try to prevent food odors or scraps from accumulating on your clothes or sleeping gear. Don't sleep in the same clothes you wore while cooking. Don't bury your garbage, either. If you used food containers such as cans, burn them in your fire or on your stove until all odor has been charred away. Crush the containers and store them in sealed plastic bags along with the other garbage you will pack out. Remember, a clean camp is the surest way to avoid a bear confrontation.

When hiking in grizzly country:

—Be alert and cautious. Look around you, not only for bears but for fresh tracks, rootings, and droppings. Be especially careful when walking through thick timber, when walking into the wind, and when hiking along streams. A bear may not hear you coming in such situations.

—Wear a bell. A metallic noise seems to frighten away bears better than human voices, which may be muffled by foliage. Don't stalk or creep. The more noise you make, the greater the probability a bear will hear you and flee.

—At all costs, avoid coming between a sow and her cubs. Seventy-one percent of all bear attacks in the backcountry of our national parks occurred when a hiker surprised a sow with cubs.

—If you see the bear first, make a wide detour on its upwind side so it can catch your scent. If this isn't practical, backtrack the trail until you are out of sight. Then start making a racket and slowly come back up the trail, making as much noise as you can.

—Leave your dog at home.

—Travel in a group if possible. Two or more people make more noise than one.

Suppose you follow all the rules and a grizzly still enters your camp or charges you on the trail? What should you do?

Wherever you are, try to be within reach of an escape tree. If a grizzly charges, you should climb at least ten feet off the ground. If there is no tree handy or if you can't reach one in time, *don't run away.* Grizzlies have very poor eyesight, and what might be construed as a charge could merely be the bear coming closer to verify what you are.

If all this fails, and if you happen to be the one person in 2 million who is fated to be mauled by a bear, try to stay calm. Curl up in a fetal position, clasp your hands over the back of your neck, and play dead. The bear may leave you alone.

With such a potentially dangerous animal roaming the woods, a logical question to ask is, "Why not carry a weapon?" The answer, quite simply, is that the regulations of our national parks prohibit the carrying of firearms. Carrying a firearm should be considered in bear territory outside a national park, however.

Poisonous Toads

Handling toads can be dangerous. The skins of some toads secrete a poison that, when conveyed to the mouth, causes drooling, convulsive seizures and serious heart disturbances.

The Colorado River toad is the most toxic toad in North America. It can cause neurological problems and even death in animals that pick it up by mouth, and in one case

almost killed a young boy. Suffering paralysis, seizures and difficulty in breathing, he required intensive care for over seven days before he began to recover.

The Real Outdoor Dangers

The Upjohn Company recently surveyed lovers of the outdoors to discover the kinds and frequency of the dangers and accidents they encounter. See how close you can come to ranking these in the order Upjohn's sample reported: contaminated water; insect bites; poison ivy; wasp stings; sunburn; food poisoning; getting lost; traumas like near drownings, major falls, violent storms, or bear attacks; deep cuts; embedded fishhooks; broken bones; snakebites; sprained ankles; sunstroke; burns other than sunburn and blisters.

Answer: Insect bites 95%; sunburn and contaminated water tied at 77%; wasp stings and blisters tied at 70%; deep cuts and traumas tied at 52%;

poison ivy 45%; embedded fishhooks and sprained ankles tied at 43%; burns 32%; getting lost 16%; broken bones 14%; food poisoning 10%; sunstroke 8.4%; and snakebites 4.8%.

Most of the percentages represent occurrences within a three-year period, but Upjohn extended the reporting time for four of the dangers—embedded fishhooks, broken bones, getting lost, and food poisoning—to a lifetime of outdoor recreation.

Interestingly, once in the wilderness, you're over 15 times more liable to be attacked by a water-dwelling parasite than to be bitten by a snake, and most snakebites could be avoided by leaving snakes alone.

SURVIVAL

Survival is largely a matter of mental outlook. The will to survive is the most important factor. Emotional problems resulting from shock, fear, despair, loneliness, and boredom will be experienced. If you are not mentally prepared, the chances of survival are greatly reduced.

Fear is a natural emotion present in all. It is a defense against hostility or the unknown. Fear heightens your senses to potential dangers and hazards. This strong emotion must be properly channeled or it can lead to panic.

Panic is the most destructive response to a survival situation. It may lead to hopelessness, which can break down the will to survive. Positive mental steps must be taken to make fear an ally and panic an impossibility. Knowledge of survival techniques will instill confidence and lead to self-control as well as command of the environment.

Loneliness and boredom come upon one quietly and unexpectedly, usually after all the basic needs have been provided for. They can lead to depression and undermine the will to survive. Keep the mind occupied. These emotions only exist in the absence of affirmative thought.

Most of all, remember the central theme of every survival situation: *Never give up.*

Surviving Without Food

When you're lost or stranded, your concerns become fundamental: shelter, food, water. Convinced they were starving to death, people have resorted to cannibalism after just a few days without food. The truth is, you can usually go about a month without nourishment before actual starvation begins. Until then, you're not starving but fasting.

For the first three days without food you'll typically experience hunger, headaches, nausea, and dizziness. Your tongue will be coated and may cause bad breath. These are not danger signs but indications that the body is ridding itself of waste materials—cleansing itself, in fact.

After three days, there are generally few further hunger pangs until about the 25th day. Ironically, if you manage to find a little food during this time, you'll be hungry constantly. Eating little is dieting, not fasting, and the body responds differently.

The return of hunger after a month or so means your body has depleted its spare resources (fat) and is beginning to consume its own protein. This is when true starvation begins.

When Ralph Flores's plane went down in northern British Columbia in 1963, he and his passenger, Helen Klaben, went without food (except for

RESCUE

Hundreds of anglers, hikers, and campers will get lost this year.

If you become lost, think of the word RESCUE and what the letters stand for:

R RELAX, never panic. Running around only uses up energy and further disorients you.

E ELEVATION. Find a hill or higher ground. Don't aim for some promontory miles away. Just get higher so that you have a better view of the situation.

S SIT DOWN. Use your map, compass, the sun's position, and anything else at your disposal to get oriented. Most of the time, you will be able to right yourself. If you still can't figure out a way back, give some thought to backtracking.

C CHOOSE a *course* of action with a *cool* head. If you haven't reoriented yourself, make camp. If you know which way's out, be sure you can make it back before sunset. If not, spend the night and rest.

U UTILIZE everything at your disposal. If you make camp, collect enough firewood for the night. Make a comfortable bed and signal with your knife or mirror as long as possible.

E ECONOMIZE on your supplies. Drink water and eat, but save enough for a possible long stay. If your county has a search-and-rescue team, a smokey fire usually spells rescue in the morning. Save food for breakfast—you may have a long hike out.

a few biscuits) for 45 days before rescue. She lost 45 pounds and he 51.

While the body can lose nearly all its fat and glycogen and half its protein without death, loss of only one-fifth of its water can be fatal (Klaben and Flores used melted snow). Without any food at all, you should drink about two quarts of water daily, more if you are exerting yourself. You lose a pint a day just through normal breathing.

So, if you're ever lost or stranded, secure water and shelter first. You have almost a month in which to obtain survival food.

DEALING WITH SHOCK

Shock is not, as many people think, a minor emotional affliction. Nor is it the condition of being psychologically stunned by a traumatic event. To the contrary, shock is a serious, life-threatening *physiological* crisis. A basic emergency medical technician's manual sums it up clearly: "If nothing is done for the patient who is in shock, death will almost always result."

That is a frightening statement, made worse by the fact that shock is a frequent response to all manner of injuries and emergency situations, from broken bones to severe cuts and burns to falls and auto accidents. From a survival standpoint—whether one is in the wilderness or along the highway—knowing exactly what shock is, and knowing how to give the appropriate first aid, can mean saving a life.

Essentially, shock is the body's reaction to circulatory disruption or failure. Our physiology requires sufficient blood flow to supply oxygen, remove wastes, and maintain a salt balance between the blood and tissues. This process of exchange is known as perfusion, and when perfusion is allayed, shock ensues. More specifically:

• If the heart is not pumping blood adequately, or if it stops, shock will develop.
• If blood vessels are cut or burst and enough blood is lost, shock follows.

It's important to understand that shock is not a single condition, but a developing process of conditions. Blood loss leads to an increased heart rate as the body tries to adjust to lowering blood pressure, which leads to more rapid blood loss and more accelerated heart activity, and so on in a downward spiral of cause-and-effect.

SYMPTOMS AND SIGNS

The symptoms can include any or all of the following: weakness, nausea and/or vomiting, thirst, vertigo (dizziness), restlessness, nervousness, fear. The signs may include some of these: profuse bleeding; shallow, rapid breathing; rapid, weak pulse; pale, clammy skin; blue lips, tongue, earlobes; vacant look in eyes, dilated pupils.

Especially watch for: increased pulse, as the body attempts to adjust to blood loss; increased rate of breathing (because of circulatory trouble, the body needs more oxygen and involuntarily tries to obtain it); restlessness, paranoia, irritability, as the victim senses deep bodily distress; and the changes in skin color and temperature mentioned above, which may become more pronounced as shock deepens.

FIRST AID FOR SHOCK

When someone is seriously injured, whether in an auto accident or with burns, cuts, or broken bones, treat with the expectation that shock will develop. Follow these steps:

1. Treat the primary trauma first; for example, stop external blood flow or splint broken limbs.

2. Have the victim lie at rest.

3. To ensure that the victim's air passage stays open, keep his/her head straight or tilted slightly back—never bent forward.

4. Keep the victim warm—with covers if possible—but don't overheat. In a cold wilderness situation, you may need to introduce artificial heat, such as a hot-water bottle or wraps of heated stones.

5. If there are no spinal injuries or pelvic fractures, elevate the lower extremities. The victim should lie flat, face up, with legs elevated eight or 12 inches. (In case of a fracture, elevate a limb only after it is securely splinted.)

6. If the victim has trouble breathing *and* is conscious and has no neck, spine, chest, or abdominal injuries, slightly raise the head and shoulders, without allowing the head to tilt forward (which, again, may restrict the airway).

7. Do not give the victim food or fluid, even if he or she is thirsty and asks for it.

8. Don't let the victim sit up or move about; restlessness can be a sign of incipient shock.

9. Fear and anxiety are likely to increase the risk of shock or even worsen it. Words of reassurance can be important.

10. Get professional medical help soon.

ALLERGY SHOCK

Allergy or anaphylactic shock is a true emergency everyone should understand and take seriously. Although dangerous allergic reactions can occur from foods or medications, the most severe outdoor threat comes from insect bites and stings—particularly those from the order Hymenoptera, which includes bees, wasps, hornets, yellow jackets, and fire ants. In the United States about 50 to 100 people die each year from insect-caused shock; many thousands suffer serious allergic reactions.

If you've been stung without serious result, don't think yourself immune; anyone can become sensitized to insect venom, even though the sensitization process might take years. If, on the other hand, you have had uncomfortable reactions to stings, consider it a warning that more severe, even fatal, allergic reactions could occur, and be prepared to deal with them correctly.

The signs of allergy shock can include severe swelling near the sting site, hives, rash, or itching skin; rapid, weak pulse rate; nausea or vomiting; dizziness, restlessness, or fainting; blue or swollen lips; and wheezing.

Beware Deer Ticks

Outdoors people should be aware of Lyme disease, which is transmitted by deer ticks. It first struck people in states all along the East Coast as far south as Maryland and has been spreading in Wisconsin and Minnesota, all the way to California and up north into Oregon.

Dr. Allen C. Steere of the Yale University School of Medicine, one of the leading authorities on the disease, named it when an unusual outbreak of flu-like symptoms culminated in severe arthritic pains in patients from the Lyme, Connecticut, area in 1975. At first it was thought to be a new viral infection. When penicillin, administered to patients during the disease's early stages, controlled the pain, it was rediagnosed as being caused by a bacteria.

Through patient screening the evidence points to the deer tick, *Ixodes dammini*. Tiny bites in the center of the rash were discovered on many patients, in the early stages of this illness. The deer tick is so small—one-sixteenth of an inch long, less than half the size of the common dog tick— that many people did not notice they had been bitten until examined by medical personnel.

Chills, high fever, sweating, nausea, headache, and swollen lymph glands are the disease's symptoms. A circular rash develops at the site of the bite and spreads, in some cases covering the entire body. As the illness progresses, patients develop irregular heartbeats and a low pulse leading to fainting spells. At times a pacemaker has to be implanted to ensure a regular heartbeat. The symptoms climax in severe arthritic pains that can plague the victims for many years.

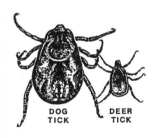

DOG TICK   **DEER TICK**

In the early stages this illness can be mistaken for a form of flu; a certain diagnosis can be made only through a blood analysis. If you come down with flu-like symptoms, check for any evidence of a tick bite or a spreading circular rash, and request the diagnostic procedures for Lyme disease.

You should be particularly careful during warm, damp, spring days when ticks lurk on the tips of foliage. These ticks are less active in the summer and disappear by mid-August.

STAY WARM

The axiom "If your feet are cold, try putting on a warmer hat" holds more truth than might at first appear. Under normal conditions, your body loses about 25 percent of its heat through your head, with your eyes responsible for about one-third of that loss. If you are dressed in warm clothes but with your head uncovered, the percentages become much higher.

Once you begin to lose heat at a rate that exceeds your body's ability to replace it, the blood circulation (and thus the heat circulation) to your limbs is cut back to maintain central body temperature. Your feet don't just feel cold, they really are.

Any time you're in cold, windy conditions, a warm hat is the best insurance against cold feet. Insulated storm hoods that protect the entire head and neck are very effective. In extreme cold, ski goggles can cut down on the heat loss through your eyes.

ON THE TRAIL

WATCH YOUR COMPASS

Certain precautions should be taken when reading your compass.

If you are carrying a rifle, the metal in the barrel can throw off the compass needle 90 degrees or more. So put your rifle down (along with any other iron or steel objects you may be carrying) and stand about six feet from these objects when taking a compass reading.

Another problem, in some parts of the country, is the deflection of a compass's needle from iron deposits in the soil. The only solution is to take numerous readings as you move along. The majority of these readings will be correct, and though your travels may be less than straight, you will eventually get to the place where you are going.

TOPO TO HYDRO

A hydrographic map is great for scouting an unfamiliar lake. Its contour lines most often represent water depths in 10- or 20-foot increments. A quick survey can save you hours of hunting for favorable fish habitat. Unfortunately, many new lakes operated by the U.S. Army Corps of Engineers have not yet been plotted for depth. However, corps lake bottom outlines can be found on standard topographic maps.

To convert topo to hydro, first call the corps' lake office and ask for the current surface elevation. If, for example, you are told that the surface is 1330 feet above sea level, all you need to do is find and then highlight the 1330-foot contour on your topo map. This becomes the shoreline of the lake. The 1320-foot contour will then indicate a depth of 10-feet; the 1310 line will indicate a depth of 20 feet; and so on.

Help Comes in Threes

When you are lost or need help in the outdoors, remember the number three. Three of anything is the signal for distress. Three shots in a row, or three shouts or whistle blasts, are all signals for help. Three lines trampled in a meadow or grass, or field of snow, or three brightly colored sleeping bags in a row also mean a call for assistance.

BUREAUCRACY WILL DO IT

We were at a mountain cabin for the opening of deer season. "What's the weather going to be like tomorrow?" I asked our guide. "Fit for hiking?"

"Don't honestly know, boy," he replied. "Used to be that a man could always judge the weather. Now the government has took it over, and you can't ever tell what the hell it will do."

HIKING TECHNIQUES

Some of us—because of our jobs or where we live—don't walk as much as we'd like. When we hit the trail—after fish or game, or on a camping holiday—we discover that our legs have forgotten the age-old motions. If this describes your relation to moving through the outdoors, or if you'd like to work on more intricate hiking techniques, the pointers below may help.

My number one piece of advice is to *go light*. If you're carrying a pack, ruthless paring is the order of the day.

My number two suggestion is to wear lightweight clothes that don't restrict your movement and, when the weather and activity permit, to wear shorts. You'll stay cooler and more comfortable.

My number three suggestion is to believe that your body is an amazing machine even when it isn't perfectly conditioned. Though a slow warm-up should always be the way to leave the trailhead, a gradual increase in pace will help you reap the rewards of increased circulation, suppler joints and a brisker overall hiking speed. This pushing of your perceived comfort limits not only enhances your hiking performance over a season but also allows you to "hit your stride" on any given occasion.

Of course, there comes a time during the day when this exhilarating feeling of being strong and powerful ends. Lactic acid, a product of exercise, stiffens your muscles and adds to your fatigue. Periodically removing your pack and gently touching your toes, as well as swinging arms and legs in opposite directions to crack your back, will alleviate some of this fatigue.

Perhaps the hardest part of "hiking" as opposed to "walking" comes when the trail grows steep or you must leave the trail altogether. If you're heading cross-country and the way goes steeply up, it does little good to make a beeline for your destination. Choose an angled course and, after heading in that direction for a while, make a switchback and reverse your heading. This longer but more economical way will significantly reduce the strain on your calf muscles; the shallower your switchbacks, the less the strain.

On particularly steep hillsides, another technique will make switchbacking easier. Instead of planting the sole of your foot flat on the terrain, so that your ankle rolls down the hill, use the outside of your boot sole to cut a shallow niche in the ground. Then stand on the edge of your boot while making your next upward step. If you've taken your first step with your right foot, when you take your next step make sure that the *inside* of your left boot sole strikes the hill. Stand on the inside of that foot while your rear foot comes forward. The "kicking steps" save energy on slopes.

No matter if you're kicking steps cross-country in this fashion or ascending a steep trail, the "rest step" will also assist in conserving your strength. Start by moving your right foot: Keeping all your weight on your straightened left leg, move your right foot forward and take a breath. It's important that your left leg stay straight, for this allows your bones to support your weight rather than your tensed muscle, which, of course, will eventually grow tired. When your right foot finds a secure place, straighten it, roll your body weight onto it, take a breath or two, then move the unweighted left leg forward.

Naturally, hills almost always have other sides, which must be descended. If the truth be known, these descents are harder than the climbs. Knees buckle under the weight of packs, toes slam into the fronts of boots, ankles twist. Try to think of going downhill as analogous to driving on icy pavement: Caution and taking the terrain slower than seems necessary will see you to the bottom safely.

In addition, you'll want to tighten the laces of your boots, and perhaps put on an extra pair of socks, to both prevent your toes from hitting the fronts of your boots.

If scree and talus are present ball bearing-sized pebbles and rocks of between two and three inches in diameter—an effective descent can be accomplished by glissading. Shuffle your feet until the stones begin to move under your boots and their sliding motion carries you slowly along. A glissade can be accomplished on some very steep mountainsides, but only after you've practiced on slopes of lesser gradients and you bear in mind that the stones can begin to move quite rapidly and carry you so quickly that you, too, become part of a rock avalanche. Be ready to step aside onto firm ground at all times.

Get the Bank Right

Which side of a stream, river, or brook is the right bank?

No, not the side where the fish are biting. According to the federal government, every waterway has permanent right and left banks, and they're not interchangeable. The designations are constant whether you're flying 3000 feet overhead, going downstream, or standing on either shore.

Give up? The right bank is always on the right side of the *direction in which the water is flowing.*

Share the Wealth

One blue-and-gold afternoon in early fall, I was driving down a slope of the Alleghenies in western Virginia when I noticed a police car following me. Just before a turn in the highway the patrolman pulled ahead and motioned for me to follow him. Soon he indicated we stop.

By the side of the road, looking down into a mountain hollow, lay a pool of still water, dappled by leaves. In the light and shadow I discerned several deer, partly reflected in the pool, motionless, the sun glinting on sleek coats.

Not a word was spoken for several minutes, then the trooper turned, touched his hat in salute and said, "Thank you, sir! I *had* to show it to somebody else."

Are Rivers Free?

Some of those clear, bubbling streams that you come across can plunge you into murky legal controversy: You think it's public water—but here's an irate landowner threatening to sue because you're trespassing.

The theory of public access and navigability started with the English, who wanted to protect both commercial and public movement on their rivers. Sometimes our federal law rules; often it's the state, and there is no uniformity among them. They can't even agree on what is "navigable." (Very broadly, that means you can fish from your boat but if you step out of it you're trespassing—you may not fish from the bank.)

The following 20 states have recognized the importance of streams for outdoors people and have included their use in standards of navigability: Alaska, Arkansas, California, Colorado, Florida, Idaho, Iowa, Michigan, Minnesota, Mississippi, Missouri, New York, North Dakota, Ohio, Oregon, South Carolina, South Dakota, Texas, Washington, and Wisconsin.

When floating or canoeing unknown water, try to check what position the law takes ahead of time. Or ask permission from a landowner if you can find him or her. Don't get into an argument even if you are sure you are right. Just quietly leave the site.

TRIP TIP

Here's a quick method for measuring distances on a map.

Bend a pipe cleaner or a piece of soft copper wire along the proposed map route, then straighten the cleaner or wire and measure it against the scale-of-miles chart in the corner of the map. This saves adding up all those short distances between small town and remote crossroads and results in a fairly accurate reading of the mileage.

NATURE'S FORECASTERS

If you're off to the wild country and you'd rather not pack a radio to monitor weather forecasts, examine local residents for clues to impending changes.

Rabbits out at strange times mean rainclouds are brewing. If a group sits looking in one direction, with ears twitching, there'll be thunder with those showers. Toads feel the electromagnetic radiation too, and hurry toward water. In the evening, large numbers of toads moving through the brush and frogs croaking enthusiastically mean rain.

Fish tend to gambol near the water's surface when rain is imminent. If temperatures are likely to be high, the fish keep to the cooler, deeper water and are reluctant to take a hook.

When the day is going to be hot and dry, spiders spin long webs in the morning. When wet weather threatens, the webs are short or they disappear altogether. Some outdoorsmen claim they've seen spiders breaking their webs before a storm. Winds are on the rise when spiders tighten the main strands.

When you find yourself brushing baby spiders off gear, that marks the beginning of a warm, dry spell.

A swarm of gnats out in the open is a clue to clear weather for the next 24 hours. When they gather in the shade, though, keep the raingear close by.

Bees, hornets, and wasps on casual flight are a sign of fair weather. If you see them crowding back into their hives, take cover yourself because a storm is moving in. Stay away from their nests—distant thunder makes them edgy and nasty.

In some places the woodpecker is called the rain bird because its laughing call is often heard before precipitation. A particularly raucous screech owl outside your tent could be a warning: It becomes more vocal with the approach of downpours.

Blame all this on the drop in barometric pressure and the rise in humidity. It causes some uncomfortable swelling of certain tissues within the bird. Incidentally, the insects birds feed on fly closer to the ground then (frisky fish can reach them hovering just above the water's surface)—that's why many birds fly lower before showers.

FIRST TRAIL RATION

The first trail ration to gain wide usage was a compact food pill developed by Greek army supply officer Philon of Byzantium in 150 B.C. About the size of a large olive, the ration was a mixture of sesame, honey, opium poppy, and a medicinal root called squill. Although crude by modern standards, the pills were reasonably effective. The honey provided carbohydrates for energy, sesame added protein, opium deadened hunger pains, and the squill had a general tonic effect. Soldiers on the move were allowed two pills daily, one at 8:00 a.m. and the other at 4:00 in the afternoon.

To tear its food into small pieces, a crocodile will grasp prey and spin its *own* body around, tearing out chunks of flesh or ripping off limbs.

TRAVELING WITH MAP AND COMPASS

The best maps are similar to the finest paintings. They don't render exactly, but they transmit the spirit of a place. Used with a compass, they make the world understandable and give power—the power of free movement—to those skilled in the craft of navigation. With map and compass you are never lost, only situated at one of countless destinations.

This serene and oriented state of mind doesn't happen automatically. It takes much practice, but it can be hastened by participating in orienteering, a sport that combines map and compass skills with hiking and running, and which can be played anywhere—city streets, neighborhood parks, the deep wilderness.

The basic gear for orienteering is simple. You need a large-scale topographic map of your area and an orienteering compass. These compasses have a transparent baseplate inscribed with a directional arrow for shooting bearings, a rotating compass housing graduated in at least two-degree increments, and a needle that floats in liquid so that readings can be taken while walking.

Before you set up or run an orienteering course, you must know how to read topographic maps. At the bottom margin of U.S. Geological Survey (USGS) topographic maps, you'll find two arrows. One points straight up, has a star at its top, and

is sometimes labeled True North; the other points either east or west of the first arrow (depending on your location in North America) and is labeled MN or Magnetic North. The angle between the two arrows is called Magnetic Declination and expresses, in degrees, the relationship between True North (the North Pole) and Magnetic North (the place near Hudson Bay that attracts your compass needle). In Maine, for instance, this angle will be 20 degrees west of North, in California it will be 18 degrees east of North. Now take a ruler and with a pencil extend the Magnetic North line up through the map. (Make sure that the declination diagram at the bottom of the map is accurate and not merely a representation of the stated angle of declination for your location.) Draw other meridian lines parallel to this line, about an inch apart, until your map is scribed with parallel lines east to west.

Using map and compass is now simple:

1) Place your compass on the map with the edge of its baseplate touching both where you are and where you would like to go. The direction of travel arrow inscribed on the baseplate should be pointing toward your destination.

2) Without moving the compass on the map and *disregarding the compass needle*, rotate the compass housing until the N on the housing dial points to Magnetic North on the map. At this point you'll note that

the bottom of the compass housing has several parallel lines inscribed on it. When these lines are parallel to the magnetic meridian lines you drew on your map, your compass is correctly aligned. What you have done is take a magnetic bearing from the map and transferred it to the dial of the compass housing. You'll now see that the tail end of the direction of travel arrow is striking a number from 0 to 360 on the compass housing. This is your magnetic bearing.

3) Hold the compass in your hand with the direction of travel arrow pointing straight ahead of you. Turn your body, not the compass, until the North end of the compass needle floats into alignment with the N mark on the compass housing. The direction of travel arrow will now point to your destination.

The standard Orienteering race, called a Line Event, can be set up to suit your needs in a large backyard if you're teaching map and compass to children, or across many miles of difficult terrain if you're interested in demanding competition. The organizers of the race place "controls"—human referees, retrievable objects, or code words—on recognizable terrain features, which are also flagged with some sort of visible marker. On a mini-orienteering course the controls can be 25 meters apart while a large course may have them separated by 500 meters. (NOTE: Measurements are metric because most orienteering games were designed in Europe. One meter = 39.37 inches.) On the contestants' maps, each control is marked with a circle around a dot. The simplest way to verify that a contestant visits all the controls is to have a code word written on a slip of paper tacked to a terrain feature. If a contestant returns with all the code words, it means he has visited all the controls.

From the starting line, each contestant takes a bearing on his map to the first control. Contestants are started at approximately two-minute intervals. After finding the first control and writing down the code word, the contestant takes a bearing to the second control and so on. The person who visits all the controls in the quickest time wins. Of course this game can be played by those of all abilities. One group may run the course while another may walk it, for the Line Event doesn't set a premium on physical conditioning; instead it tests fitness in conjunction with map reading skill A Line Event that has been planned with care should consistently highlight route-finding choices, making them both intricate and subtle and thus presenting the contestants with a wide variety of challenges.

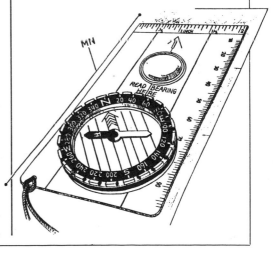

BEWARE OF HYPOTHERMIA IN SPRING

Sportsmen are well aware of what frigid conditions can do, but many ignore the fact that hypothermia can strike when it's sunny and 50°F. Hypothermia is deceptive—it occurs when there is a subnormal temperature within the central body. This results when an individual is exposed for a prolonged period to cold, freezing wind, snow or chilling rain or is dumped into water 50°F or colder.

Spring temperatures in the 40s and 50s can be deadly and are often more threatening since they are deceiving. The temperature may be 50°F, but a strong wind combined with the cool temperature from the ground can produce a windchill factor well below freezing. A cold rain makes conditions even worse.

Sportsmen are prime candidates for hypothermia in the spring. So be prepared for just about anything. Wear several layers of clothing.

A good warm wool cap and mittens or gloves should be worn on any outing in the early spring. The groin and the sides of the chest are two other areas where body heat is lost quickly. Don't forget insulated boots.

Carry some food and hot liquids with you. Chocolate is a quick energy source. Hot chocolate, coffee and soup are good warming fluids. Carry dry matches to start a fire.

Hypothermia can strike the unwise boater on a nice spring day. You can't last more than 10 or 15 minutes in cold water.

Should someone in your group begin showing symptoms of hypothermia, warm him as quickly as possible. Dizziness, disorientation, drowsiness and slurred and slowed speech are the first symptoms. When the temperature of the heart, lungs and brain reaches 90°F, unconsciousness may occur.

Time is the important factor. Get the person covered with as many blankets or articles of clothing as possible. Warm him by a fire. Make him eat something and drink hot fluids. Never give him alcohol. Get him to a doctor or hospital as soon as possible.

LIGHTNING FLASHES

When it rains and big thunderheads roll in overhead, it's time to think about lightning striking, right? Actually, it may strike at other times.

While generally associated with rain and thunderheads, lightning can also occur in snowstorms, sandstorms, and tornadoes.

Weather Reports?

Some of the old weather sayings are true. For example:

Red sky at night, sailor's delight. The dust particles in the dry air (no rain tomorrow) produce a red glow. *Red sky in the morning, sailor's take warning.* Dust-laden air is moving east and moist air is coming in from the west.

If smoke goes high, no rain comes by. If smoke rises from a fire in a thin vertical column, it indicates a high pressure system and is a sign of fair weather. *If smoke hangs low, watch out for the blow.* A low pressure area prevents smoke from rising. Low-rising smoke that is flattened out indicates stormy weather.

Swallows flying high mean there's no rain in the sky. Swallows catch and eat insects on the wing. At high air pressure, which comes with fair weather, insects are carried up high by air currents. *Swallows flying near the ground mean a storm will come around.* At low air pressure, insects fly close to the ground on heavy, moist wings. Precipitation is likely. Insect activity increases before a storm, but active bees mean fair weather as a rule.

When the dew is on the grass, no rain will pass. Dew forms when the moisture condenses on cooled-off vegetation. This happens during nights of dry air and clear skies.

BOOTLACE TRICKS

Tricks can make life with lace-up boots easier:

The ankle areas usually need to be laced loosely, to prevent binding when these joints flex. Conversely, for maximum comfort and fit, laces above and below the ankles often need to be snug. To solve the problem of maintaining both tight- and loose-fitting lace sections on the same boot, tie an overhand knot in each lace, just above the arches (see photo). This keeps the lower laces snug yet permits ankle movement. Similar knots above the ankles aren't usually needed.

For a more comfortable feel, try using flat cloth laces, rather than round cloth or rawhide laces.

To distinguish one pair of boots from an identical pair,

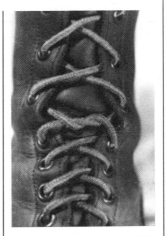

tie a granny knot in the middle of each lace in one pair.

Last, here's a military and Boy Scout trick to let you make the most of lace-up boots in the field: After walking for half an hour or so and during a noon rest, take off your boots and adjust your socks. When you replace the boots, you've automatically compensated for the inevitable foot swelling that occurs on the trail.

Untied Boot Strings

Boot laces have a tendency to come untied. If you simply roll the tops of your socks over the knots and boot tops, you've eliminated the problem. You can virtually walk all day without having to retie. It is a good idea on long treks, however, to tighten the laces after an hour of walking in order to keep your boots tight and to keep "foot slop" down.

Rotate Your Eyelets

Even with well-made boots, the constant pressure of laces on the eyelets eventually causes grooving in them. You can turn the eyelets so the laces bear on an unaffected area. Turn the eyelet over and grip the bottom side with a pair of side-cutter pliers, then rotate the eyelet.

Loose Ends

Bootlaces have a bad habit of becoming frayed at the ends long before they break. A simple, inexpensive way to mend them is to take a little Scotch tape and wrap it tightly around the end of the frayed lace—exactly where the plastic coating had been. This allows you to draw the lace through the boot eyelets with a minimum of effort and cussing.

TOUCH ME NOTS

About 90 plants can cause some form of skin irritation. The best known, of course, are poison ivy, poison oak, and poison sumac. However, two others, located across the southeastern United States, can be more devastating if touched.

The first is known as poison wood, *Metopium toxiferum*. Its local names include hog gum, doctor gum, or coral sumac.

The second, indigenous to the Caribbean Islands, has established a foothold on the sandy coast of Florida. The sap of manchineel, *Hippomane Mancinella L.*, is probably the most caustic of any known plant in this part of the world. Contact with it should be avoided; it can cause severe dermatitis, and if sap gets near the eyes, temporary blindness may occur.

ROUTE-FINDING

Years ago while lounging in my camp high in the Wind River Mountains of Wyoming, I saw two backpackers approaching. They stopped to chat and mentioned that they were heading for a lake that lay just over the ridge to the west of where we were standing. When I said I had been there the day before, they looked at me incredulously. When I said I had also caught some fish there, they dropped their packs, pulled out topographic maps, and pointed to the trail on which they were hiking, a trail that headed south down the valley, made a wide swing around the distant toe of the ridge, then reclimbed the next westward valley to eventually reach the lake in question. I said that, yes, one could get to the lake by heading down-valley and up the adjacent drainage, but one could also hike 2000 feet up the side valley before us, pass through the saddle at its head, and descend to the fishy lake in a couple of hours instead of two days.

"But you couldn't have done it," said one of the backpackers sincerely. "The map shows no trail that way."

Navigation may be an exact science; routefinding, as these two hikers displayed, is not. It takes an intuitive grasp of landscape, a sole-of-the-feet feel for country, and the willingness to backtrack. An artful routefinder can move with economy through unknown ground with the confidence that he or she won't get lost.

What differentiates the mechanical navigator from the artful routefinder? The first has a slavish dedication to the map and compass and will follow a track like an ant. The second studies the maps, calculates bearings, looks keenly at the actual landscape, and before setting out, as well as while on the move, constantly revises the route plan in accordance with what lies off the trail and away from the obvious route of travel.

Consider these examples:

• Saddles and Cols—Low points in ridge systems are called saddles if they're reasonably gentle, cols if they're high and steep. They are often the shortest distance between two points on the opposite sides of an intervening ridge. What needs to be compared is the time spent walking around the ridge from point A to point B, as opposed to the time spent climbing to the saddle or col and descending to point B.

• Contouring Game Trails in Open Country—Wild animals expend the least amount of energy for the most gain. In the mountains they stay high, contouring around edges, because it saves calories. The smart routefinder, descending a ridge and intent on heading up the drainage below, will not indiscriminately bypass the obvious sheep or elk trail that also heads up the drainage—but hundreds of feet above the valley floor.

• Opportunistic Trail Fidelity in the Woods—Contouring game trails can also be used as the quickest way home in the woods. For example, let's say camp lies to the north and west of your location and is far below you. Head downhill and west until striking a game trail that heads north. Follow this trail faithfully until it turns away from your chosen direction or peters out, then head downhill until you come across another game trail heading north. In this opportunistic, zigzag fashion, you can find a clear way through the forest until you are fairly close to your destination, at which time you can then make a beeline for home.

• Energy-Saving Topographic Features— Losing and gaining altitude, trudging through boggy bottomland and brush, or walking over tree slopes is physically and psychologically draining. Don't immediately take the shortest line between two points, for it may be filled with such obstacles. In trailless country, the saddle or col route may be inviting, but it may contain willow and alder. Hiking on gravel bars around the intervening ridge may, in this case, be longer in miles but far shorter in time and energy. Likewise, when faced with a long sidehill traverse, perhaps one with loose rock or intervening gully and ridge systems, consider hiking to the top of the ridge, where level tundra may afford swift travel.

LOOK BACK

Most goal-oriented anglers and mountaineers look ahead to their prize, not realizing that frequently the final goal is to return the way they came. Rather than agonizing between two faint trails in the waning light of dusk, turn around as you head out in the full light of day, especially at all critical junctures, so you know what the country will look like when you return. Make mental notes, and if your memory is faulty, write yourself a reminder, e.g., "Return trail is on the right side of white boulder."

>>

SNOW-SHOEING

People are snowshoeing again. Many sporting goods stores all over are getting requests for the rawhide shoes.

Anyone can learn to walk with webbed shoes in minutes. Snowshoeing is a fine way to keep in shape during the winter months. For another, snowshoeing is safe—no fractures or sprains. If you fall, the harness (or binding) lets your foot go at once.

You can go almost anyplace on snowshoes—across the snow-covered plains, up steep mountains, over gently rolling foothills. Any kind of boot suitable for winter outdoors wear will do.

Snowshoe equipment is inexpensive and in many places you can rent a good pair of snowshoes with harnesses. A coat of shellac or varnish once a year will keep your snowshoes in good repair for a lifetime. The webbing can be tightened and/or replaced with little trouble.

Here are tips to keep you from getting caught in unsafe situations:

• Don't travel during a blizzard. Always check the weather forecast before starting.
• Clear winter air makes estimating distance difficult. Underestimates are more frequent than overestimates.
• Avoid traveling in white-out conditions, when lack of contrast makes it impossible to judge the nature of the terrain.
• If you camp overnight, stop early enough to have plenty of time to build a shelter.

<<<<<<<<<<<<<<<<<<<<<<<<<<<<<<<<<<<<<<<<<<

BOARDED BOOTS

Damp boots dry more quickly if each boot has a thin board pushed down inside it. The board should extend from instep to boot top and fit snugly. Place the boots sideways to a source of heat. Warm air going down on one side of the board insert will draw cool air down the other side, creating a constantly circulating flow of drying air.

Neat for Sale

You've probably used neat's-foot oil at one time or another to soften your boots. But have you ever wondered what kind of animal that intrepid "neat" might be? And what about those feet?

No, it's not a pitiful, near-extinct furred creature of the Arctic. In fact, a neat is no more rare than the local cow. According to the dictionary, *neat* means "bovines collectively; pertaining to bovines."

The oil is obtained by boiling the feet and shinbones of many cows.

Nature Lesson

Parents have been teaching their children about nature for a long time. For example, when my six-year-old son went fishing with me I scolded him for tossing a banana peel into the stream. "The Lord doesn't like us to dirty up His rivers," I explained, just as a sudden squall came up, with thunder crashing and lightning forks stabbing all around us. We hurried back to camp through the drenching downpour. As we sat shivering miserably in our tent, soaked to the skin, my son looked out at the dark heavens, wide-eyed, and said to me, "Gosh! All that over one little banana peel!"

Keeping Warm

If you hike any reasonable distance in the winter you probably will work up a sweat. As the perspiration on your skin evaporates, body temperature is lowered and soon, you feel the discomforting cold creeping in.

Here's how to overcome this problem. Put your socks, underwear, long johns, and extra warm clothes in your pack. Wear lighter clothes for the hike up the mountain. When you get to the top, change everything.

By the time you reach the summit you will look like a steaming locomotive as your breath meets the frigid morning air.

Pack your clothing so that you can take each piece out in the order you want. Remove the light coat, shirt, and undershirt first. Dry off with a towel. Seconds later put on fresh, dry clothes.

When the morning wind howls and the temperature never climbs to zero, you will stay warm and comfortable.

IMMUNITY IMPUNITY

If you think you're immune to the effects of poison ivy because you have come in contact with it and displayed no symptoms, you may be in for an unpleasant surprise the next time you're afield.

Dermatologists caution that it takes at least two brushes with the irritable weed to be affected. The first contact merely sensitizes the body without displaying any symptoms. Subsequent contact may bring on the unpleasant, itchy rash. So don't be fooled into thinking you're immune. Poison ivy is a weed to avoid.

BEWARE OF FROSTBITE

Aside from thin ice, a winter hiker's greatest threat is frostbite. It is a skin condition similar to a burn and is caused by a combination of subfreezing temperature, humidity, and wind. Staying out too long is inviting disaster.

Most often affected are the ears, the tip of the nose, fingers, and toes. If you hike alone, it's a good idea to carry a pocket mirror to see how your nose and ears are doing as the day wears on. Should any exposed skin appear yellow-white, waxy, and cold and hard to the touch, get out of the cold. A car is a good place to warm a frostbitten area because it can be done gradually. Don't massage the affected area; rather, keep it cool until returning blood circulation thaws it from within. Applying heat directly to the frostbitten area before the circulation returns can result in clotting the blood in the blood vessels, causing that part of the skin to die, turn black, and fall off—a phenomenon known as dry gangrene.

Common sense should keep the winter hiker out of trouble. If your hands or feet get numb, or you feel a burning sensation on any exposed area followed by numbness, it's time to quit.

DEALING WITH COLD WEATHER

Most people don't like the cold. Not only do vehicles, cameras, eyeglasses, and campstoves stop working, but the human body also comes to a painful halt. However, most people's dislike of the cold stems from bad experiences: Their spectacles fog up every time they come inside; their numb fingers can't tie a knot.

Fortunately, there are ways to deal with all these cold-weather annoyances.

CAMERAS

Professional photographers sometimes "winterize" their cameras. This is an expensive procedure that is unnecessary unless you're sledding to the pole. But if you aren't careful with an unwinterized camera, it will definitely stop working. Down to zero, I leave my cameras outside, removing the lithium batteries or the motor drives and bringing them inside. If it's far below zero, the diaphragms of unwinterized lenses, left out overnight, will grow sluggish and won't stop-down properly the next day. You will then have overexposed shots, even though everything else in the camera is working. The solution is to leave the cameras in their carrying bags and place them in an intermediate-temperature zone in your cabin or tent—by the door, for example.

When it's really cold during the day—less than 20 below zero—I carry my camera inside my parka and let my body heat keep it warm. If you're exerting yourself, the camera is going to get covered with moisture, so cover it with plastic.

When it's time to take pictures, remember two important details: First, if you press your nose or your lips to the back of the camera body, they're going to freeze there. Keep your face slightly away and hold your breath. If you don't, your breath will instantly fog the eyepiece.

Second, when you load film, do it slowly. Film becomes brittle when cold and can easily fragment into many pieces.

EYEWEAR

Those who wear eyeglasses may wish to consider carrying an extra pair in an inside pocket. Don the warm pair inside.

Contact lenses work far better in really cold weather. However, lens cleaning solutions freeze at about the same temperature as water. The kangaroo pouch solves this problem.

In the winter I wear a pile pullover that has a large zippered pocket—what I call a kangaroo pouch—on the chest. Into this pocket goes my contact lens solutions, extra batteries for my camera, a couple of butane lighters—the lighters won't work if they've been sitting in your pack at 30 below—and several pemmican and chocolate bars to get extra calories into my stomach quickly.

STOKING THE FIRE

I own a pair of boots rated to −80°F. I've been toasty in them at −60°, and yet have felt as if my feet were two frozen bricks at −15°F.

How come? Simple: At 15 below, I was out of gas—I hadn't eaten in six hours, and I'd been pushing a sled over broken pack ice. No matter how good your footgear or your clothing, you won't be warm if you don't eat. Moderate that huge breakfast, which will only make you sluggish out the door, and take a lot more high-calorie food in your daypack. When you start to feel cold, don't wait. Eat then.

FOODS FOR WINTER WARMTH

FOOD ITEM	CALORIES
One tablespoon margarine (added to sandwich)	100
Milky Way bar (2.15 oz.)	280
Hershey's Dark Chocolate bar (1.35 oz.)	210
Peanuts (1 oz.)	160–180
Nature Valley pemmican bar (3.75 oz.)	420
Black coffee	0
One tablespoon sugar (added to any drink)	44
One cup hot cocoa (Swiss Miss or Carnation)	110

Sunburn Protection

If exposed skin becomes sun-burned despite precautions, try dropping two or three tea bags under the hot water tap while the tub is filling and then take a leisurely bath. Tea or even a wet tea bag can also be dabbed over the burned area—the tannic acid in the tea is soothing and healing.

THE ATTACK

From time to time, outdoors people are attacked by rabid, wild, or aggressively mean canines—wolves, coyotes, feral dogs, foxes or even some-one's pet.

Now, there is no question that if one had to face a savage canine, a 12 gauge loaded with buckshot would be the weapon of choice, but sometimes such firepower is not at hand. If the situation does not allow a safe retreat, a sharp blow with a stout stick, a broom handle, or even a clenched fist across the snout will send most canines to the ground in a stupor.

WHY ARGUE

During a field trip last year we returned to our campsite and found it invaded by several bears. One large black bear was tossing and slapping an ice chest around like a beach ball. I screamed at my husband to go rescue our chest. He watched the bear for a few seconds, then turning said to me, "That's not *our* ice chest. That's *his* ice chest."

To Avoid Rabies

Some 30,000 Americans annually undergo vaccination to prevent rabies after being bitten, usually by wild animals. The worst offenders are bats, skunks, foxes, and raccoons—dogs are last.

How do you spot a rabid animal? Veterinarians list two forms of the dread disease, which without treatment is almost certainly fatal. With "nervous" rabies the animal is very agitated and drools. The "dumb" form (common in dogs) is just the opposite: The animal drops its jaw, is slack and lackluster and at times appears to have something stuck in its throat. The *Pennsylvania Game News* suggests these safety procedures.

• Keep pets vaccinated.
• Don't handle wild animals, especially if they are unusually tame.
• Use gloves when you handle animals—alive or dead.

If bitten:
• Wash wound thoroughly with soap and water.
• Take yourself and the animal—dead or alive—immediately to a doctor if rabies is suspected.

BOTTLES GALORE

During a lull between strikes, I was sitting in the shade of a cottonwood on a sandbar. Poking around with a willow stick, I struck a solid object. A moment later I held a green bottle, the type that takes a cork, not a cap. On the round glass was embossed "A. M. Bininger & Co. No. 19 Broad St. New York." A part of the past, I thought and slipped the bottle into my creel. Back home a collector, eyes bugging, offered me $175 for my happenstance find.

Since then I've never passed up a chance to probe sandbars, or poke into thickets on the banks of lakes and streams, and have been rewarded by many important, and not so important, bottle finds.

Any embossed bottle (one with lettering worked into the glass) is a definite collectible, as are bottles showing a three-piece mold seam, placing their manufacture somewhere between 1809 and the mid-1880s. Never pass up a free-blown bottle, one with a slightly irregular shape.

Another clue to a valuable find is bubbles in the glass, which were fairly common in bottles before 1920. Many

clear bottles made between 1880 and 1910 and exposed to the sun turn purple, or amethyst, because of manganese in the glass.

Other clues to look for in bottles worth saving are pontil marks (rough glass on the bottom), inside screw threads, blob tops, unusual coloring, laid-on rings, and odd-shaped bottles.

Penalties for Poaching

Over the ages societies have viewed poaching violations with uniform disapproval. Yet despite often cruel and blatantly morbid penalties, poaching has been an unshakable part of human existence. As soon as there were game laws, there were poachers.

In ancient Greece, the twin penalties of banishment and seizure of all property were invoked upon deer poachers. In addition, they could not be buried in Attica, a fate that doomed their souls to eternal wandering and misery.

Roman poachers were simply tossed off the Torpeian Rock, their bodies abandoned.

In Britain, the fate of poachers depended on the disposition of the monarch. Under Richard II any person unauthorized to hunt for lack of family wealth was imprisoned for one year if found to have hunting gear. Under Edward II unlawful possession of any raptor resulted in a fine plus two years in prison. The sport-loving Henry VIII introduced new penalties with more bite. They included the death penalty for unlawful possession of one hawk egg.

By 1604, under James I, poaching penalties were greatly relaxed. As a result, poaching became rampant. After 130 years of trifling penalties led to dwindling game, remedial action was taken. George II in 1737 prescribed seven years banishment "in one of his Majesty's plantations in America."

Historically, game administrators were vigilant in enforcing laws. They saw to it that people were not given the chance to violate twice. Sometimes the penalty for poaching was harsher than that for murder.

Outdoor Values

I wonder if sporting people shouldn't give more thought to the esthetic values of their sport. What kind of value do we get from the pleasure of observing a dozen mallards setting their wings prior to landing on a pond? Or the thrill of seeing an 8-point whitetail emerge ghostlike from the brush; or the tug of a hefty bass on your line?

I find it very difficult to place any monetary value on them or to take these sights and sounds for granted.

Native American Philosophy

When we Indians kill meat, we eat it all up. When we dig roots, we make little holes. When we build houses, we make little holes. . . . We don't chop down trees. We only use dead wood. (Wintu Holy Woman)

BUCKSKINS FOR BRITAIN

Deer hides were once a significant item of commerce between the American colonies and England. Old customs records show that 2,601,152 pounds of deerskins were shipped just from Savannah, Georgia, to England between 1755 and 1773.

FAIR GAME AND FOWL

See if you can match these game and water birds with their common nicknames:

(1) double-crested cormorant
(2) willow-ptarmigan
(3) bufflehead
(4) great black-backed gull
(5) scaup
(6) frigatebird
(7) pied-billed grebe
(8) king rail
(9) anhinga
(10) merganser
(11) American coot
(12) American black duck

(a) dabchick
(b) shag
(c) snakebird
(d) bluebill
(e) snow grouse
(f) man-o'-war
(g) redleg
(h) butterball
(i) marsh hen
(j) mud hen
(k) coffin bearer
(l) sawbill

Answers:
1) b, 2) e, 3) h, 4) k, 5) d, 6) f, 7) a, 8) i, 9) c, 10) l, 11) j, 12) g.

Caribou Hide

Leather made of caribou and reindeer hide has the singular property of not stretching when wet. Also—as those dwelling in the Far North have known for countless centuries—when tanned with the hair on, it forms the warmest of all coverings. No other leather moccasins can even compare with those of caribou hide if it has been tanned without the use of chemicals. It makes exceptionally strong, durable thongs, fine blankets, tents, and rugs.

All sorts of storage bags, packs, and the like can be fashioned from the hide. Indeed, as is best pointed out in Farley Mowat's *People of the Deer* (a book that deserves to be better known), caribou meat and hides provide the wherewithal for meeting virtually all of life's needs in arctic regions.

Anyone fortunate enough to own items made of caribou skin has real treasures, treasures that will last, for not the least of the hide's properties is its durability.

ON THE WATER

Canoeing Moving Water

A canoe can be a stubborn critter, but there are a lot of tricks to making it go where you want in a riffle or minor rapid. They are all based on teamwork—coordination of strokes between the bow and stern paddlers.

Although it is a slight over-simplification, remembering one simple fact will help you keep a canoe out of trouble in most situations: *The person in the stern positions the canoe to set its direction. The bow paddler supplies the power to move it in that direction.*

The more experienced paddler belongs in the stern, the stronger in the bow.

LANDING WARNING

Be especially careful of snakes at boat landings. The smell of fish lingers around boats and docks, and sometimes even bits of bait or minnows are left on the deck or in the livewell. Moreover, many people pull the bow of a boat up onto the beach, leaving the stern in the water. This creates an air space just under the hull that is ideal for water snakes, so be watchful when pushing off from a bank. Few things infuriate a cottonmouth as much as a boat sliding over it!

BOW PADDLER SUPPLIES POWER   STERN PADDLER POSITIONS CANOE

DROWNPROOFING

Hundreds lose their lives each year because they can't swim. Two life-saving in-the-water rules give people a better chance of surviving:

First, *learn to swim.*

Second, learn "*drownproofing*," a technique that protects people from panic and exhaustion. It is the best way to stay alive in water for long periods of time without artificial aids, and anyone from 4 to 70 can learn the method.

The basic principle: Make the most of your body's natural buoyancy by *floating facedown in a relaxed dangling position* instead of using up energy to keep your head above water. You come up for air every 10 seconds or so. Clothes, currents, undertows, and tides all lose their fearsome aspect.

Drownproofed people should be able to survive 24 hours at sea unless there are hazards such as concussion or cramps. If you experience these, you *can* survive with just one arm or leg working.

Find out where drownproofing is taught: Check your local Red Cross or the Ys for classes, which can save lives, in your area.

HOW TO FORD RIVERS

To facilitate rocky river crossings, I always carry a pair of nylon-mesh running shoes in my pack. After taking off my boots and socks, I slip into my running shoes, make the crossing, then hang them from my pack to dry as I continue to hike.

Deeper crossings can be done more comfortably if you wear a pair of nylon running shorts with a polypro brief. Cotton underwear will stay wet long after running shorts have dried. On very cold crossings, wear long underwear instead of trousers. The body-hugging underwear offers less resistance to the current and will, like running shorts, dry with body heat as you continue to hike.

Once you've resolved your footwear and clothing problems, inspect the stream or river carefully, considering in particular the possibility that a man-made or natural bridge exists nearby.

If it's still late spring or early summer, a snow bridge made of avalanche debris may exist where the stream or river enters a canyon. Or if you're in a canyon, consider searching for a widening of the river. Here you might find stepping-stones that will lead you easily across. In addition, the current will be moving more slowly and the water will be shallower at a wide place in the river, making fording easier. If you do find natural stepping-stones, beware of slippery moss and thin films of ice.

Before crossing, unstrap your pack's hip belt and loosen its shoulder straps. You want to get out of your pack immediately if you take a spill. If you're alone, find a wading staff and use it on your upstream side as a third leg. I prefer to cross with my side to the current, offering the least surface area to the river, and move one leg or the wading staff one step at a time.

If two or more people are crossing, they can link arms and support themselves. The largest person should be upstream, to break the current. If the shallow part of the ford extends for any length upstream and downstream, crossing can be made easier by starting at the top of the shallow stretch and angling downstream with the current.

Whether alone, in a pair, or in a group, if the water is at all swift and begins to boil above your knees, you will start to lose your footing. Such swift, cold, hip-deep water is nearly impossible to ford unless you have a stout staff, are tall and well muscled, and are also brave to the point of foolhardiness. Remember, in 40°F water, humans can do only 7½ minutes' worth of useful work, and nearly everyone becomes unconscious after 30 minutes of immersion. Consider these statistics if there is any chance of your being swept away and stranded—partially submerged—on some boulder in the middle of the river.

If there is no way to avoid fording such a

stream or river, use a rope. Tent guy lines and light cord are out of the question. Climbing rope or whitewater throw rope should be used. The strongest swimmer should go across with the rope. NEVER tie into the rope. If you tie the rope around your waist and are swept away, chances are you will be held underwater and drowned. Instead, loop the rope around your waist and have one or preferably two people on the shore (one upstream, one downstream) belay you. You can lean against the rope for support as you cross. If you're swept away, however, you can quickly duck out of the loop. (To increase your margin of safety, carry a sheath knife to cut yourself free if entangled.)

Once the crosser reaches the other side, two options exist. He can anchor the rope while the other members of the party use it as a handline to support their fording. Or, if the original forder doesn't want to recross the river at the end of the fording, he can loop his end of the rope around a tree, then toss that end back to his belayers, who, after putting their end around a tree, tie their end to his end. He hauls the knot across, tensions the rope, and when everyone is done crossing, he unties the knot, pulls the rope across, and everyone goes on his way.

Needless to say, this method is involved and can often be circumvented by walking a few miles upstream or downstream to a more inviting ford. Another alternative would be to wait until early morning before crossing, when mountain rivers are generally lower.

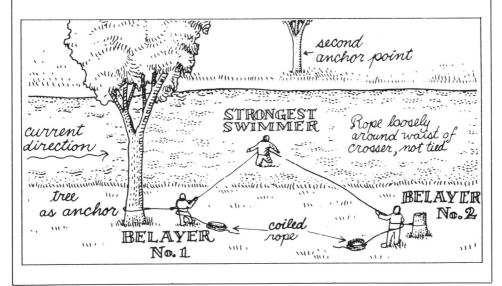

second anchor point

current direction

STRONGEST SWIMMER

Rope loosely around waist of crosser, not tied

tree as anchor

BELAYER No. 1

coiled rope

BELAYER No. 2

WAVE ACTION

Standing waves—haystacks —are a phenomenon experienced only on rivers. The fundamental difference between these and ocean swells is water movement. On a river, the waves are stationary, and water moves through them. On the ocean, waves move through the water, cresting first, then washing out on shore as surf.

It is possible to "surf" a river by riding stationary waves in a kayak or canoe—or even a surfboard. Paddlers work against the flow of current to slow down the drift of the boat, becoming stalled on the wave for a free ride.

If the waves are big enough and of the right configuration,

even larger boats such as rafts can surf. While this game is fun for experienced boaters, the risk of overturning is great. Boaters should have safety backups waiting below a surfing rapid, and they must be skilled at handling their craft in an emergency (e.g., kayakers must be proficient at Eskimo rolling).

To avoid getting stuck in a wave and possibly capsizing, river drifters must keep up momentum by paddling or rowing through big waves. Also, keep the bow of the boat pointed straight into the wave—don't let the power of a big river haystack knock the boat sideways.

RIVER RAFTING

Contrary to traditional rowboat technique, river-runners row facing forward, bow first, looking downstream to see any obstacles the river presents.

The basic *push stroke* (pushing forward on the oars) is used only for easy maneuvers by rafters, although it's a favorite of hard-shell boats that move faster. For quick response and making speed in a raft, use the *power stroke*: pull backward hard on the oars, with the raft angled stern first in the direction you're going.

A raft can be turned by pushing or pulling on one oar, but for quick, sure pivoting use the *double-oar turn*: to spin the raft left, pull hard on the left oar while you push on the right. Reverse for a right turn.

Beginning rowers should test rowing skills on lakes first, to develop the fundamentals and gain confidence. Then move on to easy streams with sluggish currents as you become adept at maneuvering the raft or drift boat forward through flat water and riffles, then back and forth across the river (*ferrying*). Gradually move to rougher rivers.

With a good boat and a season of practice, you can escape the limitations of bank-plunking to explore new, otherwise inaccessible backcountry and float a little white-knuckle water.

Basic River Rafting Safety

Practice and perfect your rowing skills before you tackle tough waters. Then work on these points:

• If your ambition is floating classified white water, seek professional instruction. Many river outfitters and public institutions offer courses in reading and running rivers.

• Know your river. Be certain of what's ahead before you commit to a route. Seek information about new rivers by asking locals and consulting guides. Keep alert for new obstacles such as strainers (trees brought down by winter storms). When in doubt, pull ashore and look before you float.

• Regardless of your rowing skills or your boat's stability, always wear your life jacket and make sure passengers do the same.

• Carry essentials: first-aid kit, foot pump, raft repair kit (with patching materials and frame-fixing tools), a spare oar mounted high on one side with quick-release buckled straps, warm clothing secured in a dry bag, and perhaps food and hot water in a thermos.

• Always keep ropes coiled or stowed in small bags.

• When the raft is about to broach a rock in fast waters, everyone should quickly move *toward* the rock. Otherwise, you may wrap around the rock like a wet sheet. (The command for this maneuver is "Rockside!" or "Jump to!")

• Rafters should remember that if they fall out in swift, rocky waters, never to try to stand up or swim. Instead, *sit in the water* with feet downstream to ward off rocks. Let the life jacket float you to quieter waters where you can be successfully rescued.

• In wild waters, all rafts should have lifelines strung around the tubes for passengers to grab hold of and flip lines to right the raft should it be overturned in rough water.

The oceans cover 71 percent of the earth's surface, harbor 80 percent of all animal life, serve as a reservoir for 97 percent of the earth's water, provide us with half of our life-sustaining oxygen and with millions of tons of food.

GROUNDING ON WATER

Lightning kills more people each year than do tornadoes, hurricanes, or floods. Boaters are particularly vulnerable to lightning strikes. There is a precaution you can take—a simple grounding system to protect the boat. Run a No. 4 copper wire from a metal rod, installed at the highest point on the boat, to one square foot of copper flashing dangled in the water or attached to the hull below the waterline.

TWELFTH-MONTH FAVORITES: STEELHEAD, BLUEGILLS, BASS

Twelfth-month fishing is a some-time thing in many states, but not to those tetched on steel-head, bluegills, and bass. Now is when those anglers are hard at it because some of the year's monsters can be had.

Wherever my travels take me in December, I'm near one of these fine game-fish. And that comforts me more than sitting inside, because I know how to garb for the elements and gear for these favorites. Let's take them in order.

Steelhead—This is a rainbow trout that decided to roam into the sea, or large lake, grow to heavyweight proportions, and re-turn to the stream of its birth. For several years it has been gorging and putting on muscle.

Two methods appear to work in rivers. One: fresh roe (spawn) draped over a hook or balled inside thin nylon mesh. This is weighted with enough sinker to keep it near bottom and bottom-bounced in deep holes. And two: drift bottom-nudging lures downstream, letting them cover the width of a hole, then dropping downstream to the next spot.

Bluegills—The farther north you hap-pen to be, the sooner the ice comes on. Many bluegillers never wet a line during "soft-water" months, preferring "hard wa-ter" which means when the lakes ice over.

And there's something to be said for ice fishing. My grandfather never thought a thing about being there and spudding a hole through one-foot ice at daybreak. I never thought much of it myself. I prefer drilling ice holes after breakfast when the sun is high.

Further, I enjoy being inside a cozy ice shanty with a fishing buddy so we can catch up on our lying about summertime fishing. It's dark, peaceful, and shirt-sleeve cozy, thanks to a small stove, even when it's zero outside. Ice shantys have a way of gathering into small cities, a sure sign of good panfishing. Just join the crowd.

A consistently good method for taking hand-sized bluegills is to use two-pound monofilament on a small rod. Said rod has about the same heft as a fly-rod tip. A tiny hook, Size 12, baited with red worms, or grubs found in horseweed galls, and jigged slightly over weedy cover will get you all the bluegills you care to clean, if they're around. If not, move until you find where the schools are located.

Bass—Now is when bass hounds in the Southeast are living it up. The tourist-anglers are absent, and natives have most of the good spots to themselves and other cold-weather bassin' people.

And now is the time to visit some outback lakes and ponds that are too weedy to fish during summer and fall months. With weeds thinned by frosts, those big lunkers can be reached if you're quiet.

Two lures pay off for me with these goliaths. When the surface is mirror-flat, a noisy top-water spinner lure seems to goad them into murdering it. It is best worked s-l-o-w-l-y, teasingly, over weed pockets and around lily pads, in five to ten feet of water. Don't ever be in a hurry; a big bass isn't.

The other is a black, six-inch salamander made by Stembridge. Rig it just like you do a plastic worm with a slip-sinker. I prefer a 2/0 Eagle Claw worm hook with the "Z" bend and a ½-ounce bullet lead to get it down quickly. Working it is simple. Let it reach bottom, then raise the rod tip, maintain a taut line, and just swim it in as you reel slowly.

Whichever one of these three you go for, do it. I can't think of a greater way to put the icing on the dull winter months. All are sporting to catch and delectable to eat. What are you waiting for? Sic 'em!

GARB FOR WINTER FISHING

When that thermometer plunges near the zero mark, it can chill you to your marrow if you aren't dressed properly, especially if there's a wind blowing, which will compound your misery.

In such extreme conditions, insulated garments on top of wool shirts and pants, on top of insulated underwear, will keep your body warm. Wool socks inside of insulated boots will keep your tootsies toasty. Top this off with a wool stocking cap, or earflap hat, and insulated gloves and you're ready for the elements.

In moderate temperatures, from freezing to the 50s, use the layer system, because you can peel a layer off should the day grow warm. This calls for insulated underwear, the waffle-weave, two-piece type.

Next come any tight-weave pants and shirt, then a loose sweater and a lightweight insulated jacket. On top of this don a soft-plastic foul-weather suit, two-piece, and one that doesn't stiffen when cold. On your head wear an earflapped hat or cap and slip light, tight-weave gloves onto your hands. Bama socks are insulated fibrous socks that wick away moisture to keep feet dry and warm. Any shoes will do to keep your feet comfy. A jug of hot coffee does a lot to maintain inner body heat.

Casting, Mending, and Making Fast

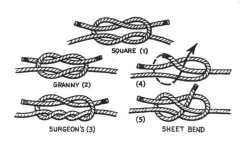

Have you ever cast a figure eight or a stevedore? In their language, sailors don't just "tie knots"—they "put in" splices, "make fast" hitches, "bend" ropes together, and "clamp on" a stopper. They "clear" a tangle or "open" a jammed knot.

Among sailors, there are four categories of knots: hitches, bends, splices, and, of course, knots. A hitch is used to tie, or make fast, a rope to an object; a bend unites two rope ends; and a splice is a multi-strand bend or loop. A knot may be a knob (tied in the end of a rope to prevent unraveling), a loop, or anything else that's not a hitch, bend, or splice.

From now on I'm going to use knot in its broadest sense to include everything. What makes a good knot? First, it should do the job it was designed for. Second, it should be easy to tie. Last, it should be easy to untie.

Outdoors people often need to tie two rope ends together. The best knots for this purpose are the square knot and the sheet bend. Use the square knot for rope ends of the same diameter, and the sheet bend for rope ends of unequal thickness.

An easy way to remember how to tie the square knot is, Left over right, and under; right over left, and under. Be sure the finished knot looks like Fig. 1, or you're likely to end up with a granny knot (Fig. 2), and a granny knot won't hold well.

A square knot can be "upset" or "spilled" by either pushing the ends toward the knot or pulling back on one end and pulling the other end through the loops. By taking an extra turn, a square knot becomes a surgeon's knot (Fig. 3). The extra turn often facilitates tying, especially when the rope ends are under tension.

For joining two rope ends of different diameter, use a sheet bend. Begin by forming a loop or bight in the larger-diameter rope (Fig. 4). Then weave the smaller rope through the eye, around the bight and back under itself (Fig. 5). Be sure to snug the knot carefully before putting it under any strain.

When you tie your shoes you are basically tying a square knot, except that you are doubling the shoelace on the second turn. That makes the knot easy to untie—slippery, in nautical terms.

WALLET SAVER

To reduce the chance of losing your wallet when afield, wrap a thick, heavy rubber band around it. This will prevent your wallet from slipping out of your pocket.

No Trip Down

When ferrying people and supplies across the killing-cold waters of northern lakes, it is better to take two safe trips than one trip with an overloaded boat. A dunking in the icy water could be fatal.

There are two forms of arrowhead plants, terrestrial and aquatic.

Patching Aluminum Boats

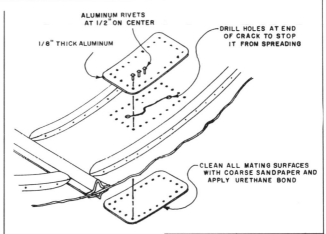

The first step is to drill a hole at all ends of the split or crack—a one-quarter-inch hole is about the right size. Use a rubber mallet to reshape the damaged area.

Next cut two patches of equal size from a one-eighth-inch sheet of aluminum. They should extend at least one inch on all sides of the crack. Use a fine-toothed plywood blade on a radial arm saw or a table saw. Round off the corners of the patches and shape them to conform to the contour of the boat. Position the patches over and under the crack, and drill a hole at one end through them and the boat. Place a rivet through the hole. Drill a second hole at the opposite side of the patches and place a rivet through them, too. With the two rivets holding the patches, drill additional holes around the edges on about one-half-inch centers.

Be sure the rivets are aluminum or they'll corrode. They should protrude through the inner patch, boat, and outer patch about the same length as the diameter of the rivet.

Clean and rough up the mating surfaces of the patches and the boat with coarse sandpaper. Liberally apply Dow Corning Urethane Bond™ to the patches and the boat. (There are other adhesives that will work equally as well.)

Work fast, before the adhesive sets. Place the rivets through the holes and peen them over with a hammer. Hold a second hammer on the head of the rivet while flattening the other end to form a second head. Keep the head of the rivet even with the patch while peening. Do a good job, and the patched crack will never leak again.

While searching for a better method of fixing my boat, I ran across a package of J-B Weld™ in an auto parts store. The package consists of two tubes, one of steel and one of hardener. Mixed together, they form a gray substance that when dry is as hard as the aluminum itself.

Two applications of J-B Weld fixed my john boat. J-B Weld can be found in most auto parts stores.

Craft Shops for Anglers?

Flytiers and do-it-yourself lure makers are always on the lookout for materials. Nothing will replace the well-stocked tackleshop for most needs, but there are other shops that stock many useful items not found in tackle stores.

Try your neighborhood craftshop. It can be a treasure trove for the imaginative or innovative angler. Marabou feathers in more colors than you can imagine, beads in a wide range of sizes and colors, yarns in a variety of colors and textures, and plastic products suitable for body material on bugs and poppers are just a few of the possibilities.

The prepackaged quantities are generous and the price is lower per unit than for the small packages sold in tackleshops. (It might pay to do some of your shopping with a friend and split the cost.)

Solving Stream Mysteries

Water and gravel and rock, and somewhere within it all, scattered here and there, are those great prize packages called trout. All too infrequently you can see them, pale waverings casting shadows on the stream floor, or mouths tilting up to sip floating insects. But mostly they lie still and hidden near bottom, living secret lives, tucked away beneath the mysterious weave of the current.

An angler approaches and wonders: Where do I cast? Where are the fish in all this water? A most serious question if you want to catch trout, a question more subtly layered than most people who fish realize.

Not that the basics are difficult. Simply, you must know what a trout requires from its environment, then find the kind of water that fulfills those needs. The requirements are three: First, a trout needs respite from the current; otherwise even the strongest fish would soon be exhausted by the continual surge of water. Second, and not necessarily in order of importance, is the need for shelter from predators, real or imaginary, human or "natural." Last is the need for a good food supply and the kind of current flow (or lack of same) that will facilitate feeding.

The best trout lies—prime lies—offer all these attributes in the same space. An example would be where a boulder breaks the force of a fast, medium-deep current. The boulder cushions the hard flow, the comparatively deep water offers protection and a sense of shelter, and the surrounding fast current carries a steady food line of nymphs, baitfish, and surface insects. On freestone streams, these are the kinds of places you should fish when there are no trout visibly feeding on the surface, or no other clue to the trout's whereabouts. Other examples of prime lies include undercut banks next to a flow; deep runs in midriver; fallen logs or trees lying parallel to the main current in water at least knee-deep; and any place marked by a "seam" in the surface flow.

A seam is where currents of different speeds meet. For instance, when a main current splits around an island and joins again downstream, the slower water at the tail of the island will form a visible seam on both sides, where it meets the faster flow. Trout love such places, especially when they're three or more feet deep. The same principle applies to inlet currents, such as where a tributary or side channel flows into the main river, or where a riffle cuts hard and fast onto the head of a narrow pool.

So much for the fundamentals. What comes next separates the true stream-readers from the mediocre ones; a gap that, once crossed, can open up a new dimension in trout fishing.

The premise here is that trout use far more of a stream than most anglers realize, although they use it very selectively. Nearly everyone fishes the pools and runs and obvious currents seams—these places get pummeled on popular waters—but there are many good lies that rarely or never get fished. An angler who works them correctly can experience nearly virgin fishing, literally amid the crowds. Let's consider some examples.

As a typical stream or river meanders, it carries the bulk of its flow to the outside bank. The water surges in a deep channel and often gouges out the bank, creating undercuts that are excellent holding areas, particularly for brown trout. Good anglers automatically work the deeper banks, and usually with some success. But few pay attention to the inner bank . . . that shallow, slow area where one suspects only shiners, fingerlings, and perhaps suckers would bother to forage. Yet on many a midsummer day an observant angler will see delicate rises occurring in these shallow inner bends. "Sippers,"

they're called, large fish rising daintily to midges or tiny mayflies. A careful, low-profile presentation to this water could result in the best fishing of the day.

Riffles are another kind of water often overlooked, particularly if they appear wide, shallow and flat. Yet the "shallowness" is relative and often deceptive when viewed from the usual human angle. If you get into the water and wade a bit and observe closely, you may find that the "foot-deep" riffle is gouged in places and cut with current seams and submerged boulders . . . all of which spell trout. A dry fly presented carefully downstream on a slack line, through these seams and over the sunken rocks, may save the day.

The point here is to widen your range of focus and possibility. Yes, fish the main pools, but pay attention to the shallower tailwaters. Work them carefully. Trout often leave the deeper water to feed in the thinner tail sections, where it's easier to rise to naturals.

Don't ignore the water near shore. Too many people are fixated on the center of the stream, in effect standing in and casting from the place they should be fishing. Even large trout will use the comparatively shallow water under, next to, or just off a bank.

Always watch the currents carefully and take pains to observe the minute details. Notice a bit of foam swirling or gathered up against a bank? Consider it a prime lie and work it carefully; where foam gathers, so do insects and baitfish and other current-delivered food items. In all likelihood, trout will be close by.

JELLYFISH STINGS

If you swim in waters where jellyfish are found, be careful.

Jellyfish toxin is rather complex and reacts on the skin rapidly. A sting requires urgent and appropriate treatment. Depending on the physical condition and age of the victim, the toxins can create a near-critical reaction.

Many remedies have been devised in the quest for rapid and effective relief—everything from sand, alcohol, vinegar, and meat tenderizers. Laboratory studies have demonstrated that certain standard solutions actually add to the discomfort when put on the wound. The result is a rupture of the nematocyst (stinging) threads that still adhere to the skin and more toxins. These false remedies include Clorox, acetone, vinegar, and ammonia. Meat tenderizer possibly gives some relief but there is concern that the concentration required might re-

sult in skin injury. A combination of vinegar and commercial antisting remedy appears to be best.

Muscle activity also adds to your discomfort by increasing the amount of toxin entering the bloodstream. So try not to move the affected area.

Approved first-aid measures include the following:

1. For sea nettle stings, liberally cover the area with baking soda to form a slurry. Use vinegar to treat man-of-war contacts.
2. If tentacles are embedded in the skin, they should be carefully removed.
3. Rest the affected limb for as long as 60 minutes.

Best idea of all: don't touch a jellyfish!

Double Your Chances for Panfish

A dandy way to catch perch and big bluegills in deep water is with a rig consisting of a trout wet fly or nymph and a soft plastic grub impaled on a 1/16-inch or 1/8-ounce lead head jig.

Tie both baits to short but separate leaders (with the fly leader about half the length of that attached to the jig) and fasten to a three-way swivel attached to your fishing line. The swivel will do a surprisingly good job of keeping the leaders from twisting together.

Fish the rig on or near bottom in deep water where perch are usually found. Retrieve in short jerks to catch those thieving nibblers that inhale and expel a lure with almost microchip speed.

This rig will attract yellow perch and bluegills, and will tempt bass as well.

HIGH WATER, LOW VISIBILITY

Any low-water period is an excellent time to chart your favorite river or stream. It is surprising how much fish-holding structure is visible during a drought or dry spell. Logs, sandbars, boulders, and holes should all be marked on a map. Strive to be as accurate

as possible, noting all landmarks well above the high-water line. Use at least two reference points to triangulate the structure precisely. Knowing the exact location of these areas when the water is back to normal will improve your angling success.

Key Ring Net Retractor

A less expensive alternative to an $8 net retractor is a device you probably remember being worn by your grade school janitor: a retractable reel key ring. You can usually get one for less than $4. Such a key ring is essentially the same device sold as a net retractor by fishing shops.

The only thing you have to be wary of is the length of the chain. Make sure the reel comes with at least a 24-inch chain so that you'll be able to pull your net all the way down to the fish when you need it.

Logging for Bait

Don't overlook rotting logs as sources of live bait, especially when they lie on wet ground. Turn the log over and check for worms, water dogs, or other critters. Then break the log apart with a hoe or hatchet to reveal grubs or larvae. Logs may hold large numbers of newts during the colder months. On pine logs, check just under the bark.

Remember, though, that snakes, especially copperheads, live around logs.

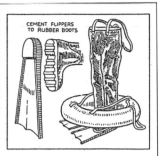

BELLY BOAT BOOTS

One of the more exasperating tasks facing anyone who fishes with a float tube is that of putting on the flippers. It is a hassle to reach around or through the belly boat. Take the easy way out: Cement the fins to a pair of high-topped rubber boots. Set the tube down over the boots, and the tops stick up in full view, making getting into them much easier.

Grabbling and the Bard

Who in the world would jump into a lake or creek, stick his arm into a hollow log all the way up to the shoulder, feel around for a catfish, and then try to pull it out by hand? More people than you might think. Grabbling (also called grappling or noodling), though an illegal practice in many areas, is permitted seasonally in much of the South.

The lowly method of fishing has a British pedigree. In fact, no less a personage than William Shakespeare refers to this rodless angling in at least two of his plays. (*Measure for Measure* [Act 1, Scene 2] and *Twelfth Night* [Act II, Scene 5]).

Legal or illegal, and by whatever name you call it, grabbling must have been a well-entrenched practice in Shakespeare's time. Otherwise, it's doubtful he would have alluded to "the trout who must be tickled" for fear that his audience might not catch his meaning. On the other hand, maybe Shakespeare had considerable personal experience with fishing by hand and didn't care whether his audience caught the joke or not. Who knows, maybe old Bill, having grown up in the country on the banks of the Avon, wasn't above doing a little grabbling himself every now and then.

Fish Bite Best

When the wind is in the East,
Then the fishes bite the least;
When the wind is in the West,
Then the fishes bite the best;
When the wind is in the North;
Then the fishes do come forth;
When the wind is in the South,
It blows the bait in the fish's
mouth.

FINDING PANFISH

When you say panfish, right off there's a mouthwatering response. The reason is simple. These are *the* favorite eating fishes all across this angling nation of ours. A panfish is just about any species small enough to fit into a frying pan and spunky enough to be fun to catch. They provide a whale of a lot of recreation—capped by that tasty payoff—for millions of Americans. So, let's take a look at our most popular panfish, their habits and habitats, and the where and how to catch them.

In the panfish category are ten members of the sunfish family: bluegill, green, longear, pumpkinseed, orange-spotted, redear, spotted, Sacramento perch, rock bass, and warmouth bass. Other panfish are white and yellow basses, white and black crappies, yellow perch, white perch, and catfish.

THE SUNFISHES

This grouping comprises the smallest members of the panfish clan, with bluegills being the biggest. But it matters not if you can't tell one from another. All have similar habits, haunts, and diets, and all are fairly easy to catch.

Where to find: Seek out weedy areas and you will find the panfishes. The things they eat are found mainly in weeds, and they can hide there from bigger predators.

The best live baits are worms, crickets, snails, grubs, maggots, mousies, grasshoppers, and catalpa worms. Dependable artificial lures are tiny 1/64-ounce jigs, spinners, poppers, small spoons, and flies of many types, both wet and dry.

When sunfish are in shallow water the best artificials are floating lures such as poppers, dry flies, and tiny plugs. In deeper water jigs and spinners, as well as wet flies, will sink naturally into panfish hangouts.

The key is to fish very slowly. Keep lines light, never more than 6-pound test and preferably 4.

After the spawning madness is over, it will require more skill to find and catch these fish. Seek them in weed fringes bordering deepening water, around lily pads where the water is six to eight feet deep, around brush piles, off deep points, and over midlake islands or humps that are surrounded by deep water.

YELLOW PERCH

The yellow perch is a delectable fish to eat and a favorite of both anglers and restaurants throughout the Great Lakes and northeastern areas of the United States.

Where to Find: There are two habit patterns of the yellow perch that make it easier to predict than other species. 1) They are bottom feeders except for odd moments of suspension, so odd that you should spend all your fishing hours probing the bottom. 2) They are daylight feeders, descending to the lake bottom at dusk and remaining there until morning light arouses them into action.

WHITE AND YELLOW BASSES

The yellow bass is much scarcer than the white bass and is found from Iowa and Illinois southward into Texas and Louisiana. The white bass has been successfully transplanted in most large reservoirs from Colorado eastward and is caught in abundance except in Florida and the New England states. It probably is the hardest hitting fish for its size in fresh water, leaving no doubt when one tags your lure.

Where to Find: Two places, near the surface and smackdab on the bottom. I'm not being facetious. These are roving, moving fish, constantly in search of minnows, their favorite food.

WHITE AND BLACK CRAPPIES

These two species look so much alike it takes an ichthyologist to identify them, though the black is usually darker than the white. The black crappie is found in all states but Alaska and Hawaii. The white crappie has made it in some 36 states, excluding Arizona, Wyoming, Wisconsin, Michigan, and the northeast coastal states.

Where to Find: Just imagine you are a minnow trying to hide from a hungry horde of crappies out to dine on your tiny carcass. You'd hide in the nearest brush pile, rocky formation, timbered area, lily pad cluster, weedy spots on midlake humps, off rocky ledges, and around deadfalls. This is where you'll find crappies.

CATFISH

Catfishes are among the easiest-to-recognize fishes because over 1000 species worldwide have two common characteristics: whiskers adorn their unhandsome faces, the dorsal and pectoral fins have sharp, stiff spines that can inflict a painful wound.

All are delicious to eat and heavily fished despite the fact that each has a poison gland at the base of the dorsal and pectoral fins. The toxic substance is exuded from the base of the fin and contaminates the spines.

Where to Find: Think bottom when you think catfish because that is where they spend most of their time, foraging for something to eat, either alive or dead. In lakes you'll find them around docks where fish are cleaned and the entrails discarded, also off deep points, in coves, old creek channels, and where streams flow in. In streams they collect to feed in the eddy water below rapids, under bank overhangs, around fallen timber or debris, and in the deeper water on the outside of bends.

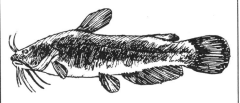

Tackle Busters in the Current

There are times when small-mouth bass and walleyes lie behind submerged rocks in the tailwater of a dam. They do it mid-river, too. Live bait or minnow-imitating lures can take these bottom-hugging fish, but getting the bait down and keeping it down is the problem.

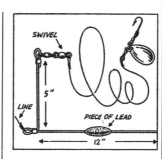

A neat device known as a bottom bouncer will take the bait down to the fish every time. And the weight keeps it in the strike zone. This nifty piece of equipment is simply a stiff wire 17 inches long with a 90-degree bend five inches from the top. The lower end remains in contact with the bottom and is about 12 inches long. A bullet-shaped piece of lead is placed about five inches from the bottom.

Connect your line to the loop at the bend. A leader is attached to a swivel that extends from the upper end of the wire. The bottom bouncer resembles an inverted L and comes in different weights. If you intend to fish fast water regularly, attach a two-foot monofilament leader in combination with a walleye rig, some crawlers, a leech or a crankbait, and you'll soon be in business.

Grass-catcher Grasshoppers

Grasshoppers are a tried and proven bait for a wide variety of freshwater game fish ranging from bream to trout. They can be readily caught in heavy grass or weeds in the cool dews of early morning, but this makes for wet, messy work. A simple alternative is available to any angler who has a riding mower equipped with a standard rear-loaded grass-catcher. Remove the empty bag from its frame, then make a rapid dragging pass of several yards through the grass. At the end of the pass, quickly flip the netting over the frame, then gingerly remove the imprisoned 'hoppers by hand and place them in a bait container. Three or four passes—a matter of a few minutes' work—should provide you with plenty of bait.

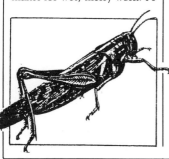

A Steady Hand for Pickerel

Be sure to maintain a constant retrieve of your lure when fishing for chain pickerel. These fish, with their long, slender bodies, rely on fast strikes to catch their prey, and are often unable to respond quickly to the jerky retrieve that is often used for bass.

If you're fishing for pickerel with minnows, it's best to allow the fish to take the bait for a few seconds before you try setting the hook. Pickerel seize their prey by its side and then manipulate the minnow head-first down the throat. And so a quick setting of the hook will often result in a missed fish.

NO HOPE

My wife and I love to fish, and we are constantly on the lookout for good new spots. Once on such an expedition, we discovered a small pond in southern Oregon that looked promising, but a sign posted there read simply: NOPE.

When we heard that the pond had a new owner, we expectantly drove up to see if the sign had been removed. It had. But in its place was a new one reading: STILL NOPE.

Hook, Line, and Superstition

The average angler has more knowledge, skill, and equipment than ever before. But for days when the best lures and favorite fishing spots yield nothing but frustration, here are some long-standing fishing superstitions that may help assuage your pain:

In some parts of England, anglers believe that to make fish bite you should remove an eye from the first one you catch and throw it into the water. It will look for other fish and draw them to your boat.

To bring them luck, anglers in Northern Ireland always spit in the mouth of the first fish of the day they catch.

Sit with your feet crossed while fishing, and you will catch a lot of fish.

A good time to fish is when the moon is on the wane. But if you see a new moon while you're fishing, look at the first coin you take from your pocket. If it's heads, you'll have good luck. If it's tails, you will catch no more fish.

According to Native American legend, a hook that has already caught fish will bring good luck.

Some anglers in England consider it lucky to quarrel with members of their families before going fishing.

People who fish in Brittany take a cat with them when they go fishing. Cats love fish and can scent them from afar.

In Iceland, people will not sing while fishing. And some anglers consider it an unpardonable sin to whistle.

HOOK, LINE, AND BAIT

When a fish takes live bait, such as a shiner or frog, the angler usually lets it run for a while before setting the hook. How long should one wait?

A large-mouth bass can take a very large shiner in only a few seconds, though many anglers wait for some time before striking. A full-grown muskie will readily take into its mouth a live sucker up to 15 inches long—but swallowing it may take several minutes. A pike or pickerel will often take a live fish crosswise, run a ways, stop, turn the bait around, swallow it, and run again. During the first run, the hook may not be in the fish's mouth, so the knowledgeable angler strikes on the second run.

Most good anglers will watch the line carefully, and many hold it lightly between thumb and forefinger as it goes out. I know one big-bass man who will tug on the line very lightly, trying to make the fish think the bait is struggling to get away. It works.

POSTMAN, BEWARE

A friend vacationing in northern Wisconsin, enjoying a successful run at a fishing hotspot, decided to send some of his catch to his family in Florida. After carefully packing it in an ice-filled refrigerator bag, he wrote on the outside of the package: "If not delivered within three days, forget it."

FINDING FISH IN STREAMS

I find it much easier to catch fish in streams than in lakes. As one of my first tutors put it: "Streams talk to you and tell you where fish live. Lakes just sit there and don't say nothin'."

To get you tuned in to reading water, I've selected 11 places where fish hang out in streams and listed the best ways to consistently take fish from them.

First, let's consider the lures that catch most river species, including largemouth, smallmouth, spotted, yellow and white basses, walleyes, pike, muskies, trout, steelhead, char, and salmon. Six stalwart stream selections are *slim minnows:* elongated bodies, lips to make them wiggle and dive, and two or more treble hooks make them deadly; *weedless spoons:* pork frogs can be attached to their single, wire-guarded hooks for added attraction; *surface noisemakers:* these include chugging or popping types, plus those with head or tail spinners; *crankbaits:* small or large lips make them dive slowly or quickly, while lipless types create a vibratory wiggle; *in-line spinners:* these work better in streams than the overhead types because of their streamlined bodies: and last, *soft lures:* plastic worms and leadhead grubs have little action but can be deadly in slow to fast waters.

When fishing from a boat, indulge yourself and take your bulging tacklebox, then have at it. Now, those 11 hotspots:

Below riffles and rapids: Rushing currents pour into deep holes here, carrying food to bottom dwellers. Use crankbaits, spinners, plastic worms, and jigs here. Cast slightly upstream, keep rod tip high, and with a taut line bottom-nudge lures to prevent snagging in V's of rocks.

Eddies: These waters flow backward, rubbing bodies with the mainstream, and are grand gathering for gamefish to skulk and pounce on anything washing past. An especially good hotspot is "the slot," where flotsam draws a static line. All six lure types are worth trying here.

Fallen trees, debris pileups: Large fish like to congregate near wreckage that borders deep water. Probe these perimeters with plastic worms and jigs (rigged weedless), crankbaits, and spinners. Flipping is an especially effective method.

Undercut banks: These shelvings provide shade and shelter for large predators. Because they are ridden with roots and snags, they are best fished with weedless spoons and plastic worms. Crankbaits with large enough lips to make them occasionally tap bottom cover are also ideal.

Backwater areas: Bays, inlets, areas behind levees, and old oxbows formed by the stream's original course offer quiet but deep waters where large fish can set up territorial lairs and spring spawning sessions. Surface lures can bring explosive strikes in these calmer waters.

Inflowing streams: Baitfish thrive in this nourishment-rich water, so large predators are also likely to dwell here. With your rod tip high and your line taut, try casting a jig upstream, letting it touch bottom as you lift and reel. Cast spinners slightly upstream and reel just fast enough to keep them from hanging on bottom. As a last resort, run upstream, rest for about half an hour to give fish time to return to spots you spooked them from, then, where the waters meet, try crankbaits, spinners, and jigs. When you reach a deep run in the main stream that is cut by the course of the inflowing stream, fish this spot slowly and deeply.

Bank riprap: These rocky stretches are natural hideouts for crayfish, hellgrammites, leeches, and other food chain creatures. Look for structure that drops off into deep water, then ply it with your gamut of lures.

Islands: These inviting spots can vary from the size of a bushel basket to that of a city block. Usually one side has faster water from the other. Fish the runs from your boat. If you don't score, beach the boat and fish from shore, using crankbaits and plastic worms in fast water, slim minnows and surface lures in calm water.

Midstream boulders: Because the water pours down the front and along both sides of these obstructions, a natural hideout exists directly behind each boulder where fish can rest from fighting current. It's also a good ambush spot for feeding fish. Use jigs, crawlers, spinners, and crankbaits are all effective.

Deep channel runs: Where streams narrow and the current has cut deeply into the bed (between high banks or through gorges, for example) is prime fish habitat. Anchor your boat, using a collapsible anchor that won't lodge in rocks, and you'll be able to cover every square yard of water with your casts. Fish may be anywhere. Deep-diving crankbaits, jigs, and weighted spinners, fished slowly and deeply, should coax fish out of hiding.

Bank-bound logs: Every stream has its share of these fish havens. But, as logs are favorite targets for fishermen, you'll have to try a different approach. Tie your boat at least 50 yards above the logs and go in on foot. Use plastic worms, weedless jigs, and spoons, and lay them in every imaginable lair. Take it slow and easy!

In larger rivers a sonar is mighty helpful in delineating courses and helpful in delineating courses and depths of original channels, submerged humps, hogbacks, bars, sunken boats, weeds, and other structures that hold gamefish.

One last tip: When rain begins to turn a stream roily, fish may go on a feeding spree. To imitate this condition in a small stream, wade in above a hole and kick up mud. Then hurry downstream and cast to the hole where fish think it's raining.

Learn how to read a stream, and you'll learn where fish live.

DOG-DAY FISHING TRICKS

T he dog days of summer is the time for that less esteemed, but always hungry triumvirate: the bluegill, crappie, and catfish. They are sporting, procurable, and far tastier than most of the other, flashier species.

But let's go for them with light tackle to increase the challenge and enjoyment, not to mention your chances to outwit the larger fish of each species.

Here are some time-tested tricks to try. They don't always work; but you'll find that the average catch will be higher.

BLUEGILLS

When you seek big ones, think deep— maybe just over a drop-off in 10 to 20 feet of water that has a weedy bottom.

The number-one lure for all times of day is as universally attractive as peanut butter and jelly to kids. It's a cricket, and you can buy it at most live-bait stores.

Take along at least 50, or better 100, because bluegills can suck these off your hook faster than scat.

Use a No. 8, long-shank Carlisle hook. Run the point down through the cricket's back just behind the head. Then bury the bar in its butt. This method is far superior to hooking it through the collar.

Use a lightweight spinning or spincasting outfit and just enough split-shot above the cricket to make it cast easily. Cast and let the cricket sink until a slack line tells

you it's resting on the bottom. Raise your rod tip about one foot, and reel in v-e-r-y s-l-o-w-l-y. Watch your line closely and if it does anything, especially if it grows taut or slack, set the hook and enjoy.

CRAPPIES

Few freshwater fish are as succulent. And because crappies travel in schools, catching one means you're among them.

So rove until you catch one, then fish that spot very thoroughly. Brush piles, weed beds, fallen trees, and lily pads are prime areas.

The best artificial lure is a ⅛-ounce white jig with either feather, hair, or soft plastic body. Cast close to the cover, let it sink until the line slackens, then retrieve it s-o v-e-r-y s-l-o-w-l-y you can imagine your hair is graying.

No one knows why, but crappies go for barely moving lures. So cater to this whim around every type of shoreline cover. But if they don't chew the lure up, then they are probably out cruising.

Run upwind and make cross-lake drifts from one side to the other. Use lively minnows, about 1½ inches long, with a bobber to hold them at various depths. As you drift, try all depths from one foot on.

Also, trim off the feathery part of the minnow's tail fin. It will help you catch the bigger crappies.

You see, the minnow has to swim

harder to stay upright and its vibrations attract the attention of the whopper crappies. When you catch your first crappie, toss over a bright-colored float to mark the spot and keep fishing there until action stops. Then start roving again.

The best crappie tackle is a spinning or spincasting rig, with four- to six-pound monofilament line. The clearer the water, the lighter the line.

The best hook is a No. 4 Carlisle. The fine wire doesn't tear the crappie's tender mouth as easily. And when hooked below a minnow's dorsal fin, it is less likely to penetrate the spine and kill the minnow.

CATFISH

Here is one of our unsung uglies in the fun-to-catch and good-to-eat class. Channel catfish, especially, are prime fare when deep fried, just done, and complemented with hush puppies.

Two baits have done in more catfish for me than all others. If fresh chicken livers or shrimp a tad too smelly to stand in the kitchen won't take Mister Whiskers, nothing will. Prime hangouts are where a stream flows into a lake, or along dark, deep drop-offs. In streams, wade the shallow side and fish the deep side.

Any kind of tackle will do, so long as it's strong enough for the size you're catching. My favorite is a fly rod and monofilament line on a single-action fly reel.

Just strip off enough monofilament to allow you to reach the hole, then use a lobbing sidecast to propel the lure. This is called spat fishing, and you can become surprisingly accurate at placing the lure precisely where you want it.

Attach just enough splitshot to hold the lure on the bottom, especially when drifting it in current. And keep moving and probing until you latch onto a hellraiser.

I'm serious when I say that playing a 10- to 20-pound catfish on a fly rod is one of my favorite ways to enjoy the most that hand-to-fin combat has to offer.

Your best hours will be from daybreak to 10 A.M., and from about 4 P.M. until dark, for all three species.

QUICK THINKING

The old-timer sat on the river-bank, obviously awaiting a nibble though the fishing season had not officially opened. I stood behind him quietly for several minutes. "You a game warden?" he finally inquired.

"Yep," I lied, figuring to scare him a little.

Apparently unruffled, the old man began to move the fishing pole vigorously from side to side. Finally he lifted the line out of the water.

"Just teaching him how to swim," he explained, pointing to the minnow that was wiggling on the end of the line.

Catch of the Century

"What was the biggest fish you ever caught?" a sportsman asked his friend.

"The one that measured 14 inches."

"That's not much," the first man scoffed.

"Between the eyes?" his friend replied.

What's in a Name

Federal involvement with game and fish control began in 1900 with passage of the Lacey Act. It regulated the importation of birds and animals and interstate traffic in game. In 1939 the Bureau of Biological Survey in the Department of Agriculture and the Bureau of Fisheries were transferred to the Department of the Interior. Combined in 1940, they became the Fish and Wildlife Service.

In 1956 the Fish and Wildlife Service was split and reorganized into the Bureau of Sport Fisheries and Wildlife and the Bureau of Commercial Fisheries. In 1970 the latter was transferred back to the Department of Commerce to become the National Marine Fisheries Service. The Bureau of Sport Fisheries and Wildlife became known as the United States Fish and Wildlife Service back in 1974.

Over the years, titles of officers in the agencies have also changed. From 1900 to 1918 they were known as inspectors, interstate commerce in game, and as game wardens from 1918 to 1928. From 1928 to 1934 they were game protectors, and game management agents from 1934 to 1973. Since 1973 they have been special agents.

Cool, Clear Water

In summer sensible anglers carry a good deal of liquid to quench thirst and prevent dehydration, but stocking a cooler is a bother. An efficient solution to this problem is supplied by any plastic two-liter soft-drink bottle. Just rinse thoroughly with warm water, fill two-thirds full with fresh water, and add four or five slices of fresh lemon. Replace the cap and put the bottle in the freezer overnight.

About a half hour before you leave on your fishing trip, remove the bottle from the freezer and set it in the sun to begin thawing. During the trip, be sure to keep the bottle in the shade. As the water gradually defrosts, it will offer you a source of cool and tasty refreshment.

CATCH AND RELEASE

If your fishing philosophy is catch and release, here are a few hints on returning fish to catch another day.

• Do not wear out the fish—land it as soon as you can.

• If possible, leave the fish in the water. Do not touch it with dry hands.

• Gently remove the hook; do not put your fingers in the gills or squeeze the fish.

• Cut the line if the hook is too deep or hard to remove.

• Release the fish in quiet water only after it can stay upright on its own. If the fish needs help recovering, wet your hands and gently move it back and forth in the water to help it breathe.

• Here is the best part: Come back another day and try to catch the fish again.

PEDAGOGICAL INGENUITY

An ingenious teacher new to Grangeville, Idaho, and unfamiliar with the fishing potential and hot spots of her new area, hit on a novel solution to the problem. Assigning her 35 students a 200-word theme entitled, "My Three Favorite Fishing Holes," she got the inside dope on over 50 spots.

The assignment required the students to list the best lures or baits, the sections of the streams or lakes which were best, the species and sizes of fish, and the best roads or trails to take. Within a week, she had learned about areas that even old-timers weren't aware of. She gave 35 As!

LANDING FISH BARE-HANDED

Using your bare hands to bring fish aboard is probably the surest way to put that rascal in your possession, yet there are nearly as many different ways of doing this as there are people to argue about them. Each angler has his pet way, and this is fine as long as it works for you.

Landing Net: Play the fish until it is tired enough to allow itself to be led, or pulled, in a straight line. Only then reach for that net. Ease the net into the water and lead the fish into it. If you decide to go for this method, just be sure to get a net big enough to do the job.

The Snatch Method: Just like it sounds. You just snatch the fish out of the water, using your rod as a hoist. When properly done, it is an effective maneuver.

Anglers use from 14- to 20-pound line on a gutty rod. This will easily snatch fish up to five pounds. The trick is in the timing, and here is how it's done.

With smaller fish you simply let the bend in your rod lever the fish into the boat. This works well on fish up to two pounds, maybe three, depending on the actions of the individual fish.

With larger fish, up to five pounds, you play the fish and can drag it over the surface. Then you just shorten your line, covert the drag into lift, and hoist the fish into your boat.

Let's break it down into two categories:

1) fish without teeth, and 2) fish with teeth.

Fish without teeth include: bass, bluegills, catfish, crappies, perch, etc. Lacking dentition, these fish have jaws that are rimmed with rasplike borders for holding whatever they grab. These are not sharp enough to puncture your flesh, so the jaw is a safe place to grab.

The Jaw Grip: This is the safest, surest, most humane way to land a fish, especially if you plan to release the fish and want it to survive. To handle a fish elsewhere, especially around the gills and body, is to inflict it with hand acid which can cause fungal or bacterial infection and death.

Here's why the jaw grip is so effective: after you subdue the fish, reach down and lay your thumb over the lower jawbone. At the same time, curl your forefinger directly under the fish's lower jawbone. Pinch with both fingers and lift the fish so it hangs suspended.

The fish is paralyzed because suspending it over your forefinger causes the tongue to pull upward on the internal organs. This puts pressure against the central nervous system and immobilizes the fish. It will not flop and is safe to handle while extracting hooks.

Gill-Compression Grip: This method is advisable when the hooks of a lure are exposed outside the fish's mouth. This is dangerous because should the fish thrash as you reach for its jaw, you could wind up with you on one hook and the fish on the other, in which case the fish becomes the hooker and you the hookee.

The safest way to handle this situation is to subdue the fish, reach down, and grasp the fish over its head with your thumb on one gill cover and your four fingers on the other. Squeeze firmly and lift the fish into the boat.

But suppose you latch onto the fish whose head is too large to span with your hand for the gill compression. Then, use the belly lift.

Belly Lift: This works on all soft-belly fish I've tried it on, especially bass. Subdue the fish and bring it close to the boat.

Slowly raise your middle finger and exert upward pressure on the fish's soft belly. Balance the fish with the other fingers and lift. Again, the pressure of your middle finger against the fish's innards paralyzes it.

Ease it into your boat and it will hang there, immobile, until you can grab its lower jaw in a safe place for hook removal.

So much for handling toothless fish. Now let's talk about those with teeth that can wound you painfully if not properly handled. These include pike, muskellunge, pickerel, walleyes, etc.

Obviously, the jaw grip is out. All the other methods can be used, plus one more.

Slot Lift: This is used on toothy fish so large you can't grasp them over the gill flaps, and when you have no net. All fish have a slot, or opening, on each side under the lower jaw.

However, here's a word of caution:

pike, muskies, and pickerel have teeth all over the insides of their mouths. And their gillrakers are mighty rough. So, as I said, *ease* your fingers into the jaw slot and feel your way to a safe gripping surface.

The Jolt Release: This is my best method for releasing fish with the greatest certainty for survival. I rarely keep fish and use this 90 percent of the time. It works on any fish where you can reach the hook with a pair of long-nose pliers, and when the hook is imbedded anywhere except in the gills. Your hands never touch the fish.

Play the fish until it's docile. Hold the line in one hand and the pliers in the other with the fish still in the water. Raise the fish's head above the water and firmly grip the shank of the hook that holds the fish.

Lift the fish a few inches above the gunwale, outside of and close to the boat. Lower the fish suddenly, letting the pliers strike the gunwale with a sharp impact. The pliers and hook stop, but the fish keeps on going, untouched and unharmed.

Choose the method that best fits the species of fish you normally catch. You're bound to like one of them.

CHINESE FISHING

The Chinese long ago devel oped great ingenuity in the methods used to catch fish. One, a sort of angling equivalent of falconry, involved trained cormorants. (This practice also enjoyed some popularity in England—in medieval and Renaissance times—when the master of cormorants was an officer of the royal household.) A special strap or collar fastened about the cormorant's neck allowed it to move and breathe freely while preventing its swallowing the catch. A good

cormorant could take astounding quantities of fish in a short period and was a highly prized possession.

A second method used by the Chinese involved inducing mullet and perch to jump into boats. Done in calm water on moonlit nights, it worked by what amounted to optical illusion. The craft were built with a very low freeboard, and a white plank about three feet in height was erected along one side. On the opposite side was a gradually sloping shelf, also painted white, the lower edge of which met the water. Apparently, moonbeams reflecting off the white boards induced fish to jump at them, and they conveniently landed in the bottom of the boats. At any rate, it was a remarkably effective technique.

THE TIE THAT BINDS

A good knot often makes the difference between a fish in the boat and a "you should have seen the one that got away" story. Yet how well a knot is tied is often more important than the type of knot used. Here are some useful tips on how to tie good, strong knots for fishing.

—Make sure the line at the knot isn't nicked or abraded.

—See that the coils of the knot form smoothly.

—Lubricate the knot with saliva before drawing it up tight.

—Slowly draw the knot up as tight as possible.

—Never use heat to seal a knot—this weakens the line.

—Clip the tag end carefully and be sure you don't nick the knot or line.

PARTS OF A HOOK

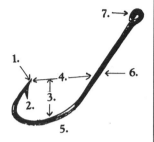

A fishhook is made from one continuous length of tempered wire. Design variations are created by changes made in seven areas. Some alterations hold certain baits better, fit mouths of certain fish differently, or stay stuck once the hook is embedded.

These seven areas of the hook are called the throat, point, eye, barb, bend, shank, and gap.

Can you assign these names to the proper hook areas?

1. _____
2. _____
3. _____
4. _____
5. _____
6. _____
7. _____

Answers: 1) point, 2) barb, 3) throat, 4) gap, 5) bend, 6) shank and 7) eye.

Fishing IQ: Water

Some people may only mix it with whiskey, but fish have to live in it. Check out the ways that water affects fish by diving into these 10 questions:

1. During summer months, impounded fresh water often settles into three layers. This process is called _____ _____.
2. The middle layer is the: a) hypolimnion. b) dypolimnion. c) epilimnion. d) thermocline.
3. Many gamefish prefer this middle level because it provides enough dissolved oxygen and a suitable temperature range. True or false?
4. The three layers are mixed by the _____ _____.
5. Using the Fahrenheit scale, water is densest at: a) 39°. b) 42°. c) 51°. d) 68°.
6. As water temperature decreases, a fish's metabolism quickens. True or false?
7. Dissolved oxygen is often measured in parts per: a) 10. b) 100. c) 1000. d) million.
8. The pH level of water indicates: a) dissolved oxygen content. b) salinity. c) alkalinity. d) pollution index.
9. A high level of photosynthesis among aquatic plants increases this pH level. This makes the water _____.
10. Sound travels more quickly through water than through air. True or false?

Answers: 1) thermal stratification. 2) d. 3) true. 4) fall turnover. 5) a. 6) false. 7) d. 8) c. 9) alkaline. 10) true.

International Angler's IQ

Trout fishing in Yugoslavia, Kenya, or Tierra del Fuego represents only a fraction of international angling action. So let's see if you can match these foreign words, which mean fish, with their respective languages:

1. Arabic	a. poisson
2. Chinese-Mandarin	b. fisch
	c. pez
3. Farsi	d. pesce
4. French	e. samaka
5. German	f. icthys
6. Greek	g. peixe
7. Hebrew	h. mahe
8. Irish	i. fisk
9. Italian	j. sakana
10. Japanese	k. yu
11. Portuguese	l. reba
12. Russian	m. iasc (isk)
13. Serbo-Croatian	n. dag
14. Spanish	o. samaki
15. Swahili	
16. Swedish	

Answers:
1-e, 2-k, 3-h, 4-a, 5-b, 6-f, 7-n, 8-m, 9-d, 10-j, 11-g, 12-l, 13-l, 14-c, 15-o, 16-i.

HOOKS QUIZ

The plain fishhook has evolved to conform to specific fishing situations. Each of the following hooks has a particular name. Try to identify them. Answers are listed below.

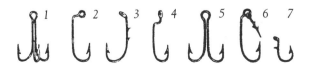

Answers: 1) treble hook, 2) jig hook, 3) bait hook, 4) worm hook, 5) double hook, 6) weedless worm hook, 7) salmon egg hook.

CHAPTER THREE

RECIPES FROM THE FIELD

C ooking in the field can be a challenge, if you're not prepared. Compiled in this chapter are a wide variety of recipes created by outdoors people especially for the campsite. Here you'll find wonderful suggestions for making delicious meals by campfire.

By foraging the wild fruits of the forest or learning new ways to prepare and preserve the daily catch, you can whip up meals that are even more exciting and tasty than those at home. This chapter offers ideas from which you can create entire menus: there are fish and meat entrées, breads and biscuits, vegetables and side dishes, and drinks—all of which an enterprising chef can concoct in the field.

FORAGING TIPS

JUNIPER BERRIES

Juniper berries are not true berries but are small cones that only rarely open to a cone shape. Each berry contains one hard seed, though some varieties do have more than one. The common juniper grows widely in Europe, temperate Asia, North Africa, and North America and varies from a low, spreading shrub to a 20-foot tree.

Juniper berries are used as a pepper substitute and as flavoring for sauerkraut dishes; they are also fermented to make beer and brandy. In southern Europe the berries are picked in great quantities for commercial use: The dried berries are distilled to produce an oil that is widely used as flavoring in soft drinks, condiments, meat products, liqueurs, and, of course, gin.

Although juniper berries can be purchased at fancy prices in specialty stores catering to gourmet cooks, they are free for the picking in many places in the United States. Berries from the Rocky Mountain or Utah juniper keep well indefinitely with no special treatment. This species pro-

duces bountiful numbers of large, silvered, purple berries. From late August into October (in most places) they are at their best. Enough can be picked in ten minutes to last for several years.

After picking, spread the berries in a single layer on shallow pans lined with paper towels in a suitable warm place to dry for several hours. Sort them and remove any imperfect or wormy berries. Store in small, airtight glass jars.

A little experimenting will tell you the number of berries you will prefer in your meat dishes, sauces, and so on. Four to five berries added to a meat stew will impart just the right bouquet to suit most tastes.

MINT TEA

If you have ever been downwind from a bed of spearmint, you know its delightful fragrance. Did you ever track down the source and pick a few leaves for steeping a pot of fresh tea?

Spearmint, *Mentha spicata*, is one of a variety of mint plants that grow over the eastern half of the United States. Many are so closely allied that it is difficult to distinguish them, but all have the characteristic square stem and pungent aroma.

Spearmint is one of the more common mints that grows in or near open meadow streams. Be sure to gather a handful of leaves because nothing caps a meal of trout, especially one of meadow brook trout, like steaming mint tea.

MUSHROOM POISONS

Despite what the dictionary says, there is no difference between a mushroom and a toadstool. All mushrooms are toadstools and vice versa. For centuries it was thought that toads were poisonous and when they sat on toadstools, toadstools became poisonous.

There are hundreds of different mushrooms in this country, but only a small percentage are highly toxic. The chemistry of the poisons is very complex, and the effects and degrees of poisoning vary a great deal.

Some poisonous mushrooms contain toxins that affect the nervous system; other toxins affect the digestive system and some attack the body's protoplasm. Some contain disulfiram, which, incidentally, is used to treat patients with alcoholism.

Depending on the toxin ingested, symptoms of poisoning may occur within 10 minutes or up to 24 hours later. Some toxins can cause hallucinations, others severe vomiting, diarrhea, sweating, and profuse salivation. The pupils may constrict, the pulse rate slows, and blood pressure drops. Some toxic deaths occur because of heart-muscle paralysis and the cessation of breathing. There may be delirium, severe muscle spasms, conditions similar to intoxication, depression or elation, and visual disturbances. The most dangerous poisons cause death by injury to the heart muscle, liver, and skeletal muscles some time later.

In every case of mushroom poisoning, even suspected ones, call a physician immediately and rush the person to a hospital or poison control center. If possible, take along the mushrooms for identification so that correct treatment can be given.

Tips for the Woodland Forager

If you are depending on wild plants for food, you must know which are in season and if you like them. Not every plant that is considered edible actually tastes good. In fact, some taste downright awful. Skunk cabbage sprouts are listed as edible in many foraging guides, but no matter how long you cook skunk cabbage, it tastes and feels like rubber.

Be aware of pollutants. This is particularly important when taking plants from streams and lakes because they can absorb toxic chemicals from surface water. Pollutants do not have to be man-made to affect water plants. Some natural poisons are water-soluble and can be absorbed by plants downstream from the source. Sampling a small portion of an aquatic plant is highly recommended before using it to make a main course.

The modern-day forager must be concerned about the environment. Some edible plants are rare, and a few are threatened with extinction.

Even common plants should be picked with caution. Don't pick every edible plant you find—leave at least 10 for every one you take with you.

HUNTING WILD MUSHROOMS

Mushroom hunting can be as absorbing as any other form of hunting, but in different ways. For one thing, the season is always open. Any time the ground isn't frozen, you can find good, edible mushrooms in abundance if you know where to look.

By late spring mushrooms drop both in number and kind to their lowest point, but new kinds appear with summer.

Not long after this comes the amazing shaggy mane, which emerges with such power that it can lift a layer of asphalt along the shoulder of the highway. Most often you will find it beside an old manure pile. Shaggy manes are unmistakable, with reddish brown scales over soft flesh.

Summer is still with us, but there's a hint of autumn in the air when big puffballs suddenly appear in the grass of meadows or along ditches or streams. They're the big game of mushroom hunting. A single puffball is enough for your whole family. It's a mushroom for the beginner, too, because nothing else is quite like it except for stalked mushrooms that haven't yet burst out of their sac (when you're an expert, you'll call it the "universal veil"). Once you locate puffballs, you'll generally find them in the same spot year after year. Be sure you harvest them while the inside is still nice and white. When the flesh turns yellow, they're past eating; by then, chances are they'll be shot through with wormholes.

When waterfowl season approaches, mushrooms begin to pop up all over. Now is the time for the glorious suillus and other boletuses, for the cup-shaped chanterelles and for the shelf-like polypores that are attached to trees.

Unlike other kinds of hunting, there's no bag limit on mushrooms. Gathering them doesn't subtract a bit from the next harvest. What you pick is simply the fruit; the plant itself, a network of thread-like mycelia (if you want to get technical), is all underground. But there is danger in mushroom hunting, for you certainly don't want to eat a poisonous one. The way to eliminate that danger is to learn to know mushrooms, one at a time, and for that you need a book.

With book in hand, the next thing to do is to go out hunting with an old-timer (the older the better, for good reason). He can show you the best ones for the beginner.

The first thing to do in safeguarding yourself is to learn the amanitas so well that the sight of one makes you nauseated. The amanitas are generally big, showy mushrooms, always associated with trees. If you are doubtful about any, don't eat it without consulting an authority.

Learning the mushrooms is no chore, though; in fact, it's much of the fun. On a hike through the fall woods, you'll find a dozen kinds. Take plastic bags with you so you can keep each kind separate, or else study them on the spot and discard the questionable ones. If in doubt, be sure to dig deep enough to get the base of the stem; a cup-shaped "volva" is one mark of an amanita. Check all mushrooms for wormholes, and, finally, before dropping your catch into your sack, cut off the bottoms to keep out sand or soil.

Unlike most other kinds of hunting, there is no need to travel far for mushrooms. I found my biggest haul of morels in a friend's backyard in New Jersey. Each summer I pick a meal of slippery jacks from around the little jack pines on my way to the mailbox.

Mushroom hunting gives me an excuse for a walk through the woods, alone or with friends. Some of the bleakest places I know have been loaded with mushrooms. The straggly moors of Newfoundland were dotted with boletes, and the otherwise lifeless tundra across the river from Churchill, Manitoba, was crowded with morels.

Mushroom hunting, I guarantee, is going to add savor to your meals, and to your life too. Happy hunting!

How to Cook Mushrooms

Why not stake out a reputation as a great mushroom chef? The field is wide open, and mushrooms are easy to fix. Take puffballs, for instance. First you cut through them to make sure they aren't stalked mushrooms that haven't broken out yet. At the same time, check for worms or any

yellowing of the flesh. The thinner you make your slices, the more butter they'll absorb. Fry them to a golden brown and serve.

At your steak fry, add slices of boletus a few minutes before the meat is ready, cutting the mushrooms so the form of the stem and parasol or cap will show. The flavor is so delicate that you'll barely detect it, but they make any steak look special.

I like pickled mushrooms. Mix three tablespoons or so of wine vinegar in half a cup of olive oil, add salt, pepper, and an herb such as tarragon, then toss in the mushrooms and let stand for a few hours, until it's time to serve.

Mushrooms fried with eggs are great. Try dousing mushrooms with cream, a little sherry, and a quarter cup of butter with lemon juice and chopped parsley, and spoon over toast. That's a favorite in the commercial mushroom-growing area at Kennett Square outside Philadelphia.

Mushrooms dipped in a batter of breadcrumbs, butter, and onions make a fine dish, especially when you're short of mushrooms and need to extend them.

Then, when you've tried everything else, check through cookbooks for such gourmet dishes as broiled stuffed mushrooms, mushrooms stuffed with liver, mushrooms stuffed with snails, and mushrooms under glass.

After any of those dishes, you'll probably have friends clamoring to join you—by now an old-timer yourself!—on your next hunt.

Wild Strawberry Surprise

Some folks claim that wild strawberries (*Fragaria virginiana*) are among the sweetest tasting berries in all the world. The tiny red berries grow on small stalks along sunny hillsides and beside meadow streams and are found over all of eastern North America.

On a day in late June or July, if patches of wild strawberries grow nearby, pick a few!

Wild strawberries make delicious jams and jellies and, like other berries, can be preserved by drying.

Wild strawberry leaves are rich in Vitamin C. Shred a handful, boil about 15 minutes in a pint of water, and let stand overnight. Strain the water and add to other fruit juices or ades for a highly palatable beverage.

BRAMBLE STRATAGEM

Larry Kline is a man of few words, and he usually makes them count. A master chef, he now cooks for Alaskan oil crews, but he used to forage for natural foods back home in central Pennsylvania. One July morning, he pulled on a worn-out pair of waders and set out to fill a couple of pails in his favorite black raspberry patch. Pretty soon he found himself sharing the patch with a middle-aged couple who skimmed the high berries while trampling the low ones. The wife noticed Larry's boots and remarked on how smart he was trying to protect himself that way from the thorns. Without pausing, Larry replied, "They also protect me from the rattlers and copperheads." The last he saw of the couple, they were running as fast as they could.

Morel Mushrooms

The morel is one—perhaps the only—mushroom that almost any amateur mushroom hunter can identify. It is better known as the sponge mushroom, for obvious reasons.

Morels are among the best-tasting and least perishable of the wild mushrooms and so can be prepared in a number of ways that wouldn't do for many of the more delicate species. Most cooks season morels with salt and pepper and sauté them in butter. My preference is just in butter, without salt or pepper. The morels can also be dipped in a batter of eggs, milk, and flour before frying. Fritter batter can be substituted.

Because of their many folds, morels may harbor small insects. Rinse them thoroughly under running water, then soak in lightly salted water for an hour or two. Larger mushrooms can be quartered or cut into smaller pieces before being soaked. The smaller ones need only be cut once, along their length.

PREPARING AT HOME

Tips from the Camp Cook

Freshly caught fish, if not filleted, will usually curl while frying. The next time you fry trout or pan-sized fish at streamside, score the skin with three or four diagonal slashes on each side. This cuts some of the muscles that cause curling and allows the heat to penetrate deeper, thus cooking the fish more evenly.

Butter is the best fat for frying fish because it imparts a fine flavor. When you're cooking a whole fish or thick fillets, however, butter will usually burn before the fish is done. To avoid this, use half butter and half butter-flavored cooking oil to get the flavor without burning. But just use all butter for thin fillets or very small panfish.

When camping, cook your extra fish. Cooked fish keeps longer than fresh fish. A good use for leftover fish: Flake it and mix with mashed potatoes, some chopped onions, and an egg. Form into cakes and fry. Add some shredded

cheese, if you like. This is excellent with scrambled eggs.

To make a soup or stew, or even hash brown or potato salad, old-time camp cooks *never* peel potatoes or scrape carrots. They just scrub the skins thoroughly and cut them up as desired.

Don't throw away celery tops—they add flavor to soups, stews, and stuffings. Or toss them in a salad.

Potatoes will cook up deliciously brown if dusted with flour before frying. Dip in water and shake off excess. Then toss in a paper bag with seasoned flour. Use bacon drippings for extra flavor.

BACKPACKING EGGS

To keep eggs fresh without worrying about breakage, follow these easy directions: Fill a thermos with crushed ice the night before your trip. In the morning pour out all the ice. Break the eggs one at a time into a cup, making sure they're whole, then pour into the thermos and seal. The eggs will stay fresh for about a week and can be poured out one at a time as needed.

Brew a Flapjack

Many outdoor people have devised various uses for beer in preparing food. This one was passed on by a camp cook, and it's great for breakfast: When mixing pancake batter, leave out the milk and use beer instead. It adds great color and taste to the flapjacks and acts as a leavening agent. Besides, beer is easier to carry to the hunting camp than milk.

Bread Box Oven

An old metal breadbox can be easily converted into a reflector oven for camping. If enameled or painted, remove paint to bare metal with steel wool buffing pad attached to electric drill. Just install a stove grill inside, drill a few holes near the top back for ventilation, and it's ready to use. Place oven close to campfire to bake pies, muffins, and delicious campfire biscuits.

DUTCH OVEN PIES

Baking pies in a dutch oven often leaves a sticky mess difficult to clean up. If the fire is not strictly controlled, the pie cooks unevenly and portions of it often burn since it is placed directly on the bottom of the oven. To avoid this, place the pie pan on top of three small rocks in the dutch oven. Hot, dry air can then circulate around the pie, as it does in your home oven. Not only will you have a well-baked pie, there will be little if any mess for you to clean up.

PRACTICE MAKES PERFECT

Anyone who has a fireplace at home can easily practice camp cooking. You can purchase special books, racks, and other gadgets for fireplace cooking, but these are not necessary. You do not need your camp frying pan, dutch oven, reflector oven, skewers, and so on to re-create the campfire experience.

When fireplace cooking with frying pans and dutch ovens, pull some coals out a ways onto the hearth to cook on. Never try to balance a pan or pot of hot grease on logs or rocks over the main fire. In case of a flare-up, let the utensil burn in the fireplace instead of trying to take it outside. A little baking soda tossed into the pan or pot will put out even a roaring grease fire very quickly and safely.

Be sure to use well-dried hard wood, such as oak or hickory for your cooking fire.

FLOUR BARREL

To make your camp cooking both simpler and more versatile, carry a flour mix from which you can quickly prepare biscuits, pancakes, muffins, pan breads, or even cookies or cakes. The basic mix calls for the following:

2½ lb. all-purpose flour
1⅛ cups powdered milk
⅜ cup baking powder
¼ cup sugar
1 tbsp. salt
1 lb. vegetable shortening

Combine the dry ingredients in a large bowl and mix with a wire whisk. Then cut in the shortening until the mixture has a crumbly texture. Store in doubled plastic bags in the camp grub box. Mix does not need refrigeration. Recipes for the camp cook are easy:

Biscuits or pan bread: 3 cups mix; ¾ cup water.
Pancakes: 1½ cups mix; 1 egg; 1 cup water.
Muffins: 3 cups mix; 1 egg; 1 cup water; ¼ cup sugar.
Cookies: 3 cups mix; 1 egg; 1 cup water; ¼ cup sugar; ¼ cup shortening; 1 tsp. vanilla; 1 cup chocolate chips or raisins.
Cake: 4 cups mix; 2 eggs; 1⅓ cups water; 2 cups sugar; 2 tsps. vanilla extract.

These recipes are especially suited for cooking in cast-iron frying pans or dutch ovens. They can be halved or doubled. Cooking times will vary.

TRAIL SNACKS

Trail Salad

Outdoors people who love salad are often stuck when trying to assemble the proper ingredients because lettuce and other greens are perishable. Here is a salad made entirely of nourishing ingredients that don't spoil quickly and are easy to transport.

2 cans (17 oz.) peas, drained
2 eggs, hard-boiled and peeled
½ medium onion
1 small can pimientos, drained
1 tbsp. dried parsley flakes
salt and pepper to taste
½ cup mayonnaise

Place drained peas in bowl. Chop eggs, onion, and pimientos, and add with other ingredients to peas. Mix well. Mayonnaise can be added just before serving. (Note: Mayonnaise in a jar once opened is highly perishable without refrigeration. Carry tubes or the smallest jar you can buy.)

Optional additions are finely chopped celery, carrots, radishes, garlic, sliced mushrooms (fresh or canned). Serves four people.

NUTTY GRANOLA

1 cup honey
¾ cup vegetable oil
5 cups rolled oats (old-fashioned)
1 cup shredded coconut
1 cup raw wheat germ
1 cup dry milk (may be omitted)
1 cup seeds (sesame or shelled sunflower)
1 cup chopped nuts (your choice)
1 cup raisins (optional)

Warm the honey for easier mixing and stir into vegetable oil. Combine remaining ingredients, except nuts and raisins. Pour the oil and honey mixture over them and mix well. Spread mixture thinly on three large lightly greased baking sheets. Bake at 275°F for about 35 minutes; stir after first 15 minutes, again after another 10. Add nuts and raisins and finish baking. Stir once or twice while cooling. Cool completely before storing.

One teaspoon of salt may be added to the granola for taste before mixing.

Sourdough's Lunch

An old Alaska sourdough always carried a cloth sack of flour in his gear, and in the middle of the bag was his ball of nearly dried-up sourdough starter. On the mornings when campers would feast on his pancakes, Andy always made a sourdough's lunch to be carried in our pockets for the midday meal.

Instead of Andy's sourdough, all you need is a box of complete pancake mix. When you're having pancakes, mix up some extra batter. After you're through with breakfast, add a little extra milk or water to the leftover batter, to thin it just a little. Grease a hot skillet and pour in enough to make five- or six-inch pancakes. Brown nicely on each side. While the pancakes are still warm, spread on soft butter or margarine and sprinkle liberally with sugar and cinnamon, or spread on jam or jelly.

Then roll them up and wrap in waxed paper or plastic wrap. Stick them in your pocket, and you've got a handy lunch.

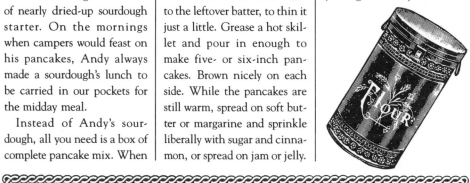

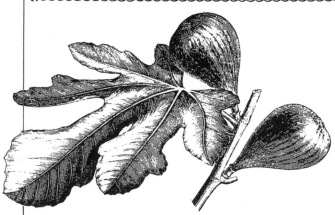

TRAIL FOOD

1 box seeded raisins
1 box pitted prunes
1 package dried figs
1 cup dried apricots
½ cup chopped lemon peel
1 cup or more sweet cider

The raisins, prunes, and figs should be ground coarsely and put into a large bowl; then add coarsely chopped apricots and lemon peel. Slowly pour the cider over the fruit until it is workable. Knead, then press mixture into a shallow cake pan lined with wax paper and refrigerate until solid.

When firm, slice into bars and wrap each in wax paper. Store in a cool place.

Dates may be used, but sugar crystals have a tendency to form on them, drying out the bars—the moist consistency of the fruit bar is one of its best features.

BROWN-BAGGING EGGS

Eggs can be cooked easily at camp without frying pans or boilers. And they are very good, too. Simply wrap each egg in four layers of wet brown paper, the type grocery bags are made from. Cover in hot coals for 10 minutes or until the outer layer of paper begins to char. It is very important that the brown paper be quite wet because the steam will help cook the egg without cracking the shell.

Lacking salt, the north-central Native American tribes used maple sugar as a flavoring agent.

COOKING AND PRESERVING YOUR CATCH

KEEPING FISH

With ice, refrigeration, and rapid transportation readily available, we sometimes forget the traditional ways of preserving our catch. Yet the methods used by fish catchers before today's technology are worth knowing. Sooner or later most outdoors people will find an occasion to use them.

Fish being kept for table purposes should be killed instantly. This reduces stress and the buildup of body acids that impart a bad taste.

The fish should be carefully cleaned. Remove the blood, gills, and eyes, and then dry the fish thoroughly. Using a sharp knife, split the backbone from the inside to the skin; fill the split with salt. Allow the fish to cool overnight if the temperature permits (anything above 75°F is too high), then fold them in dry towels or cloth so that none of the fish touch. Form a package of all the fish and wrap it in muslin or strong cheesecloth.

How a Naturalist Developed Frozen Foods

Great technological breakthroughs are often accidental. Such was the case with Clarence Birdseye. In 1912 the naturalist went ice fishing while on a trapping expedition in Labrador for the U.S. Fish and Wildlife Service.

In the 20-below-zero temperature, fish froze instantly as they were pulled from the sea. Birdseye took his string of fish back to camp and tossed one of them into a bucket of plain water. To his astonishment, the fish revived and began to dart back and forth. It gave him the idea for quick-frozen foods that, when defrosted and cooked weeks later, would still taste fresh, revolutionizing food-storage methods.

After World War I, Birdseye founded the Freezing Company and launched the industrial freezing of foods.

SPOON SCALER

If you ever find yourself without a fish scaler, try using an ordinary tablespoon. Simply grip the bowl near where the handle begins. Now, with the edge of the spoon resting on the fish and the hollow facing toward its head, make a smooth, deliberate stroke. The scales have a tendency to gather in the hollow, making them easy to dispose of. It isn't necessary to lift and strike repeatedly so that scales fly every which way. A smooth, even stroke is all it takes. Also, in any scaling job, you'll find that it helps to keep the fish wet.

Keeping the "Fresh" in Frozen Fish

• Cook frozen fish as soon as possible; it loses its flavor after prolonged freezing.

• Fish keeps longer if it is frozen in a container of water (milk cartons are perfect for this) or with its skin on. These measures also help to prevent dreaded freezer burn.

• Grayling should not be frozen. Because of its acid content, the meat tends to become very soft after freezing. A good alternative to freezing is to have it smoked.

• Northern pike is the fish least affected by freezing, but care is needed in cooking because it tends to dry out more than other fish.

• Soaking trout in whole milk for an hour before cooking will remove most of its strong-tasting oil.

How to Freeze Bluegills and Other Small Fish

Freezer burn ruins too many fish, especially panfish, which are difficult to package satisfactorily. If you put them into a bag, or try to wrap a batch of them with freezer paper, there will be too many air spaces. Freezing them in water contained in milk cartons is the best bet, but the cartons can take up a lot of room.

One trick is to put the fish into a loaf pan or plastic container with smooth, sloping sides, then barely cover them with water. Freeze solid, then

remove the block from the loaf pan and quickly wrap it in freezer paper, aluminum foil or plastic film. Label the contents on the end of the package. The blocks can now be stacked up like bricks, taking up a minimum of space and preventing freezer burn.

PICKLED FISH

Ever consider pickling fish? It's a tasty change from smoked, baked, or fried fish, especially on a hot summer's day.

Almost any type of fish can be pickled; some people even prefer pickled salmon to smoked salmon. However, bony fish are most commonly prepared this way because the pickling solution dissolves the bones.

It's best to scale, gut, and cut off the head and tail of smaller fish, while big fish should be filleted and cut into bite-sized pieces. Soak in a brine solution of two cups of un-iodized granular salt to one gallon of water for up to 48 hours. Then drain and rinse. Now make a mixture of half water, half vinegar and add about ½ teaspoon black pepper, white pepper, mustard seed, and tarragon, plus a bay leaf and perhaps a clove of garlic. Mix this all together and pour over the fish which have been packed in alternating layers of fish and chopped onion in a large glass jar.

The fish should pickle eight to ten weeks in a refrigerator before you try just a little piece. Once you've opened the jar it takes a lot of will power to keep from emptying it right then and there.

Easy Pickled Fish

Pickled fish in sour cream is an appetizer befitting a king, and is easy to prepare.

Clean, skin, and cut your choice of fish into bite-sized pieces (this is the hardest part). Fill a quart jar half full with white vinegar. Add 1 cup sugar, ¼ cup salt, 2 tbsp. pickling spices, and shake until the sugar and salt dissolve. Slice a large onion and alternate layers of fish and onion in the pickling solution. Cap the jar, refrigerate for two weeks, and then get ready to enjoy a treat. Pour off the vinegar and add sour cream.

I usually use crappie fillets because that's what I have the most of, but any fish will do.

CANNING FISH

Although herring are great-tasting fish, the chore of picking bones from the cooked fish is enough to try severely the patience of any otherwise sane soul. In addition, there is the greater problem of how to preserve a large quantity of fish to savor the delectable flavor many months after a herring run is complete.

Most people will salt them down in tubs or barrels. This preserves the fish for a good length of time, but the herring have an extreme salty flavor, and in addition, there are still the bones to contend with. A better method is to pressure-cook the fish. The results are so good that this method can be used to can and preserve different types of bony fish that you may want to freeze. Using this method almost all bones are dissolved, with the possible exception of the backbones in large fish, which may be discarded when the jar is opened.

Clean the fish thoroughly, wipe dry, and cut into chunks or lengths that will fit into pint jars. Fill jars to within one inch of the top and adjust lids. Place jars in a pressure canner and cook at ten pounds pressure for approximately one hour and 40 minutes. Remove cooker from heat, and after cooling store jars away from sunlight or heat. (Note: Required pressure pounds and cooking time vary from cooker to cooker.)

When a jar is opened, the fish are seasoned to taste and warmed. Another favorite method is to make fish cakes which are delicately fried to a golden brown in an open cast-iron skillet.

Ten Minutes an Inch

Here is a reliable method for determining how long to broil large fish fillets or steaks:

Measure the fillet at its thickest place and allow 10 minutes' cooking time for each inch of thickness. Add an extra five minutes to the overall cooking time if you wrap the fish in foil or cover it with a sauce. Double the overall cooking time if the fish is frozen. It's done when you can flake it easily with a fork.

COOKING WITH CANS

If the grill you use for cooking over open campfires is without legs, don't use stones to prop it over the flames. Rocks sometimes explode from heat, they are uneven, and their soot-blackened remains are a major form of camping litter everywhere. In a pinch you can devise a sturdy grill support with four beverage cans set upright under the corners. When you leave, just squash the blackened cans flat and dispose of them properly.

Deboning Small Fish

Many people like to eat small fish but refuse to dig tasty morsels from a mass of bones. When fish are too small to be filleted in the normal manner, you can cook them and pull away the backbones, but irritating small bones still cling to the meat.

My method of removing bones can be mastered in minutes. The fresher the fish, the easier your job. Clean the catch. Using a sharp, thin-bladed knife, lightly scrape once or twice along the bones lining each side of the abdominal opening to loosen them a bit. Sever the backbone behind the gill covers, leaving the head attached. Make a cut through the skin to the bone on both sides of the fish near its tail.

Using your thumb and forefinger, grasp the severed backbone and gently strip it and the rib cage down and out of the abdominal slit, holding the fish firmly upside down with one hand. Slice off at cuts in front of the tail. Discard the skeleton, to which the tail will be attached. Gently press along the inside of the filleted fish, and you may feel several additional clusters of bones that were pulled free and remained in the meat. These can easily be scraped out or cut free.

Do not cook small fish too long. When done, pull out the dorsal fins. With this technique your fish should be tasty and relatively bone-free.

CUTTING FISH STEAKS

When cutting steaks from round-shaped fish such as salmon, don't mash the fish while trying to cut through bone. This usually happens when you place a fish on its side before cutting. Lay the fish on its belly instead so that the backbone is facing up. Cut straight down, and more often than not the knife will find its own way between the vertebrae of the backbone.

Fish Stock

After filleting a fish, always save the backbone and head to make stock for soups and for casseroles.

To prepare basic fish stock, toss the heads and backbones into a pot, cover with cold water (do not add any flavorings yet), and bring to a boil. Lower heat, cover, and simmer for one hour, skimming off any scum that comes to the surface. Let cool and then strain through cheesecloth into plastic containers, one cup per container. Freeze stock for later use. Discard the heads and backbones.

Use the fish stock to make rice soup: For each serving

bring four tablespoons of rice to a boil in one cup of fish stock. Salt and pepper to taste. Add a pinch of thyme, one heaping tablespoon of diced onion, and one half of a garlic clove. Cook until rice is done.

Try adding one cup of fish stock to a packet of dried onion soup, boil, and serve.

You can use fish stock instead of water in any dish where the flavors are compatible.

FISH COOKERY IQ

Getting your catch to the table in prime condition requires different skills from landing them. Test your basic fish-cooking savvy with these questions:

1. Keepers usually taste better than trophy-sized specimens. T/F?
2. Physiological stress releases decay enzymes in fish. So to preserve the best flavor, quickly land 'em, kill 'em, and ice 'em down. T/F?
3. The flavor of fish caught in muddy or murky water can often be improved by skinning them. T/F?
4. Poaching is an effective method for cooking fish that have a low fat content. T/F?
5. Bread crumbs, cornmeal, cereal, or flour not only add flavor but also form a shield to prevent fish from drying out when fried. T/F?
6. Fish cooked in a paper bag is being a) broiled, b) baked, c) fried, d) prepared uncooked.
7. Oily fish do not freeze well for extended periods, but they are prime candidates for barbecuing, smoking, or home canning. T/F?
8. Court bouillon is normally associated with a) poaching, b) broiling, c) frying, d) baking.
9. Fish are more often harmed by a) overcooking or b) undercooking.

Answers: 1) T, 2) T, 3) T, 4) T, 5) T, 6) b, 7) T, 8) a, 9) a.

FISH IN FOIL

An excellent method of cooking fish that requires little equipment involves heavy-duty aluminum foil.

Tear off a piece 15 inches square. In the center, place enough filleted fish for one person. Add salt, pepper, a slice of diced bacon, and slices of onion and lemon. If you want to be fancy, sprinkle lightly with dried tarragon. Then wrap the foil over the fish, roll the edges to form a tight seal, and fold up the ends.

Push the package close to the coals of a burned-down fire and in about ten minutes rotate a half turn. Check a time or two (until you are familiar with the method) because the fish cooks quickly and there's nothing worse than overdone fish.

The food can be eaten directly from the package or emptied onto a plate. It is a welcome change from fried fish. I also prepare it at home on a grill if the fish is fresh.

King Ludwig's Favorite Fish Recipe

King Ludwig II of Bavaria is known as the Crazy King who almost bankrupted Bavaria by building castles in the Alps. But in addition, he loved to eat wild game and fish. His favorite fish recipe was for pike, Hechtenkraut.

A pike was baked and then chilled. The bones were removed and the meat cut into small pieces. Sauerkraut was cooked with finely cut, browned onions and butter. A fireproof dish was greased and lined with bread crumbs. Alternate layers of fish and sauerkraut were laid in the dish, topped with bread crumbs and more butter, and then browned in the oven.

Bass or any other filleted fish works just as well.

Gourmet Fish Batter

Chances are that in your kitchen you have three of the four ingredients needed to make the quickest and most delicious fish batter recipe ever concocted. Concocted with tender loving care by professional chef and fishing guide Stan Nelson of Litchfield, Minneapolis, this fish batter will draw friends like geese to a cornfield.

    1½ cups of flour
    1 tsp. salt
    1 tsp. baking powder

Mix in enough inexpensive white wine (not cooking wine) to create a pancake-batter consistency. Salt and pepper the fish fillets and dip them in the batter. Deep fry in hot cooking oil (vegetable oil is preferred).

BRANDIED FISH

You can prepare an out-of-this world marinade for barbecuing your catch. Mix equal parts of brandy and melted butter, and soak fish in it for about 30 minutes. Barbecue the fish in aluminum foil on a rack over the campfire. You won't believe that anything that simple can taste so wonderful.

FOOD VALUES OF FRESHWATER FISHES

Have you ever wondered about the nutritional value of certain species of fish you may have caught? It is interesting to note that allied species have different food values. Listed here are four of the more popular domestic foods that can be used as a yardstick for comparison. Note: All values are based on a three-and-a-half-ounce serving.

ITEM	CALORIES	OZ. OF PROTEIN	OZ. OF FAT
Sirloin Steak	288	0.55	0.86
Ham	259	0.47	0.79
Chicken (fried)	165	0.85	0.12
Ground beef	177	0.72	0.35
FISH—Freshwater species, wild (not hatchery or commercially grown)			
Bass, largemouth	104	0.66	0.10
Bass, smallmouth	109	0.67	0.11
Bass, striped	196	0.76	0.29
Bass, white	98	0.63	0.08
Catfish, bullhead	84	0.57	0.06
Catfish, channel	103	0.62	0.11
Crappie	79	0.59	0.03
Perch, white	118	0.68	0.14
Perch, yellow	91	0.68	0.03
Pickerel	84	0.66	0.02
Walleye	93	0.40	0.04
Salmon, king	222	0.67	0.55
Salmon, pink	119	0.71	0.14
Salmon, silver	153	0.73	0.27
Shad	170	0.66	0.35
Trout, brown	101	0.68	0.07
Trout, lake	168	0.64	0.35
Trout, rainbow	195	0.76	0.40
Whitefish, lake	155	0.66	0.29

⊞⊞⊞⊞⊞⊞⊞⊞⊞⊞⊞⊞⊞⊞⊞⊞⊞⊞⊞⊞⊞

Food Values of Saltwater Fishes

Listed below are popular saltwater species of fish and shellfish. Four common domestic foods have been included for use as a yardstick. Note: All values are based on a three-and-a-half-ounce serving.

ITEM	CALORIES	OZ. OF PROTEIN	OZ. OF FAT
Sirloin steak	288	0.55	0.86
Ham	259	0.47	0.79
Chicken (fried)	165	0.85	0.12
Ground beef	177	0.72	0.35
Saltwater Fish & Shellfish (wild—not commercially grown)			
Bluefish	117	0.72	0.12
Butterfish	169	0.62	0.34
Clams	54	0.30	0.03
Cod	78	0.62	0.01
Crab (steamed)	93	0.60	0.07
Flounder (baked)	202	1.05	0.29
Haddock	79	0.64	0.004
Halibut	100	0.73	0.04
Kingfish	105	0.64	0.11
Lobster	91	0.59	0.07
Mackerel, Atlantic	191	0.67	0.43
Mackerel, Pacific	159	0.77	0.26
Ocean perch, Atlantic	88	0.63	0.04
Ocean perch, Pacific	95	0.67	0.05
Oysters (raw)	66	0.30	0.12
Pollock	95	0.71	0.03
Red snapper	93	0.70	0.03
Sardines	311	0.73	0.86
Scallops	240	0.49	0.70
Sea bass	96	0.75	0.02
Shrimp	91	0.64	0.03
Swordfish	118	0.68	0.14
Yellowtail	138	0.74	0.19

⊞⊞⊞⊞⊞⊞⊞⊞⊞⊞⊞⊞⊞⊞⊞⊞⊞⊞⊞⊞⊞

FISH CAKES

No matter how carefully you cut the meat from the bones of fish, you will still leave some attached to the backbone. You can scrape the meat off the vertebrae with a spoon or a knife and use the bits of flesh in a variety of ways. Here is one of them.

SCANDINAVIAN FISH CAKES
1 cup raw, chopped fish
   (any species)
1 cup milk
1 egg
2 tbsp. potato flour (or
   dehydrated potato
   flakes)
1 tsp. salt
¼ tsp. nutmeg
1 tbsp. minced onions
   (optional)

Put all the ingredients except the fish in a blender and spin until thoroughly mixed. Add the fish and blend until the mixture is a smooth consistency. Shape the batter into silver-dollar-sized cakes about three-eighths of an inch thick, or into one-inch balls, and fry them in butter or shortening until they are brown. Serve the cakes hot, alone or with a white sauce.

Refrigerated they keep well. When hungry simply warm the cakes by frying them in butter. For a quick snack on the trail you may eat them cold; they taste best when eaten with crackers, or bread and butter.

These Fish Don't Last Long

Want a great fish-eating treat? Here's how professional fishing guide Bob Snook does it on the banks of Oregon's Rogue River. He fillets a salmon or steelhead (a big trout will do) and cuts the fillets into chunks four to five inches long.

Snook builds a fire and lets it die down until the coals are just right. He tests them by holding his hand a few inches above the coals and counting, "One hippopotamus, two hippopot—" About then the coals get too hot, and he jerks his hand away. Two hippopotamuses are just about right. One is too hot; three is too cool to cook properly.

Snook places the pieces, flesh side down, on a grill just off the coals and cooks them until they're done about one-fourth of the way through—you can tell when the pink meat turns tan. He flips the fillets, places a dab of butter on each, and sprinkles them with lemon pepper, and cooks them until done. The skin will char, but the meat won't burn.

Of the three main types of clawed lobsters, the American lobster is the largest, and its greatest rival is the crab.

Smoking Fish Is Easy

A pot-type grill, such as a Weber, is a natural smokehouse for anything from fish to fowl.

When smoking fish, such as salmon or trout, remove skin and trim off fatty areas along the back, sides, and belly. Cut the fish crosswise into steaks one to two inches thick. Place steaks in brine and refrigerate for eight to 10 hours.

BRINE
   2 qts. water
   ½ cup pickling salt
   ½ cup brown sugar
   2 tsps. onion salt
   2 tsps. pickling spice
      (cloves, allspice, etc.)

Wash brine with cold water; dry on paper towels.

Pile 10 or 12 charcoal briquettes on one side of the grill and light them. When coals are gray (usually in 10 to 15 minutes), pile two handfuls of damp hickory chips on the coals. Arrange steaks on the grill opposite the fire. Keep all air vents of the grill in an open position and close cover. About every hour, add eight briquettes and two handfuls of hickory chips. Smoke for about three hours.

Do not use too much charcoal—you don't want to cook the fish over intense heat. You are curing with heat and smoke steaks.

Steaks not eaten after smoking should be refrigerated or frozen.

Fish for Breakfast?

The American public is awaking to the nutritional advantages and gastronomical merits of fish. My family has always eaten a lot of fish, and my father breakfasted on salt mullet, served with grits.

Salt mullet, with or without grits, is a bit strong for early morning eating, but this simple, tasty dish can be prepared from leftover fish.

Flake the fish and stir in with eggs. Melt a bit of butter in a skillet. Pour in the mixture and scramble until the eggs are done. Season to taste.

Fish flakes can be used to advantage in omelets. The leftover fish can be fried, baked, or broiled. (If the fried fish have a thick batter, scrape it off first.)

Fresh or frozen fish can also be used. Poach it for a few minutes and flake it with a fork. This breakfast is high in protein and lower in salt and cholesterol than the usual bacon or ham with an omelet or scrambled eggs. Try it!

Fish Soufflé

Prepare a seven-inch soufflé baking dish (any straight-sided dish will do) by greasing it with butter and dusting with flour. Make a collar for it by wrapping foil (shiny side out) around the outside. The collar should extend three inches above the top of the dish to hold any soufflé expansion.

Preheat the oven to 325°F as you mix the following:

3 tbsp. butter
3 tbsp. flour
1 cup milk
1 cup cooked flaked fish
¼ cup chopped carrots
¼ cup chopped celery
2 tbsp. pimiento
3 egg yolks
3 egg whites, beaten until stiff
1 tbsp. lemon juice
salt, paprika, parsley

Melt butter in a double boiler and sprinkle in flour. Stir until it forms a smooth paste, then slowly add milk, stirring until sauce is smooth and thick. Remove from heat and stir in fish, carrots, celery, and pimiento. Mix in egg yolks and season with lemon juice, salt, and paprika. Have ingredients at room temperature before folding in egg whites and parsley.

Place soufflé inside another baking dish that contains two inches of water and bake for 35 minutes. Garnish with parsley. Serves two to four.

FISH COOKERY, 1869

"Fish cannot be made a constant substitute for butcher's meat without considerably impairing the muscular, and perhaps the mental, force . . ."

This blunt statement comes from the "Fish and Its Preparation" chapter of a book called *The Philosophy of Housekeeping* by Joseph Lyman, first published in 1869.

Lyman does, however, acknowledge that "when freshly caught and properly cooked," fish is quite a suitable alternative for certain groups of people. Among these are "invalids, jockeys, prisoners, soldiers, and those whose occupations are sedentary."

Try some of his recipes:

1. To prepare smaller kinds of freshwater fish, cut three or four slices of salt pork, then soak overnight. Fry the pork until crisp, then remove it, keeping the fat hot. Roll the fish in flour or cornmeal and lay in the pork fat. Cook five minutes on each side, then remove quickly. Lyman's tip:

"The finest of fish can be utterly ruined by allowing the flesh to become soaked with rancid or burnt fat."

2. To cook fresh shad, salmon, or mackerel: Since these fish have a definite flavor all their own, they must be "unmixed with baser matter" and broiled. Use no fat or pepper, just a pinch of salt and a few drops of lemon juice. Put the fish in a folding wire gridiron, then broil until crispy on the outside. Tip: "Cooling is fatal to enjoyment."

3. To bake flounder, halibut, or turbot, melt four ounces of butter in a baking dish, sprinkle in a teaspoon of flour, then stir. Add a pinch of salt and pepper, nutmeg, chopped parsley, two or three chopped mushrooms, and three pounds of fish. Pour a glass of vinegar over this mixture. Cover and bake in a moderate oven until done. Tip: "Very flavorful for breakfast."

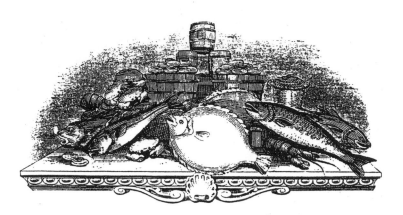

CLASSY COOKING

Korbel vintners of California, producers of champagne, have sent us these recipes for fish that Almanac readers might enjoy experimenting with for a real taste treat.

CHAMPAGNE FISH GRATINEE
  1 onion, finely chopped
  2 tbsp. minced fresh
    parsley
  4 oz. mushrooms, sliced
  ½ cup dry bread crumbs
  4 fish fillets
  salt and pepper, to taste
  ¾ cup champagne
  ½ cup shredded mozzarella
    cheese

In a greased baking dish, place half the onions, parsley, mushrooms, and bread crumbs. Place the fish fillets on top. Season with salt and pepper and cover with the remaining vegetables. Pour the champagne over this mixture.

Bake in a 375°F oven ten minutes. Sprinkle with the remaining bread crumbs and the cheese. Bake 15 minutes longer. Serves four.

OVEN-BAKED CHAMPAGNE
SOLE
  1 onion, thinly sliced
  2 fillets of sole (or other
    firm white fish), 6
    ounces each
  ½ cup champagne
  salt and pepper, to taste
  ½ cup butter, softened

Spread the onions in a greased baking dish, just large enough to hold the fish in a single layer. Place the fish over the onions. Add the champagne and season with salt and pepper. Bake the fish, covered in a 400°F oven for 15 minutes.

Strain the cooking liquid into a saucepan (keep the fish warm). Cook until reduced to two tablespoons. Add the butter and stir until melted. Serve the sauce over the fish. Serves two.

BARBECUED FISH IN FOIL
For each portion:
  1 small whole fish or fish
    fillet or steak
  salt and pepper, to taste
  1 slice lemon
  1 bay leaf
  1 tbsp. butter ·
  3 tbsp. champagne
  1 sheet aluminum foil

Place the fish on the foil and raise the sides slightly. Season with salt and pepper and place the lemon and bay leaf on the fish. Dot with butter and sprinkle with the champagne. Seal the foil well. Cook over hot coals for about 40 minutes.

FISH LOAF

After filleting your catch, don't throw away the backbones. A fair amount of meat is attached to these bones and can be used to make a delicious fish loaf. Begin by either baking the backbone scrapings in a 350°F oven or by steaming them over boiling water until they are cooked. While the fish is cooking, gather the following ingredients:

1 cup toasted bread cubes
1 small onion, diced
2 stalks celery, diced
1 tsp. salt
1 egg, beaten
½ cup tomato sauce
¾ cup grated cheddar cheese
paprika
1¼ cups cooked, flaked fish (from the scrapings described above)

Mix all ingredients except paprika and ¼ cup of the grated cheese in a large bowl. Work in the flaked fish until a uniform texture is attained. Spoon the mixture into a 9 × 5-inch breadpan and shape it into a loaf. Spread the remaining grated cheese over the loaf and sprinkle paprika on top. Bake the loaf at 350°F for one hour. Let it cool 5 to 10 minutes before cutting.

Since some fish have a very mild flavor, you might want to add a little zip to the loaf by adding some chili peppers or sprinkling in a dash of hot pepper sauce.

While fish loaf makes an excellent main dish, it is also very good as an open-faced sandwich. Cut a one-inch-thick slice from a cold, cooked loaf and place it on a piece of fresh bread or an English muffin. Sprinkle on a small amount of grated cheese and broil until the cheese melts.

Fast and Fancy Fish

About 2 lb. fish fillets (bass, crappie, or perch but not trout)
½ cup French dressing
2 tbsp. margarine
2 tbsp. cooking oil
1 small onion, chopped
1 lemon
Tartar sauce

Heat margarine and oil in a large skillet over moderate heat. Dip the fish fillets in the French dressing and add them to the skillet. Sprinkle onion over fillets. Cook three to four minutes, turn and repeat. Serve with lemon wedges and tartar sauce. Serves four to six.

A good substitute for tartar sauce can be made by adding pickle relish to salad dressing.

Thousand Islands Shoreside Lunch

Allen Benas, a restaurateur and fishing guide, serves just about the best traditional shore lunch in the Thousand Islands. Here's how he does it:

Fry a couple of pounds of fatty bacon crisp and cook onion slices in the fat. Toss a salad (with Thousand Island dressing) and serve bacon-and-onion sandwiches with the salad as an appetizer.

Slice thickly two scrubbed potatoes per person, leaving the skins on. Heat cooking oil with the bacon fat until very hot, and brown the potatoes.

Allow a fillet from a three-pound pike or two fillets from a one pound bass for each person. Shake the fillets in a paper bag with flour, salt, and pepper, and fry quickly.

For dessert, dip slices of bread in an egg-and-milk batter and fry them in oil. Butter and serve with one capful each of maple syrup, cream, and brandy.

Last, bring three quarts of water to a light boil in an open pot. Mix an egg with a half-pound of freshly ground coffee and add to the pot. Bring to a rolling boil. Add three or four ice cubes to settle the grounds.

A young shark is called a pup.

BAKED STRIPED BASS

1 lb. onions, sliced
6 tbsp. olive oil
½ cup currants
½ cup pine nuts
¼ tsp. cinnamon
¼ tsp. allspice
1 tsp. salt
¼ tsp. pepper
4 tbsp. chopped parsley
2 tbsp. lemon juice
½ cup tomato sauce
¼ cup dry white wine
1 lemon, thinly sliced
1 striped bass, about 3 lb.

Scale and clean the bass. Fillet it butterfly-style so the fillets remain attached to each other. Wash and place in a baking dish.

Sauté onions in oil until transparent. Add currants, pine nuts, and seasonings, stirring all the while, then add parsley and lemon juice.

Fill fish with the sautéed mixture, spreading evenly.

Mix the tomato sauce and wine, then pour this over the closed fish. Put lemon slices on top. Bake at 375°F for about 45 minutes, or until the flesh flakes with a fork. Excellent when served cold as a buffet dish. Makes six servings.

TROUT CREPES

While few will argue that the best trout is pan-fried and fresh, sometimes you may want to try something exotic. The following recipe is easier than it looks and tastier than it sounds.

PLAIN CREPES
¾ cup flour
⅛ tsp. salt
3 beaten eggs
2 tbsp. melted butter
¾ cup milk (more or less)
butter to brush the pan for each crepe

Beat flour, salt, and eggs together with a wire whisk or egg beater until batter is smooth. Add butter and mix thoroughly. Add milk until batter has the consistency of heavy cream. Let stand a few minutes and beat once more.

Heat a six- or seven-inch crepe pan (a heavy skillet will do) and brush with butter. Pour in about 2 tablespoons of batter and tilt pan so the bottom is covered completely. As soon as edges begin to brown or bottom appears dry, loosen edges, flip, and cook other side until slightly golden. Makes about 12 crepes. Store in waxed paper or aluminum foil until needed. They can be made ahead and frozen, or refrigerated and then reheated when they are filled.

TROUT FILLING
2 tbsp. minced onion
4 tbsp. butter
4 tbsp. flour
1 cup milk
1 cup chicken stock
2 tbsp. white wine (optional)
salt and pepper to taste
2 cups cooked, boned trout
½ cup chopped mushrooms
½ chopped cooked green pepper

Sauté onion in butter until golden. Stir in flour, then milk and chicken stock. Stir and simmer until thickened. Add wine, salt, and pepper. Set aside ½ cup of this sauce.

Add trout, mushrooms, and green pepper to remaining sauce. Simmer briefly, then fill and roll crepes. Tuck in the ends and place in a shallow baking pan. Glaze with reserved sauce. If you are home, broil for a few minutes. Otherwise, warm on any heat source. Serves four to six.

(A quick version of this recipe can also be made by substituting canned cream of mushroom soup for the milk, chicken stock, and mushrooms.)

BASS COOKERY, 1859

The Young Housekeeper's Friend by Mrs. Cornelius gives this recipe for stuffed baked bass: First, make a cracker-crumb stuffing out of finely crumbled crackers, seasoned with salt and pepper and a sprinkle of cloves, and moisten it with a beaten egg. Stuff the body cavity of the fish with this mixture, and sew it closed. Place in a baking dish, sprinkle with nutmeg and crumble a few crackers over the fish. Drench with melted butter and bake for one hour. Take your bass directly from the oven to table, and serve it in the same dish in which it was prepared—for best flavor, if not looks.

She further recommends, "If a fresh fish of any kind is left of dinner, it is a very good way to lay it in a deep dish and pour over it a little vinegar, with catsup, and add pepper or any other spice which is preferred."

CRAWDAD BOIL

In late September and early October, when water temperatures reach 50°F, crayfish become active, and they can be caught with a length of string and a chunk of leftover breakfast bacon. They make a great camp meal for hungry outdoors people.

Raid the spice rack for the following:

¼ cup mustard seed
¼ cup coriander seed
2 tbsp. dill seed
2 tbsp. whole allspice
1 tbsp. ground cloves
4 dried hot red chilies, stemmed and crumbled
3 medium-size bay leaves, crumbled

All of this equals about one cup of mix and will easily fit into a sandwich bag, which in turn will fit into a hip pocket to tote along for the makings of a campfire feast.

To three quarts of water, add 3 tablespoons or so of the mix. Bring the water to a boil over high heat, then cover and reduce heat to boil for 20 minutes.

Rinse the crawdads in fresh water. When the mix has boiled its allotted time, add the live crawdads and boil uncovered for five minutes until they turn bright red.

Remove the meat by gripping the tail between the thumbs and forefingers of both hands and applying pressure to crack the shell. Crawdads taste very similar to lobster.

This is also a great boil for lobster, crab, and shrimp.

SWIMMING FOSSIL

The lake sturgeon is a prehistoric freshwater fish with no skeleton or backbone. Instead it has a cartilaginous spine called a notochord. Its tail resembles that of a shark, and its mouth is similar to that of a sucker and is well suited to bottom feeding.

Sturgeon have been known to swim as far as 125 miles upstream to spawn. A male doesn't reach maturity until 15 years of age, and will only spawn every other year. The female sturgeon, also a late bloomer, doesn't reach sexual maturity until 25 years; then she will only spawn at five-year intervals. She will lay approximately 700,000 eggs during her spawning run. The male sturgeon releases his sperm by bumping against hard objects in the river such as rocks and logs. Of the 700,000 eggs layed, it is estimated that only two sturgeon will reach maturity due to predation and other mortality factors.

Lake sturgeon are so lethargic during the spawning period that poachers seeking their highly prized eggs for caviar need only to reach into the water and pluck them out. This has led to intensive law enforcement in order to protect this species of fish.

Bag Your Bass

At fancy prices, swanky restaurants cook pompano in a brown paper bag and call the dish *Pompano en Papillote* or some such fancy name. An ordinary bass, or walleye, cooked in a plastic baking bag might not be as quaint looking, but it can taste just as good as pompano—or better. Here's what you'll need:

2 lb bass fillets, skinned
1 large bell pepper
1 large onion
¼ cup butter, melted
1 tsp. salt
¼ tsp. pepper
1 clove of garlic
sweet paprika (optional for garnish)

Set the oven to 375°F so that it will be ready. Peel the onion and slice it into rings. Slice the

pepper into rings, removing the seeds and inner pith. Peel and mince the garlic and mix with pepper and onions. Dip the fillets in the melted butter. Mix the salt and pepper, then sprinkle onto the buttered fillets, covering both sides. Place the plastic baking bag in the center of a baking pan and open it wide. Place the onions, pepper rings, and garlic in the bag, making a bed. Carefully place the fish fillets on top. Pour the remaining melted butter on top. Close the bag and puncture holes in the top, following the manufacturer's directions.

Put the baking dish into the hot oven for 20 minutes. (Fillets from larger fish, four pounds or over, will require an extra five minutes.) Remove the pan from the oven, slit the bag on top, and carefully transfer the fillets directly to individual serving plates. Sprinkle the fillets lightly with paprika, then arrange the onion and pepper rings around them. Serve with hot bread.

Poached Salmon

1 salmon, 4 to 6 lb.
1 small onion, cut into chunks
1 celery rib, cut into chunks
1 carrot, cut into chunks
2 bay leaves
½ cup dry white wine (optional)
parsley or watercress sprigs
lemon and/or lime slices

Put enough water into a large roasting pan or fish poacher to cover the salmon. Add the onion, celery, carrot, bay leaves, and white wine to the water.

Cover and bring to a boil. Lower the heat and simmer for 15 minutes. Place the salmon on a rack or in a double thickness of cheesecloth and lower it into the bubbling water. Bring the water back to a boil, then lower the heat until the water is slowly bubbling.

Cover the pan and poach the fish for 10 minutes per inch thickness. (Measure the fish at the thickest place on the back to determine cooking time.) Most salmon will require about 25 to 30 minutes. Be sure the water is bubbling before starting to time. The fish will flake easily on the back when it is cooked.

Lift the fish from the liquid and place on a heated platter. Strip off the top skin and garnish with greens and lemon or lime slices. Serve immediately, or cool and serve. Serves five to eight.

FISH CASSEROLE

2 lb. boneless fish fillets
2 cans condensed cream of celery soup
3 cups milk
10 small potatoes peeled and halved
7 tbsp. diced ham
5 tbsp. diced onion
6 slices American cheese
4 tbsp. grated cheese

Coat inside of two-quart casserole dish lightly with oil, then lay in fillets. Place potatoes along the sides. In a saucepan heat and mix soup, milk, onions, and ham, then pour over fillets and potatoes. Sprinkle on grated cheese and bake in a 200°F oven for three hours. Then lay cheese slices on top and heat until melted. Any sort of fish can be cooked in this fashion. Serve bubbling hot with a loaf of rye bread and white wine.

Canadian Fish Chowder

On our northern lake camping trips we always plan a hearty chowder for dinner at least once a week. The following recipe was acquired on Canada's Lake Nipigon about 30 years ago. It is a simple one-pot meal.

4 medium potatoes
2 medium onions
1 carrot
4 slices bacon
1 lb. fish fillets
1 13-oz. can Milnot or condensed milk
1 can cream-style corn
salt and pepper

Dice the vegetables, add salt and pepper, barely cover with water, and simmer until tender. Dice and add the bacon and simmer 10 minutes. Dice the fish into bite-sized pieces, add, and simmer 10 minutes. Add the Milnot or condensed milk and simmer 10 minutes. Add the corn and simmer 10 minutes while stirring frequently to prevent sticking. Serves four.

Fricassee of Frogs' Legs

Fried frogs' legs are hard to beat as a gourmet's delight, but as a change of pace, Fricassee of Frogs' Legs makes an unusually tasty meal.

The hind legs are the only part used for the table. The bullfrog, leopard frog, and pickerel frog produce the largest and meatiest legs. (Consult a field guide for species descriptions.) Cut them off the same way you would chicken legs. Pull off the skin—it is loose and comes off like a sock. One pair of large frogs' legs weighs about one-half pound.

6 pairs large frogs' legs
2 tbsp. butter
4 slices onion
1 bay leaf
sprigs of parsley
a few celery leaves
1 whole clove
flour
salt and pepper
1 cup evaporated milk
1 tbsp. lemon juice
⅛ tsp. ground nutmeg
slices of toast
watercress

Wash the frogs' legs and pat dry. Dredge with flour seasoned with salt and pepper.

Melt the butter in a large frying pan. Add onion. Tie bay leaf, celery leaves, parsley, and clove into a cheesecloth bag and add to pan, stir, and then push to one side. Adjust heat to moderate and cook legs until delicately browned, turning frequently. Remove from pan, add the milk, and stir over gentle heat until sauce is smooth and slightly thickened. Replace the frogs' legs and reheat, adding lemon juice and nutmeg just before removing from heat. Serve on hot buttered toast, garnishing with watercress. Serves six.

GRAVLAX

You can make the Scandinavian hors d'oeuvre called gravlax (marinated salmon) quite easily at home.

GRAVLAX
- 3 lbs. of fresh salmon fillets
- fresh dill
- 2 tsps. vegetable oil
- 4 tbsps. salt
- 4 tbsps. sugar
- 2 tsps. crushed black pepper

Place the salmon fillets, skin side down, over a thick bed of fresh dill in a shallow dish. Brush the meat with the oil. Gently rub salt-and-sugar mixture into the flesh. Sprinkle the pepper over the meat.

If you have two fillets, place one on top of the other, flesh side to flesh side, and cover the pieces with a generous layer of fresh dill. If you only have one fillet, place it in the dish, skin side down, cover with dill, and then place plastic wrap over the top to keep the meat from drying out.

Marinate the fish in the refrigerator for two or three days. If you have two fillets, turn them over from time to time, always keeping the skin side down.

After the fish has cured, scrape the dill and the seasonings off the flesh. With a very sharp knife slice the fish diagonally to form long, thin slices. Serve on rye bread spread with cold mustard sauce. Garnish with fresh dill and lemon wedges.

MUSTARD SAUCE
- 3 tbsps. prepared mustard
- 1 tbsp. sugar
- 1 tbsp. white vinegar
- 5 tbsps. vegetable oil
- fresh dill, finely chopped onions, and chopped, hard-cooked egg yolks
- salt, pepper

Blend the mustard, sugar, vinegar, salt, and pepper in a bowl. Add the oil drop by drop, while stirring with a wooden spoon. Just before serving, add some fresh dill, a little onion, or some chopped egg yolks.

Maple Leaf Trout

- 4 trout, 10 to 12 inches
- 2 tbsps. maple syrup
- ⅓ cup milk
- ¾ cup cornmeal, seasoned with salt and pepper
- 2 tbsps. butter
- 2 tbsps. cooking oil

Dry the cleaned trout with paper towels. The heads may be removed. Mix the maple syrup and milk in a shallow dish and dip the trout in the mixture, allowing some to seep inside the stomach cavity.

Roll the trout in cornmeal, coating the skin thoroughly. In a large, heavy frying pan, heat the butter and oil over medium-high heat. Fry the trout for 5 minutes on each side until they are nicely browned and flake easily when probed with a fork at the thickest point on their backs.

Serve immediately on a heated platter. Serves four.

Pine-smoked Trout

The simplest method of getting a nice smoky flavor when cooking trout is with a wire holder. Be sure that the holder will hold the trout securely so it can be turned over—like the type made to hold hot dogs or hamburgers over barbeque grills.

Cut several pine boughs, place them on your campfire, and lay the holder with your trout directly on top. Light the pine boughs. The fire will sear, cook, and smoke your trout in about a minute before burning itself out. Turn the holder over to sear the other side, add a

couple more pine boughs, and light your fire again. Naturally, if the trout are bigger, you'll need a bigger fire so the fish cook longer. I have found that a couple of pine boughs and less than a minute for each side is perfect for each half-pound trout.

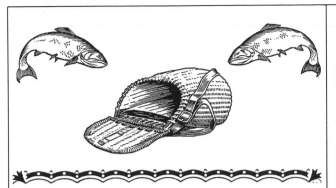

Leftover Fish 'n' Eggs

No matter whether it be fried, baked, boiled, grilled, steamed, broiled, or raw, never throw out leftover fish. Flake the meat and freeze it in units of two cups. The following is one of my favorites for breakfast or a light lunch of leftovers:

2 cups fish flakes
6 large eggs
2 strips salt pork (bacon size)
1 tbsp. butter
½ cup chopped green onions (with part of tops)
¼ cup red bell pepper, diced
1 tsp. Worcestershire sauce
salt and pepper
toast (prepared separately)
cold sliced tomatoes (optional)

After removing the rind, dice the salt pork finely. Melt the butter or margarine in a frying pan and sauté the salt pork on medium heat until browned. Add the chopped onions and diced pepper, and set heat on low until the onions begin to turn clear. Pour off excess fat. Whisk the eggs in a bowl and pour them into the frying pan. While stirring, add fish flakes, Worcestershire sauce, salt, and pepper. Cook and stir until the eggs set. Serve with toast and cold sliced tomatoes. Serves four.

Note: The above dish is even better when made with fresh fish or crawdad tails. Dice fresh meat and sauté it along with the salt pork. For cooking in camp, omit Worcestershire sauce, red pepper, and green onion. Instead, use a little chopped wild onion, puffballs, elder bloom, or root tip sprouts from cattail plants.

PICKLED BLUEGILLS

Note: Use a stainless-steel pan for this recipe. Any other type may give an unpleasant aftertaste.

Cut up your bluegills into small pieces—you will need five cups of fish. Soak in one quart of water and one cup of salt for 48 hours. Rinse the fish in cold water and drain. Pour two cups of white vinegar over fish and refrigerate for another 48 hours, then pour this off.

Cook the following mixture for five minutes and let cool:

2 cups white vinegar
1½ cups sugar
1 tsp. whole black pepper
1 tsp. whole allspice
1 tsp. whole cloves
4 bay leaves

When cool, pour over the fish; place slices of lemon and onions on top. Refrigerate for five days, then remove the spices and pack the fish into jars. It makes three pints.

Optional: If you prefer, put some onions in the jar with the fish and place a slice of lemon on top. Cover fish with the marinade. Place in refrigerator and let marinate for another five days or more before eating the bluegills. Delicious!

Killer whales have been clocked at 35 mph, porpoises at 37 mph.

Armenian Baked Fish

3 lb. whitefish (any white-
fleshed bland fish may
be substituted)
3 fresh tomatoes or small
can tomatoes
1 clove garlic, mashed
1 tbsp. flour
1 cup water
4 tbsp. minced parsley
½ cup olive oil
juice of 1 lemon
1 tsp. salt
½ tsp. pepper

Fillet and rinse fish. Spread the fillets, skin side down, in a buttered baking pan.

Cover fish with the tomatoes, garlic, and the flour mixed with the water. Sprinkle with parsley. Season with salt and pepper. Pour oil and lemon juice all around fish. Bake at 325° for 20 to 40 minutes, depending on the thickness of the fish. Spoon pan juices over the fish several times while baking. May be served hot or cold. Garnish with sliced lemon. Serves six.

BARBECUED PANFISH

3 to 4 lb. crappie,
bluegill, or perch fillets
2 tbsp. chopped onion
1 tbsp. shortening
1 cup catsup
2 tbsp. vinegar
dash of pepper
¼ cup lemon juice
3 tbsp. Worcestershire
sauce
½ tsp. salt
1 tbsp. butter

Place fish in greased shallow pan and sprinkle with salt. Using another pan, lightly brown onion in butter, and add remaining ingredients. Simmer for five minutes, then pour over fish.

Bake in hot oven (425°F) 35 to 40 minutes. Garnish with lemon.

Serves six to eight people.

Fish Steaks Peking

1 egg white
3 tsp. cornstarch
2 lb. of fish steaks
2 tbsp. cooking oil
½ cup chicken broth
¼ cup dry sherry
1 tbsp. dark corn syrup
¼ tsp. salt

With a fork beat egg white and one teaspoon of the cornstarch until blended. Dip fish steaks in this mixture, coating all sides. Heat oil in a large skillet over medium heat. Add fish and sear on both sides, about two minutes. Remove fish from skillet. Stir broth, sherry, corn syrup, remaining two teaspoons cornstarch, and salt in a skillet and bring to boil over medium heat, stirring constantly until thickened. Return fish steaks to skillet and cook about two minutes on each side until done. Remove from skillet and pour sauce over steaks. Serves four.

During the summer the arctic fox will kill and store small rodents in rock crevices for its winter food supply. Throughout summer the fox feeds on a variety of things including eggs, fish, and any carrion it finds.

MEET RECIPES

SCOTCH EGGS

Scotch eggs are a popular pub food served in parts of Canada and throughout Great Britain. They make a great pocket lunch to carry on a field trip.

½ lb. hamburger
½ lb. bulk sausage
½ tsp. salt
1 tsp. prepared mustard
1 egg, slightly beaten
½ cup dry bread crumbs
6 hard-boiled eggs, peeled
crumbs for coating

In a bowl mix hamburger, sausage, salt, and mustard. Stir in beaten egg, then bread crumbs. Scoop out about two tablespoons of meat mixture and form around each boiled egg, pressing firmly to make an even covering. Roll in fine dry bread crumbs, cracker meal, or crushed corn flakes. Cook over medium heat in a lightly greased skillet. Turn frequently until browned all over. Serve warm right out of the skillet, or cool and wrap in plastic wrap or foil for a pocket lunch. Serves four to six.

An ethologist studies animal behavior.

NAVAJO STEW

3 or 4 lbs. lamb or mutton, venison, or beef
2 onions, sliced
10 oz. can tomatoes (or tomato sauce)
3 or more juniper berries
1 or 2 cloves garlic
salt, black pepper, or peppercorn
1 to 3 tbsps. chili powder
8 oz. can whole kernel corn
1 lb. can pinto beans
8 oz. can chick peas (garbanzos)
1 can mixed vegetables or leftovers

Snowshoe à la Barbecue

The snowshoe hare is famous for its ability to leg it out in front of the dogs, and this can result in pretty tough tablefare. Here's my recipe for tender hare.

Start with two good-sized hares cut into serving pieces. Season with salt and pepper, and roll in flour. Brown lightly in two tablespoons of bacon fat in a frypan. Add two sliced onions and a cut-up green pepper. For the barbecue sauce, mix the following:

Brown meat in heavy saucepan or dutch oven. Add onions and brown slightly. Add seasoning and cover meat with water. Pour tomatoes over meat, cover, and simmer until meat is tender. Add the vegetables and beans. Heat well. Serve hot with squaw bread, tortillas, or hard rolls. Serves six to eight persons.

¼ cup red wine
¼ cup catsup
1 tbsp. mustard
1 tbsp. brown sugar
1 tbsp. lemon juice
1 tsp. Worcestershire sauce
5 (or more) drops Tabasco sauce

Pour this over the meat and simmer *gently* for two hours, covered. At the two-hour mark, add a half pound of sliced fresh mushrooms, return cover, and cook another 30 minutes, or until meat is tender. Serves four to six.

SAUSAGE, WILD AND LEAN

Making sausage is one of those crafts that seem to be shrouded in mystery. Indeed, most of us turn to the supermarket and buy ready-made beef and pork sausage. Nearly all commercial sausages also contain sodium nitrite and/or sodium nitrate, both known to be carcinogens.

Some sausages do take time and patience to make. Others are simple to produce. One that requires no implements other than those already found in your kitchen is breakfast sausage patties. Throughout the year these can be made in small lots from ground meat (burger will do nicely).

BREAKFAST SAUSAGE PATTIES

    2 lb. ground venison
    ½ medium onion, chopped
    ½ clove garlic, finely pressed
    4 tbsp. fresh parsley, finely chopped
    ½ tsp. salt
    ½ tsp. crushed dried red pepper
    ½ tsp. freshly ground black pepper
    ¾ tsp. cumin
    ¾ tsp. ground allspice

Mix all the ingredients, roll the meat into the shape of a log, wrap it in aluminum foil, and refrigerate or freeze.

Increase the pepper if you want hotter sausage. Increase the allspice if you want a nuttier flavor. Depending on the chewiness you want, chop onions coarse or fine.

If you care to make breakfast link sausage, salami, or pepperoni, you'll need more elaborate tools, such as a sausage stuffer, sausage casings, and binding ingredients. Some people claim that salami cannot be made without a cure and, furthermore, if you attempt to cook or smoke sausage at low heat without the use of a cure, you'll risk contracting botulism.

However, a small segment of the commercial meat industry routinely makes these very cooked and smoked meat products without the use of nitrites or nitrates. For example, Bob Markholt, the president of Seattle's The Meat Shop, produces USDA-approved, nitrite-free pepperoni, jerky, wieners, salami, bacon, and ham. In a recent telephone interview, he told me, "I've been making sausage without sodium nitrite for years, and it comes out the same [as sausage] with sodium nitrite. . . . It just doesn't have the bright red color." On the subject of botulism, Bob went on to say, "Botulism is a scare word, like terrorism. Any time someone sees the word, they think, 'Oh no, I'm playing with fire here.' But the fact of the matter is [that] I have not been able to run down, in 20 years in this business, any documented case of botulism with uncanned, cured meat."

Dr. George Wilson of the American Meat Institute in Washington, D.C., was able to unravel the issue for me. The

USDA has given its stamp of approval to numerous sausage makers who do not use nitrites or nitrates in their products, Dr. Wilson said. However, labeling laws do not permit these products to be called salami or pepperoni, titles traditionally reserved for those products that are created with the use of nitrite or nitrate cures. These chemically free products must bear the label "nitrite-free salami" or "nitrite-free pepperoni."

I have made this cooked salami with both elk and antelope meat and have also tried both nitrite and nitrite-free versions. With the cure, they were bright red and also saltier than the nitrite-free product.

Below is Dick Kutas's venison salami recipe, without added fat or cures.

NITRITE-FREE VENISON SALAMI
  1½ to 2 pints ice water (depending on
    how moist you want the final
    salami to be)
  4 tbsp. salt
  2 cups soy protein concentrate
  1 tbsp. ground white pepper
  2 tbsp. nutmeg
  2 large cloves fresh garlic, finely
    pressed
  6 tbsp. corn syrup solids (for binding
    and sweetening)
  2 tbsp. powdered dextrose (for tang)
  2 tbsp. liquid smoke flavor
  10 lb. ground venison

Mix all the ingredients together. Soak one-half dozen 2¼-inch fibrous sausage casings in tap water for a half hour. Place the salami mixture in a sausage stuffer and push into the casings, sealing the ends by tying with string or, more efficiently, with hog-ring clips and a hog-ring pliers (available from The Sausage Maker). Let the salamis season overnight in the fridge. The following morning, place them in a 160° to 170°F oven. Use an accurate oven thermometer to maintain this temperature. Also place a meat thermometer in the center of one of the salamis. Cook until the internal temperature of the test salami reaches 152°F—9 to 15 hours. As soon as the test salami reaches 152°F, remove the salamis and immerse them in a sink or tub of cold water for 30 minutes. Keep fresh, cold water running into the bath. Dry the salamis and return them to the fridge overnight. In the morning they can be sliced. Although these salamis should be kept refrigerated, they can be carried on most camping trips for many days without spoiling.

SWEET ITALIAN SAUSAGE
  5 lb. ground venison, elk, or
    antelope
  2 tbsp. salt
  ½ to 1 pint ice water
  1½ tsp. fennel seed
  1 tsp. freshly ground black pepper
  ½ tbsp. sugar
  2½ ounces soy protein concentrate

Place the mixed ingredients in a sausage stuffer and press into 38mm to 42mm natural hog casings. Tie off the links at six- to eight-inch intervals, using string or the casing itself. Eat immediately, refrigerate, or freeze.

Hunters' Dutch Oven Stew

Any game meat may be used in this recipe:

3 lb. meat
1 onion, chopped
1 green pepper, chopped
2 cloves garlic, chopped
½ tsp. basil
3 tbsp. ketchup
2 drops liquid pepper
    seasoning
1 cup liquid (wine, broth,
    tomato juice, or water)
½ tsp. each salt and black
    pepper

Cut up meat and brown in hot skillet. Place pieces and other ingredients in dutch oven.

Dig a pit in the ground about two inches wider and two inches deeper than the dutch oven. Line it with ashes, then live coals. Place oven in pit and heap more coals and ashes on top. Cover with dirt, being sure to leave bail of oven upright. Leave it about 8 to 10 hours, dig up, and enjoy. Serves six to eight.

Squirrel Stew

3 squirrels, cut up
2 qt. water
2 tsp. salt
black pepper to taste
4 potatoes, peeled and
    cubed
4 carrots, cut in "pennies"
1 large onion, chopped
1 stalk celery, cut into
    1-inch pieces
1 recipe of dumplings from
    biscuit-mix package

Cover squirrels with salted water in six-quart dutch oven or stewing pot. Bring to boil, reduce heat, cover, and cook slowly (just bubbling) until squirrels are fork tender (30 to 45 minutes). Remove meat and set aside. Increase heat to bring water to a boil. Add vegetables, reduce heat, cover, and simmer 30 minutes. Add pepper. Return meat to the pot and increase heat to keep water just bubbling. Drop dumpling dough by spoonfuls into the water. Cook the stew uncovered for 10 minutes; then cover for another 10 minutes. Serves four.

Chuckwagon Cooking

Here is a high-protein recipe that can be cooked over a campfire, on a charcoal grill, in a boat or RV galley. Preparation time is only minutes, and it will feed four.

TEX-MEX BURGERS
1½ lb. lean ground beef
1 cup crushed corn chips
1 large egg
1 tsp. Mexican-style chili
    powder
½ tsp. ground cumin
½ tsp. salt

In a large bowl, combine all ingredients and mix until well blended. Divide into four portions and shape into thick patties. Cook over medium coals or in a greased skillet until all of the burgers are browned on both sides.

Robin Pie
In 1874, robins were subject to hunting 5½ months of the year in North Carolina, from October 15 to April 1. They were considered a game and food bird, and robin pie was a common meal for most tables.
—John D. Lusk.

VEGETABLES AND SIDE DISHES

Serve Them Fritters

Fritters are a special treat almost any time, but especially when camping out. They're easy to make and can be cooked on a campstove or over a campfire. When combined with a meat or vegetable, they round out a meal.

BASIC FRITTER BATTER
1¾ cups all-purpose flour
3 tsp. baking powder
1 egg, slightly beaten
1 tsp. salt
1 tbsp. sugar
1 cup milk
1 tbsp. melted fat or oil

In a bowl, mix dry ingredients. Add egg, melted fat or oil, and milk. Beat until well blended and smooth. Fold in whatever meat, vegetable, or fruit you desire. Drop the mixture by tablespoons into deep hot fat. Fry until well browned on both sides. Serves four.

The key to making good fritters, crispy on the outside and moist on the inside, is to be sure your cooking oil or fat is hot enough to form an instant seal that keeps the fat from seeping through. They are probably easier to cook in deep fat but can be cooked in a skillet with little fat or oil.

For main dish fritters, those with meats, seafoods, or vegetables, omit the sugar. Drain all canned foods before adding to the fritter batter. For dessert fritters, in some cases you may want to add some more sugar to the fruits.

FRITTER VARIATIONS
SHRIMP: Add 1½ cups chopped, cooked, shelled, and deveined shrimp. If desired, add ¼ cup finely chopped onions. Serve with coleslaw.
MIXED VEGGIES: Add one can (16 oz.) cooked mixed vegetables, drained. Serve with any cooked meat.
APPLES 'N' NUTS: Add 1½ cups diced apples and ½ cup chopped nuts. Eat as is or dusted with powdered sugar.
BLUEBERRY: Add one to two cups of fresh blueberries or one can of drained blueberries. Dust with sugar.

Rub The Spud

Little can compare gustatorily to a potato wrapped in foil and baked deep in the coals of a campfire.

Sadly for some of us, the skin of such potatoes is often too crisp to be enjoyed. The solution: Rub the spud with cooking oil, lard, or butter (margarine will do fine) before wrapping it. The oil will keep the skin moist and prevent crispiness and hardening.

HEARTY HASH

For an easy camping recipe that really gets the taste buds going, dice two large potatoes and one large onion into a skillet. Add enough water to barely cover the vegetables, one large tablespoon of prepared mustard, pepper, and a dash or two of Tabasco sauce. Simmer until the vegetables are almost tender, then break up a can of corned beef into the mixture. Adjust the seasonings, stir well, and simmer, uncovered, until the vegetables are done and the mixture is of the desired consistency.

INSTANT APPLESAUCE

The French word for potato is *pomme de terre*—apple of the earth. Everyone knows about cooking that kind of apple wrapped in aluminum foil over a campfire, but here's a variation, using real apples.

Core apples and grease with butter, margarine, or a little cooking oil. Place each on two layers of aluminum foil (to prevent burning). Add a dash of cinnamon to each. Wrap and place near embers, being careful that the fire is not too hot. Unlike the pomme de terre, the "pomme de tree" will cook in about 15 minutes.

Raisins may be inserted to replace the core if care is taken so that they do not spill out. Sweetener may be added along with the raisins, but it is safer to wait until the apples are completely cooked.

HOMEMADE SAUERKRAUT

Nothing goes better with many game dishes than a healthy serving of sauerkraut. Try this recipe for a gustatory treat:

Shred five or six pounds of cabbage (preferably with a food processor) and layer in a crock or plastic bucket. Press down firmly every three or four inches and sprinkle on an ounce of noniodized (pickling or kosher) salt. Continue until the crock is full. Additional spices can be added in with the salt layers if desired— bayleaf, red pepper, garlic powder, and caraway seed give added zest. No water— cabbage juices provide the necessary liquid.

After the final layer of salt and spices is added, the container must be sealed because air will spoil the fermenting process. One way to do this is to insert the container into a plastic bag filled with water.

Store in a cool, dark area, and be patient. It takes a few months to get a prime product. Fermentation will be speeded up at higher temperatures but with a resulting decline in quality. If mold should appear around the edges, simply remove it and reseal. When ready to eat, the kraut has a yellowish cast. Put in a colander to wash off the brine and prepare it to go with one of your favorite dishes.

APPLE STUFFING FOR DUCK

Take four or five sour apples, peel, core, and quarter. Stew in a small amount of water until just tender. Add one cup of bread crumbs, a sprinkle of chili pepper, salt, and one teaspoon of sage. Mix well and use to stuff your duck.

Mount Rainier Squaw Corn

Try this quick, delicious, nourishing main or side dish, which can be easily prepared.

2 cans (16½ oz.) cream-style corn
6 slices bacon
seasonings

Cut bacon in one-inch segments, and sauté in deep 12-inch skillet until it is nearly crisp. Drain off all but two tablespoons of fat, and add corn. Stir and heat thoroughly. Add salt, pepper, Worcestershire sauce, or any desired seasoning. Serves two as an entrée, four as a side dish.

Variations: Add one-quarter cup finely chopped onion to the bacon. Or add one-quarter cup chopped green or red pepper. Another variation is to add one-half cup grated cheddar cheese with the corn. All these may be used together, along with one tablespoon chili powder.

BREADS AND BISCUITS

Homesteader's Biscuits

You can prepare enough basic biscuit mix to feed a bunch of hungry campers for nearly a week for about half the store price. It takes but a few minutes, and stored in containers the pre-mix will keep for months. Take along what you will need on a camping trip in a heavy plastic bag. For a fair-sized batch, use:

6 cups regular flour
3 tbsps. baking powder
1 tbsp. salt
⅓ cup shortening, chilled

Place about half the flour in a large bowl and add the shortening. Mix well, using your fingers, until it has the consistency of fine crumbs. Dump the balance of the flour into a medium to large paper bag, along with the salt and baking powder. Add the flour/shortening mix and fold the top of the bag over two or three times (leaving lots of empty space). Tumble mix until well blended. Store in empty coffee cans.

Use this mix for rolled biscuits, drop biscuits, shortbread, and fruit cobbler toppings (add a bit of sugar), or drop spoonfuls into a simmering stew for dumplings.

Two cups of the mixture, combined with water to create a soft dough, makes about 10 or 12 biscuits. Just press out with the heel of your hand to about a half-inch thickness on a floured board, then cut into two-inch squares and bake on a pie tin.

Streamside Hush Puppies

Try this homemade mixture and take a batch or two on your next trip.

½ cup complete buttermilk pancake mix
1 cup self-rising cornmeal
2 tbsps. minced onion flakes
¼ tsp. garlic salt (optional)

Measure ingredients into a pint-sized freezer bag, close top, and mix by tumbling. Seal with a twist tie. At camp add enough water to the bag to make a stiff dough, and mix right in the bag. Preheat cooking oil or bacon drippings in a skillet. Take a heaping teaspoonful and roll by hand into a slender egg shape. Drop into hot skillet and fry until a golden brown, turning often. You can cook 'em at the same time you're frying the fish. Serve warm. Makes about 16 to 18.

BEER BREAD

Beer is often the liquid ingredient of hot cakes and coating batters. It can also produce a tasty loaf of bread. No salt or shortening is used.

3 cups all-purpose flour
1 tbsp. baking powder
3 tbsps. sugar
1 12-oz. can beer

In a suitable pan or bowl combine flour, baking powder, and sugar; stir in beer and blend well. Turn dough into a well-greased loaf pan and bake at 350°F one hour. Turn out on a wire rack and cool before slicing.

Note: If self-rising flour is used, no baking powder is needed.

An experienced camp cook can bake beer bread in a dutch oven over coals, with coals piled on the lid to brown the bread. In a dutch oven the dough will spread and therefore bake in less time, usually about 45 minutes.

For the less experienced, or if a fire is not practical or forbidden, the bread may be "baked" in a heavy frying pan or skillet covered with a lid on the camp-stove burner. The heat must be watched closely to avoid burning the bread; keep it moderately hot or toward a lower setting. Preheat the skillet, grease well with lard or shortening, and spoon in the dough. Cover and bake 30 to 35 minutes or until firm

to the touch and no longer shiny on the surface. Flip the bread over, cover, and bake 20 to 25 minutes more. Prepared thus, it is heavier but very good.

If a skillet is used for baking the bread, the dough can be divided into four or more equal portions and shaped into buns. These may be turned as soon as they are firm and have lost their gloss—20 to 25 minutes on one side and 15 to 20 for the second.

Try placing a generous slice of cheddar cheese atop a slice of beer bread, pop it into a heated oven or skillet to melt the cheese. Serve with, what else? Beer.

BUTTERMILK BISCUITS

2 cups all-purpose flour
⅔ tsp. baking soda
¾ tsp. salt
¼ cup shortening
¾ cup cultured buttermilk

Sift together flour, baking soda, and salt. Cut in shortening by drawing two table knives scissors-fashion repeatedly through the mix until it has a crumbly texture. Gradually add buttermilk, blending it into the mix. Knead the

dough lightly on a floured surface and roll to about one-eighth-inch thickness. Cut out circles with a biscuit cutter and place on a greased cookie sheet. Bake at 450°F for 10 to 12 minutes. This recipe makes 24 small buttermilk biscuits.

Eastern Shore Corn Bread

2 sticks margarine
1½ cups yellow cornmeal
1½ cups sugar
1 cup all-purpose flour
4 tsps. baking powder
1½ tsps. salt
2½ cups milk
2 eggs, beaten

Melt one stick of margarine and pour into a 9x12-inch baking pan. Mix the dry ingredients, milk, and eggs in a large bowl. Melt other stick of margarine and add to the other ingredients. Pour into the baking pan. Bake at 425°F for approximately 20 minutes.

BEVERAGES

Drink Hearty

Before coffee became so easy to buy, people went to great lengths to concoct a substitute beverage. Various parts of available plants were dug, dried, ground, roasted, and boiled to provide a hearty dark brew. With chicory (*Cichorium intybus*), dandelion, (*Taraxacum officinale*) and burdock (*Arctium minus*), they used the roots. Wild sunflower seeds (*Helianthus annuus*) were simply harvested and toasted, but acorns required extensive leaching, sometimes in wood ashes, to be potable.

One unusual plant that was used was couch grass (*Agropyron repens*). Its long, pale yellow roots were dug, dried, and ground for "coffee." In more recent years, wheat bran, rye, and even soybeans were mixed with sweetener, roasted, and brewed.

The memoir of a pioneer woman of the late 1850s tells of a wedding at which the inventive hostess "turned out some delicious coffee, made of dried carrots."

COLD-WEATHER BEVERAGES

Anyone looking for the perfect cold-weather antifreeze is not likely to find it at the liquor store. Alcoholic beverages act as vasodilators to open the blood vessels, causing a surge of blood to the capillaries near the surface of the skin. That surge causes the sensation of warmth once thought to be beneficial. In fact, there is a big price to be paid for that moment of warmth. The heat released to the skin is coming from the core of the body, so the overall body temperature declines.

In cases of extreme temperature loss—hypothermia—alcoholic beverages can be life-threatening. Chilled people may slip into comas or die when given liquor.

The best cold-weather beverages are still hot liquids. A cup of steaming soup or tea will go a lot farther toward making that 10-below-zero day bearable than will a snort of Old Gut Shot.

It is estimated that over 95,000 cubic miles of water are circulated between the earth and sky each year. Some 80,000 cubic miles evaporate from the oceans and 15,000 cubic miles from the land masses. The average annual rainfall around the earth is 40 inches; the major rainfalls, over 80 inches, fall in the region of the equator.

COFFEE

Simmering on a Coleman stove, balanced on the dashboard of a pickup, poured from a vacuum bottle, coffee is a part of our sporting traditions. Unfortunately, the adage "It smells better than it tastes" too often hits the mark. This doesn't have to be the case. Coffee made with care, and from high-quality beans, sets the nasal passages as well as the taste buds alight.

The importance of beginning your brewing process with these fresh, whole beans cannot be emphasized enough. The coffee bean is the repository of the coffee flavor, but it is a fragile and temporary vehicle. As the roasted bean sits on the shelf, its flavor seeps inexorably.

Beans that are ground lose their flavor even more rapidly, since the volatile oils are exposed to the air and immediately begin to evaporate. In fact, after the bean is ground, 65 percent of its flavor-producing oils is lost within 24 hours.

Vacuum containers, like the ones in which coffee is sold in supermarkets, help to delay this process but cannot stop it.

It is best to buy beans in small quantities (only as much as you use in a week), to grind only what you will brew, and to store the beans in the refrigerator in an airtight glass jar with a rubber seal on the lid—canning jars are ideal.

Grinders (either hand or electric) make this process easy. Hand grinders are my favorite since they can be used on camping trips and don't heat the beans, as do some inexpensive electric grinders. This heat causes a rapid evaporation of the essential coffee oils before water can get to the grounds.

As a rule of thumb, grind your coffee beans as fine as possible (just short of powder is how I like it), for as the grind becomes finer, the contact between the water and essential coffee oils increases.

You have bought fresh, whole beans. You have stored them properly and not for a long time. You have ground your coffee beans cool. But if your water is poor, you still will not get a decent cup of coffee. If you don't like the taste of your tap water (for instance, it may have a sulfurous tang), the coffee it makes will be little better. I also find that heavily chlorinated water imparts an unpleasant taste. You may, if you are a perfectionist, want to use bottled water.

No particular brewing method can be said to produce the perfect cup of coffee. Some methods create more muscular, hearty, powerful brews; others leave a smoother, more delicate product. Your tastes will steer you to the right method, or like some coffee fanciers, you may want to use one method in the morning, one during the day, and still a third for the evening or special occasions.

At the bottom of the brewing list is the

percolator. Fundamentally, the percolator boils water and sprays this boiling water, repeatedly, over the grounds. In the process, it vaporizes much of the coffee oils and sends them into the air rather than into the water. The coffee smells great but lacks taste.

Every other method of coffee preparation does what cowboy coffee has done for over a century: steeps grinds in hot water. The cowboy, or campfire, method is still one of the best ways to make the stuff, whether at home or in the field. Boil water. Take the pot off the flame. As the water is still rolling, toss the coffee (if you've got the eye, a handful or more of grounds to the pot) to break their surface suspension. You can also filter the coffee through a specially made cotton coffee sock. In a pinch I have used my bandanna.

Unfiltered, a mug of cowboy coffee is a rich, chewy mouthful. Some people love this taste; others detest it. For those who enjoy such muscular coffee and would like to brew it at home with more elegance, a plunger-type coffee maker may be a worthwhile purchase. This device has a beaker covered by a lid in which sits a plunger. Coffee and hot water are placed in the beaker and brewed for three minutes. The plunger is then pressed down, trapping the grinds at the bottom of the beaker. The coffee, rich in suspended material and full of coffee oils, is then decanted into cups.

In many ways filtration grew out of the older drip method, which was invented in France around 1800 and which is still a fine way to brew a strong, tasty cup of coffee. Grounds and water are placed in the upper chamber of a two-compartment device. The coffee-imbued water drips through a strainer into the lower chamber. In addition to large drip pots, many coffee shops sell one-cup drippers, which produce a far better tasting brew than any instant coffee and take only a few more minutes to do so.

The automatic filter drip method has been technology's attempt to streamline the filter/drip brewing process. Since these brewers are powered by electricity, they aren't as useful in camp situations.

There are three great coffee-growing regions: Latin America; Arabia and Africa; and the Pacific Basin, including Indonesia, New Guinea, and Hawaii. Not only do coffees grown in these different regions taste different from one another, but they can also be roasted to varying degrees of darkness. Roasting companies will mix the coffees of different regions to produce a palatable blend whose ingredients complement each other.

In the Pacific Basin category there are such well-known coffees as Hawaiian Kona and Sumatran. Kona has a very powerful, rich, almost flowery aroma. Sumatran is known for its full body and bite, which is pleasant rather than bitter. In the Arabian/African variety there are Ethiopian Harrar, a racy, light coffee that some coffee connoisseurs describe as tasting like wine, and Kenyan, which has a dry, sunbaked taste that lingers on the palate.

CHAPTER FOUR

BACK HOME

A fter returning home from a successful trip into the wilderness, it might seem as though there is nothing left to do but to wait for the next expedition. This need not—indeed, should not—be the case. There are a number of projects that will help you keep your gear in great shape during the off months and prepare you for another wilderness adventure.

First, of course, all of the clothing and equipment used on your trips should be cleaned thoroughly before being retired for the season. Here are suggestions for ways to clean some of the toughest stains, such as pitch, and hints for handling problem garments, like down-filled sleeping bags.

Each piece of field equipment—from boots to fishing rods—should then be put away for the time being. Various storage methods, which should help keep your gear safe during the indoor months, are reviewed.

Tips for Cleaning and Storing Your Equipment

BABYING YOUR BOOTS

To recondition waterlogged or muddy boots, remove the laces and wash and dry them separately. Then use warm water and a small brush to take off the caked-on mud. Saddle soap is useful in renewing badly stained areas. Be sure to clean grime from the crevices around the seams and stitching. Wipe the boots dry with a clean rag.

Warm several sheets of newspaper in the oven or near the fire. Crumple them into balls, and stuff loosely inside the boots. The heated paper will speed drying and help the footwear to retain its shape. Place the boots where the air is circulating and away from direct heat. Excessive heat can cause damp leather to shrink, crack, and stiffen.

When the boots have dried, apply several coats of waterproofing compound. Stay away from silicon-based products because they may cause your feet to sweat. Use a small brush (an old toothbrush is ideal) to work the substance into seams and stitching.

If your boots have taken on a locker-room smell, seal them individually in plastic bags and place in the freezer overnight. The cold temperature will kill odor-causing bacteria.

When you're out on the trail, there's even more incentive to properly restore wet boots: Your feet have to go back into them in the morning. Clean them, using as little water as possible. Wipe dry and place each one upside down on a stick driven into the ground. Put them in the sunshine or near (but not too near) the campfire.

When your evening chores are completed, warm a panful of dry pebbles over the fire and pour them into the boots. Shake occasionally. When the stones cool off, reheat them and repeat the process.

If you didn't pack a waterproofing compound, rub a softened candle over leather and stitching while the footgear is still warm. Bacon grease or other animal fats can be used as waterproofing in an emergency, but make sure it's really an emergency. In warm weather the fat will become rancid and will sweat out and onto your socks and feet.

RUST-FREE KNIVES

Never store a quality knife in its scabbard. Leather cured with tannic acid will, over time, draw moisture and stain even the finest steel, no matter how well oiled.

At the end of the season, clean your knife thoroughly, removing all the dirt and residue. Then rub on a light coat of Vaseline. Wrap the knife in waxed paper and store in a dry place. The scabbard can be cleaned and rubbed well with Neat's-foot oil and stored separately.

Clean-Up Hints

Tired of your outdoor duds looking like something the cat dragged in? These simple tips can help get them clean again:

• Apply meat tenderizer with cool water on blood stains. Let it set for 30 minutes or so, and then sponge the spot clean and wash as usual.
• Boil underwear, socks, and T-shirts in water with a little lemon juice. They'll come out white again.
• Use warm vinegar water to remove perspiration odor.
• To remove berry stains, stretch the clothes over a bowl and from a height of two feet or so pour boiling water down through the stain. Then wash as usual.
• Spray-starch white tennis shoes to keep them looking white.
• Soak chewing gum spots in white vinegar, or rub with egg-white, before washing. If that doesn't work, try freezing the offending garment and then chip or scrape the gum off.
• Dry mildewed cloths in sunlight, then add a half cup of Lysol to the water.
• Loosen stubborn zippers by rubbing them with graphite from the "lead" of a pencil.

Handy Boot Hanger

Wet boots can spoil a day's outing. Here is an easy-to-make boot hanger that allows them to dry out and keeps them out of the way when not in use.

You will need a piece of one-half-inch plywood 12 inches wide and eight feet long. This size rack will accommodate seven pairs of boots.

First draw a line 6¾ inches in from one long side. Next, make a cardboard template 6¾ inches long and 3¾ inches wide with one end rounded off. A coffee can can be used to mark off the rounded end.

Starting three inches from one end, use the template to outline a boot slot every three inches. Then cut out with a saber saw.

Attach a piece of 1 × 12 planking or plywood 10 inches long to each end of the plywood with screws. Now your boot hanger is ready to install where circulating warm air can do its job.

Fasten to open ceiling joists or to two pieces of 2 × 4 affixed to the ceiling. If securing to the 2 × 4s, cut the top portion of the 1 × 12 at an angle to obtain a 1½-inch slope across the board's width to keep the boots in place.

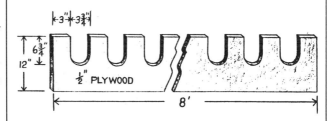

EASY CLEANUP

When I've backpacked to my favorite trout stream or have been camping off the beaten track, I cook most of my meals on a wire grill over a wood fire. I don't want a soapy taste in my

dinner, so I don't soap my nesting aluminum pots. Thus, it used to take me hours to scour and scrub them after I got home. My wife came up with this helpful suggestion: When you return from camping, simply fill a pail with plenty of *hot* water, or six to eight inches of water in a laundry tub. Add a generous slug of laundry detergent and immerse the pots and pans.

Then forget them for at least 48 hours or longer (don't attempt this with cast-iron pots or coated pans).

Later on, just drain off the grimy water and scour the pots with soaped steel wool pads. The crud will literally float off with a minimum of effort.

A deer cools itself by belching.

How To Sharpen A Knife

Sharpening a knife is simple if you follow the correct steps. The process described below is for sharpening with a whetstone, but the method is basically the same whether Crock Stick–type designs, steels, or stones are used.

If a knife has been abused, or was poorly designed with a fat "shoulder" just behind the cutting edge, it may require grinding or tapering back before the final sharpening process. Use a coarse, highly abrasive material to taper the blade, and keep an angle of only 10 to 15 degrees—less than you'll use for the final sharpening. Work the blade over the hone, in either a circular pattern or with one-direction strokes along the entire blade length from hilt to point. The object of this initial effort is to thin the shoulder behind the knife edge. Chicago Cutlery recommends the pyramid system for this tapering process. Take five strokes on each side of the blade, then four, then three, etc. Apply fairly heavy pressure.

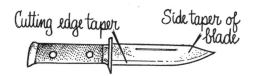

Cutting edge taper   Side taper of blade

If your knife is new and well designed, or has been maintained regularly, skip the above and proceed to the final sharpening process. For this, use a coarse material for the initial stage, then switch to a harder, finer material.

Honing oil can be used, or lubricate the stone with water. The angle you choose for the final edge of the blade depends on the edge the knife came with and what use you'll be putting it to. Some pocketknives, fillet knives and blades used for delicate caping or slicing have a thin taper, such as 10 to 15 degrees. A better taper for an all-around camping or hunting knife is 18 to 25 degrees. If you'll be doing rugged work, 25 or 30 degrees may prove useful. Whatever angle you choose, maintain it consistently as you sharpen both sides and the entire length of the blade.

To sharpen a knife on a stone, place the blade flat against one end of the stone with the cutting edge away from you. Raise the back of the knife off the stone to the chosen angle.

Using light, even pressure, stroke the blade along the stone diagonally, sweeping it so that the entire surface from the hilt to the tip makes contact. Do this five times, then turn the blade over and repeat, slicing toward you and maintaining the same angle. Use the pyramid system: five strokes on each side, then four, then three, etc. Use a soft material first, then finish on a harder one using fewer and lighter strokes. If you have trouble holding the precise angle needed, try using an angle-bracket.

How fast your knife takes on a good cutting edge will depend on the hardness of the material used in the blade and the

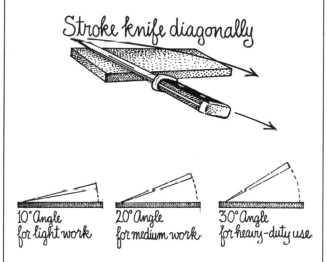

Stroke knife diagonally

10° Angle for light work   20° Angle for medium work   30° Angle for heavy-duty use

hardness of your hone or steel. A diamond-covered sharpener will bring an edge to the knife much more quickly than a natural Arkansas stone. A knife blade made of carbon steel is soft and will take an edge more quickly than those made of harder stainless steel (but will require more frequent sharpening to maintain its edge).

As a final step, if you want the ultimate edge, consider polishing or smoothing the honed blade with a strap. Once you've completed sharpening your knives, clean the steels and hones using a household scouring powder such as Ajax or Comet, with water and a nylon bristle brush. Rinse them off and either air-dry or pat with a cloth and store in a dry location.

The sharpened knife blade should be oiled lightly with mineral oil, cooking oil, petroleum jelly, or a household lubricant, then wiped.

STRIPPING PITCH

Nothing is quite so relaxing as sitting on a log near a campfire, your finger wrapped around a warm mug—until you stand up and discover that sticky pitch has left the log and stained your pants!

A ready remedy is available in the camp box: a pat of butter or a teaspoon of cooking oil. Dabbed on the pitch and patted off with a paper towel or cloth, it will remove the tarry stuff. Wash as you would normally. It's a simple solution for the wood gatherer, campfire builder, and Christmas tree cutter.

Pitch strips easily from your hands after you drop a small amount of oil on them, rub gently, and wipe with a paper towel.

ROD STORAGE

Before storing your fishing rods for the winter, be sure to wash them with soap and water and a soft scrub brush or sponge. When dry, check the guides for wear with a cotton swab. If the wraps are exposed, coat them with rod lacquer. Lubricate the reel seat with WD-40 or a similar product. Hang the rod in a rod rack without the reel; reels place undue pressure on the blank and consequently may cause the rod to warp.

Four Steps to Waterproofing Boots

A steady rain, a long hike, sodden boots, and wet feet—who hasn't sworn to do a better job waterproofing next time! Well, here's the A to Z:

One. With a brush and sponge, remove all mud, sand and gravel from the boots. Adding some warm water can speed this job along. Another way to remove dirt is to wait until the boots are dry, then brush them briskly with a heavy-duty brush.

Two. To dry boots internally, stuff them with newspaper. Use an electric hair dryer on their outsides, or put them by a woodstove or other heat source, but no closer than you can comfortably keep your hand. When the boots are dry, insert shoe trees.

Three. At room temperature, rub your waterproofer into the boot uppers with your hand, a cloth or a paper towel, making sure to stuff it liberally along the welt so a caul-like seam is created over the stitching holes. (When using a waxlike waterproofer, I often liquefy it over a low flame, then rub it on the leather as above. You can use a teaspoon to pour it on the welt.) Let the boots stand overnight. Rub off the excess waterproofer in the morning. If the waterproofer has completely disappeared, you may wish to add another coat.

Four. Be warned that the sup-

port of a fine pair of boots can be ruined by too much waterproofing. The wax and oil in the waterproofers will soften the leather until it becomes pliant and yielding. If your boots won't keep your feet dry after a few attempts at waterproofing, perhaps they're not designed for very wet conditions. Rather than destroying them with mistaken kindness, buy more suitable footgear.

Camping Preparation

The time to start preparing for your next camping trip is the day you get back from your last one. Clean all your gear: Air out your sleeping bag, sweep out the tent, carefully wash all the pots, pans and utensils in your camp cooking kit. If your stove and lantern use white gas, refill them. If you use propane, make sure the canisters are full; if they aren't, replace them. Check the mantle on your lantern, and replace it if it shows the beginnings of a hole (but don't burn the new mantle in until you get to a new camp; that way it will survive the most brutal trip).

Replenish the staples in your camp grub box: salt, pepper, sugar, and flour.

A Better Way to Hang Waders

Hanging wet neoprene waders by their shoulder straps causes undue stress on the seams. A pants hanger, available at any department store, can be clamped to either the chest section of the waders or, in the case of inner dampness due to condensation, the feet end so the waders dry inside and out. As with all such products, ultraviolet rays from the sun cause more damage than anything else, so be sure to hang your waders away from sunlight.

Care and Storage of Flylines

Modern flylines don't need much care, but they do require occasional attention if you want them to deliver optimum performance. To prolong the life of your line, for example, avoid casting without a leader, stepping on the line, pinching it between the frame and spool of your reel, snapping it in the air behind you by starting your forward cast too quickly, and allowing it to make contact with insect repellent, gasoline, and suntan lotions.

The only care necessary to keep your line in top condition is occasional cleaning. You may see a dirty film developing; the flyline may stick in the rod guides and not shoot as well as it should; or, if it's a floating line, it may begin to sink. In all of these cases a cleaning is in order, since al-gae and microscopic particles of dirt have likely built up on the line. These attract and hold water and reduce the line's buoyancy and shootability.

Some flylines come with cleaners and conditioners. If yours didn't, you can buy several types for only a few dollars, use soap and water, or apply an auto vinyl upholstery cleaner such as Armor All™.

Flylines do not require any special care during the off-season. You can remove the line from the reel if you like and store it in larger loops around a wooden peg, but the easiest storage method is to simply leave it on the spool. Be sure not to put the spool in an airtight container while it's still wet, or mildew may develop.

Care and Maintenance of Axes and Hatchets

• Rub boiled linseed oil into the handle to keep it from drying out. Sand periodically.
• Should the head loosen, coat it with petroleum jelly and soak handle and head in water. The wood will swell, lightening the head. Rewedge if the handle loosens again.
• If the foot of your ax handle comes to a sharp point, cut off a half inch to produce a flat. You can tighten a loose head by rapping this flat foot on a rock.
• In subzero weather, warm the blade lightly before using it so the metal will not chip.
• Hold an ax just behind the head when walking. Keep it on the downhill side in steep terrain. If you fall, pitch the ax away from you.
• Always carry an ax in a sheath.
• Don't use an ax unless you know what you are doing, for axes will bite you bad. Do not split wood that you prop up with your foot in the classic woodsman's pose. That is an invitation to much more than a nail clipping.
• Keep your ax sharp. A sharp ax is safer than a dull one. File on a primary edge; with a stone, hone on a secondary.

STORING ALUMINUM BOATS

Though this information's on the level, the way you store your aluminum boat or canoe should *not* be, according to technicians at Grumman Boats. Level storage might permit meltwater or condensation to puddle inside hollow extrusions used for ribs, thwarts, and gunwales. Freezing water can cause extensive damage by expansion and split the extrusions.

Such damage can be expensive and difficult to repair. But the cure is easy: Simply make sure that one end is slightly higher than the other—about an inch or two—so water can't collect.

It isn't a bad idea to make sure that one *side* is higher by a like amount. Don't cover the hull, but let it rest on wooden sawhorses. Wet canvases and ropes can cause pitting.

The cleaner the metal and the fewer things in direct contact, the better the hull will come through the rigors of the winter. That goes for lashing it down to the sawhorses—remember wet ropes against the metal hull?

Easing a Clean-Up Chore

When it comes time to scrub accumulated grime from the plastic-coated fabrics of camping equipment, what is the best method to use without scrubbing off the waterproofing or permanently damaging color and finish?

Well, there is a cleaner especially formulated for use on the airtight material of inflatable boats that is great for removing soil and stains from air mattresses, ponchos and rain suits, tarps, tents, covers, fabric waders, waterproofed duffel bags, and rod and gun cases. Called Seapower, it works three ways: a cleaning agent's sudsing action floats soil from deep in fabric pores; a gentle abrasive safely removes stains; and two polymers recondition the surface.

OAR STORAGE

To a boater few things are more frustrating than hearing a loud crunch when backing out of the garage and discovering you've just run over a brand-new ash oar. Or to uncover a canoe paddle that has warped during the wet winter months.

Your equipment can be protected and kept neatly out of the way with an inexpensive storage system that can be put together in just minutes.

For oars, nail a short piece of 2 × 4 on both sides of the

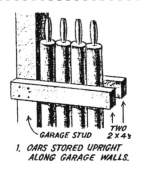

1. OARS STORED UPRIGHT ALONG GARAGE WALLS.

garage wall studs. Then stand each oar upright between these two support boards.

Paddles can be conveniently suspended from garage rafters by nailing two board scraps close enough together to insert a paddle handle sideways. Then rotate the paddle so that its T-shaped handle rests over the boards.

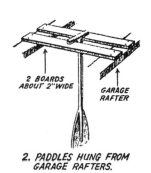

2. PADDLES HUNG FROM GARAGE RAFTERS.

THE OL' IRON SKILLET

One of the best utensils for general camp cooking is the old-fashioned cast-iron skillet. Because of its weight it heats evenly, and unless you're downright careless, you seldom burn food in one. Still, it can get mighty cruddy with baked-on grease. An Alaskan sourdough uses this trick to solve this kind of problem.

He did all of his cooking on a wood-burning kitchen stove, and his pots and pans were often blackened with encrusted grease. But every year or so, he'd take his iron frying pans and place them inside the firebox of the stove, on top of a good fire. He added a few sticks of wood, opened the draft on the stove, and left the pans overnight.

Next morning, after the fire had burned itself out, he simply retrieved his prized iron pans, gave them a good washing, and dried them well. Then he'd reseason them with bacon grease and start again.

Since you may not have a wood-burning stove, try your camp skillet in a fireplace. You may have to extract the skillet with the fire tongs in order to add more wood, but it will work like a charm! As the frying pan reddens in the fire, bits of encrusted grease will crack and pop off. Move the pan a few times, heating all encrusted sections, until the metal is clean.

In the morning remove the skillet from the ashes, wash it clean, and dry it well. Then reseason it by coating it lightly with cooking oil (or bacon grease) and heating it in a 350°F oven until almost smoking. After cooling, wipe with a paper towel, re-oil, and reheat the pan. This procedure, done two or three times, will give you a perfectly seasoned iron pan. After a final wiping with a paper towel, you'll have a black, nonstick surface, and the pan is ready to be used for cooking again.

Winterizing Outboard Motors

Manufacturers say that the best time to winterize an outboard motor is immediately after use. Here's how to do it:

Drain and flush all fuel tanks, remove spark plugs, and squirt in a drop of lubricating oil. Replace plugs finger-tight after turning the engine over once or twice to distribute oil over cylinder walls.

Drain and replace the lower-unit gear grease, clean all outside surfaces, check all fuel lines, clean sediment bowl (if present), and remove the battery. Clean battery posts with baking soda and water, and check all electrical connections from battery to motor. Store the battery in a cool, dry place on boards off the floor. Add a trickle charge to the battery during winter, and your outboard will be ready in the spring.

In England *beck* is a small stream; in Scotland it's a *burn*.

Chainsaw Brush

Cleanliness is important to the efficient operation of a chainsaw. But cleaning the external parts, especially the hard-to-reach places, can be a tedious and time-consuming job.

To make this task easier, use a six-inch-wide, inexpensive whitewash or utility brush that can be purchased at any paint shop or hardware store.

Since, the brush has a handle, you will avoid soiling your hands and also nicking your skin on sharp protrusions while cleaning the saw.

ACKNOWLEDGMENTS

Our thanks to the Field Editors of *SPORTS AFIELD* whose articles and features have been reprinted in this compendium of helpful outdoor tips and facts:

Anthony Acerrano
Homer Circle
George Harrison
Ted Kerasote

Our thanks, also, to Glenn Wolff, John Flagg, and all of the other talented artists whose delightful artwork fills these pages. Their work has not only contributed to the look of *SPORTS AFIELD*'s Almanac, but has shown, in clear visual form, how some of the more complex techniques actually work.

We regret that we are not able to credit all of the other contributors whose material has been reprinted from the many past editions of *SPORTS AFIELD*'s Almanac. It is because of their innovations and efforts that many other outdoor enthusiasts have been able to benefit and enjoy our heritage—America's great outdoors.